£4

Everyman, I will go with thee, and be thy guide,
In thy most need to go by thy side.

This is No. 511 of Everyman's Library. A
list of authors and their works in this series
will be found at the end of this volume. The
publishers will be pleased to send freely to all
applicants a separate, annotated list of the
Library.

J. M. DENT & SONS LIMITED
10–13 BEDFORD STREET LONDON W.C.2

E. P. DUTTON & CO. INC.
286–302 FOURTH AVENUE
NEW YORK

EVERYMAN'S LIBRARY
EDITED BY ERNEST RHYS

BIOGRAPHY

AUTOBIOGRAPHY OF EDWARD
GIBBON · EDITED WITH AN INTRO-
DUCTION BY OLIPHANT SMEATON, M.A.

EDWARD GIBBON, born in 1737 at Putney. Educated at Westminster School, Oxford and privately at Lausanne. Toured Italy, 1764–5, and conceived the plan of his 'History.' Settled in London in 1772 and sat in Parliament from 1774–83. Lived in Lausanne, 1787–93, and died in London in 1794.

AUTOBIOGRAPHY

EDWARD GIBBON

LONDON: J. M. DENT & SONS LTD.
NEW YORK: E. P. DUTTON & CO. INC.

INTRODUCTION

IF Gibbon's *Decline and Fall of the Roman Empire* now justly takes rank in the domain of history among those select masterpieces of genius to which the common consent of succeeding epochs has assigned a place not to be disturbed by later criticism, his *Autobiography*, in its own department, may claim as a work of art, a station little less distinguished. The remark made by Dr. Birkbeck Hill in his edition of the work, if it held true then, does so with increased cogency now, that " for one reader who has read his *Decline and Fall*, there are at least a score who have read his *Autobiography*, and know him, not as the great historian, but as a man of the most original and interesting nature." In other words, many know of Edward Gibbon the historian through his *Autobiography* who are innocent of knowledge of his *History*. That being so, there must be qualities of more than average excellence to keep the memory of such a work green for over a century.

The question has been asked times and oft wherein lies the charm of this *Autobiography?* It is more easily asked than answered. Perhaps, however, this analysis, by those familiar with its contents, may not be judged far from the truth—that in these pages we have the most accurate literary portrait ever drawn of the great historian. Not one of his little foibles and peccadilloes but peeps out in that pre-eminently truthful representation, though the lines are limned by the subject of the portrait himself. Mark Pattison has aptly said that Milton and Gibbon are the two men " who are indulged without challenge in talk about themselves." In

Gibbon's case we positively welcome the harmless vanity
and self-esteem which chronicles such details as:—"The
favourable judgment of Mr. Hayley, himself a poet and
scholar " [on Gibbon's *Critical Observations of the Sixth
Book of the Æneid*].

These little outcrops of egotism are by no means
wholly repellent. By revealing how very human the
historian was they interpret him to us. Had he not
betrayed some such little foibles, the colossal greatness
of the writer would overshadow the natural quality
of the man. In addition, we now live in an age when
personal details regarding the life, habits, appearance,
and pursuits of our leading authors, artists, musicians,
singers, etc., lend zest to our appreciation of their art,
just as the minutiæ we learn of the individual predi-
lections of Nelson, Wellington, and Livingstone impart
flesh-and-blood *vraisemblance* to the literary portraits
of the men themselves. Not the great qualities of head
or heart are those that arouse and retain our sympathetic
interest, but those minor traits, oftentimes those foibles
which reveal the fact that the popular idol is no demi-
god, but merely a man of like passions with ourselves,
are the attributes that capture and keep our interest.

The *Autobiography of Edward Gibbon* is one of those
books without which no library can be considered complete. Sir John Lubbock (Lord Avebury) in his list of
" One Hundred of the Best Books " contained in his
Pleasures of Life does not include it. In that I consider he is untrue to his own principle of selection. For
he has ranked the *Decline and Fall of the Roman Empire*
among the indispensable works in the historical section;
yet how can we adequately understand that masterpiece
without learning from the *Autobiography* the principles
on which its author proceeded in planning it and in
carrying the plan into execution.

There are passages in this book throwing a flood
of light on the methods of composition pursued by
Gibbon, which should be read with care by all

who contemplate the study of the *Decline and Fall of the Roman Empire*. The *Autobiography* is practically the key to the latter, and he will essay the latter work with increased zest and understanding who has previously perused the former, mastering thereby the great historian's method and obtaining an insight into his mind and character. For Gibbon's mode of working was all his own. Methodical as he was in many matters, he was also exceedingly desultory in others, albeit the whole scheme was subject to rules which suited the aim he had in view.

His retentive memory was a talent upon which he never seemed to set sufficient store. To few men has the gift been given of possessing an endowment at once so capacious and so reliable. Seldom did it ever play him false, and then only in one or two minor instances in his later years after the burden and heat of the day of life had been borne for long.

Of course we must remember that the *Autobiography* in its present state is only a fragment. Practically pieced together by Lord Sheffield from the materials left by Gibbon, it was not only left incomplete, but it never received that final revision in proof form which to the writer often reveals, better than aught else, much that is faulty and infelicitous in his work.

Some critics have blamed Gibbon for saying so little regarding his contemporaries, or amusing the reader with a gallery of portraits and a collection of anecdotes. To have done so would have been foreign to his plan. He was preparing an *Autobiography* or a record of his own life, and to have acted otherwise than he did would, as Dr. Birkbeck Hill says, have lessened its perfection as a whole. It is the life of the author of the *Decline and Fall of the Roman Empire*, and his life alone, that we read from the first page to the last.

Gibbon is always the supreme artist, and as such he reveals himself in every line of his work. One cannot, however, add that he also portrays himself as an entirely lovable man. He is too vain to be natural, and though the revelation of these foibles imparts *vraisemblance* to the work, it also lowers our respect for him, despite all his candour.

While we admire the genius of the great historian and the conscientious industry of the careful craftsman who will take no fact on trust, while we are compelled to praise the indefatigable zeal which sustained him amid the toil of examining mountains of material in which only a pebble or two might reward his sifting, while finally we reverence the noble impartiality which enabled him to hold the scales of critical judgment with un-biassed fairness save in cases where the claims of Christianity and the Christians entered into the problem, we cannot say that Edward Gibbon was a character whom we should have rejoiced to know because of the love we bore to his qualities of heart and head. Nay! His vanity and his self-love prompted a hypocritical insincerity which deals death to the respect whereon love must be based. As Dr. Birkbeck Hill remarks:—

" Whether we like him is another question—love him we certainly do not. . . . He had too much of the 'rational voluptuary' to be able to win our affection. His self-indulgence we are the more inclined to despise as in his later years it rendered his person ridiculous through its unwieldy corpulence. He had besides other and greater failings. In a young man in the full flow of his life we are less ready to forgive untruthfulness than when we come across it in one who is stricken with the timidity of age. . . . We are set against him moreover by the indecency of his writings however much he ' veiled it in the obscurity of a learned language.' We might have found some excuse for a wantonness which sprang from strong passions; but who can forgive *une obscénité érudite et froide ?* "

To such opinions nine out of every ten readers will add their assent. We admire, we commend, we like, but we cannot love the character of Edward Gibbon!

OLIPHANT SMEATON.

The following is a list of the works of Edward Gibbon:—

Essai sur l'Etude de la Littérature, 1761; an English translation appeared in 1764; Mémoires Littéraires de la Grande Bretagne (with Deyverdun), 2 vols., 1767, 1768; Critical Observations on the Sixth Book of the Æneid, 1770; The History of the Decline and Fall of the Roman Empire, vol. i., 1776; vols. ii. and iii., 1787; vols. iv., v., and vi., 1788; his Vindication, 1779; Antiquities of the House of Brunswick, edited by Lord Sheffield, 1814; Memoirs of my Life and Writings, edited by Lord Sheffield, 2 vols., 1827; by H. H. Milman, 1839; G. Birkbeck Hill, 1900.

Among the editions of the History are:—
Oxford Edition, 8 vols., 1828; edited by H. H. Milman, 12 vols., 1838, 1839; by Dr. W. Smith (with notes by Milman and Guizot), 8 vols., 1854, 1855; Bohn's British Classics (with variorum notes), 7 vols., 1853-5. Many later editions, among them Lubbock's Best Hundred Books, 1892; An Abridged Edition, by J. Adams, 1789; Student's Gibbon, by Dr. W. Smith, 1857; French edition, annotated by M. and Mme. Guizot, 1812.

The Miscellaneous Works, which include the Memoirs, Letters, etc., edited by Lord Sheffield, 2 vols., 1796; new edition, 5 vols., 1814; Letters (1753-1794), edited by R. E. Prothero, 1896.

LIFE.—J. C. Morison (English Men of Letters); 2nd edition, 1878; Algernon Cecil, Six Oxford Thinkers, 1909; Gibbon's Antagonism to Christianity, by S. T. MacCloy, 1933; Edward Gibbon, by C. Dawson, 1934; Edward Gibbon and His Age, by Edmund Blunden, 1935; Robert W. Mowat, Edward Gibbon, 1936.

MEMOIRS

OF

MY LIFE AND WRITINGS

In the fifty-second year of my age, after the completion of an arduous and successful work, I now propose to employ some moments of my leisure in reviewing the simple transactions of a private and literary life. Truth, naked, unblushing truth, the first virtue of more serious history, must be the sole recommendation of this personal narrative. The style shall be simple and familiar: but style is the image of character; and the habits of correct writing may produce, without labour or design, the appearance of art and study. My own amusement is my motive, and will be my reward: and if these sheets are communicated to some discreet and indulgent friends, they will be secreted from the public eye till the author shall be removed beyond the reach of criticism or ridicule.[1]

[1] This passage is found in one only of the six sketches, and in that which seems to have been the first written, and which was laid aside among loose papers. Mr. Gibbon, in his communications with me on the subject of his Memoirs, a subject which he had not mentioned to any other person, expressed a determination of publishing them in his lifetime; and never appears to have departed from that resolution, excepting in one of his letters, in which he intimates a doubt, though rather carelessly, whether in his time, or at any time, they would meet the eye of the public.—In a conversation, however, not long before his death, I suggested to him that, if he should make them a full image of his mind, he would not have nerves to publish them, and therefore that they should be posthumous. He answered, rather eagerly, that he was determined to publish them *in his lifetime.*—SHEFFIELD.

A lively desire of knowing and of recording our ancestors so generally prevails, that it must depend on the influence of some common principle in the minds of men. We seem to have lived in the persons of our forefathers; it is the labour and reward of vanity to extend the term of this ideal longevity. Our imagination is always active to enlarge the narrow circle in which nature has confined us. Fifty or a hundred years may be allotted to an individual; but we step forward beyond death with such hopes as religion and philosophy will suggest; and we fill up the silent vacancy that precedes our birth, by associating ourselves to the authors of our existence. Our calmer judgment will rather tend to moderate, than to suppress, the pride of an ancient and worthy race. The satirist may laugh, the philosopher may preach, but Reason herself will respect the prejudices and habits which have been consecrated by the experience of mankind. Few there are who can sincerely despise in others an advantage of which they are secretly ambitious to partake. The knowledge of our own family from a remote period will be always esteemed as an abstract pre-eminence, since it can never be promiscuously enjoyed; but the longest series of peasants and mechanics would not afford much gratification to the pride of their descendant. We wish to discover our ancestors, but we wish to discover them possessed of ample fortunes, adorned with honourable titles, and holding an eminent rank in the class of hereditary nobles, which has been maintained for the wisest and most beneficial purposes, in almost every climate of the globe, and in almost every modification of political society.

Wherever the distinction of birth is allowed to form a superior order in the state, education and example should always, and will often, produce among them a dignity of sentiment and propriety of conduct, which is guarded from dishonour by their own and the public esteem. If we read of some illustrious line, so ancient that it has no beginning, so worthy that it ought to have no end, we sympathise in its various fortunes; nor can we blame the generous enthusiasm, or even the harmless vanity, of those who are allied to the honours of its name. For my own part, could I draw my pedigree from a general, a statesman, or a celebrated author, I should study their lives with the diligence of filial love. In the investigation of past events our curiosity is stimulated by the immediate or indirect reference to ourselves; but in the estimate of honour we should learn to value the gifts of nature above those of fortune; to esteem in our ancestors the qualities that best promote the interests of society; and to pronounce the descendant of a king less truly noble than the offspring of a man of genius, whose writings will instruct or delight the latest posterity. The family of Confucius is, in my opinion, the most illustrious in the world. After a painful ascent of eight or ten centuries, our barons and princes of Europe are lost in the darkness of the middle ages; but, in the vast equality of the empire of China, the posterity of Confucius have maintained, above two thousand two hundred years, their peaceful honours and perpetual succession. The chief of the family is still revered, by the sovereign and the people, as the lively image of the wisest of mankind. The nobility of the Spencers has been illustrated and enriched by the trophies of Marlborough; but I exhort them to consider the *Fairy Queen* as the most precious jewel of their coronet. Our immortal Fielding was of the younger branch of the Earls of Denbigh, who draw their origin from the Counts of Habsburg, the lineal descendants of Eltrico,[1] in the seventh

---

[1] Or Ethics of Alamania.

century Duke of Alsace. Far different have been the fortunes of the English and German divisions of the family of Habsburg:[1] the former, the knights and sheriffs of Leicestershire, have slowly risen to the dignity of a peerage; the latter, the Emperors of Germany and Kings of Spain, have threatened the liberty of the old, and invaded the treasures of the new world. The successors of Charles the Fifth may disdain their brethren of England; but the romance of *Tom Jones*, that exquisite picture of human manners, will outlive the palace of the Escurial, and the imperial eagle of the house of Austria.

That these sentiments are just, or at least natural, I am the more inclined to believe, as I am not myself interested in the cause; for I can derive from my ancestors neither glory nor shame. Yet a sincere and simple narrative of my own life may amuse some of my leisure hours; but it will subject me, and perhaps with justice, to the imputation of vanity. I may judge, however, from the experience both of past and of the present times, that the public are always curious to know the men who have left behind them any image of their minds: the most scanty accounts of such men are compiled with diligence, and perused with eagerness; and the student of every class may derive a lesson, or an example, from the lives most similar to his own. My name may hereafter be placed among the thousand articles of a Biographia Britannica; and I must be conscious that no one is so well qualified as myself to describe the series of my thoughts and actions. The authority of my masters, of the grave Thuanus, and the philosophic Hume, might be sufficient to justify my design; but it would not be difficult to produce a long list of ancients and moderns, who, in

---

[1] The descent of the Fieldings from the Hapsburg family has been proved to be an error by Mr. J. H. Round.

various forms, have exhibited their own portraits. Such portraits are often the most interesting, and sometimes the only interesting parts of their writings; and, if they be sincere, we seldom complain of the minuteness or prolixity of these personal memorials. The lives of the younger Pliny, of Petrarch, and of Erasmus are expressed in the epistles which they themselves have given to the world. The essays of Montaigne and Sir William Temple bring us home to the houses and bosoms of the authors: we smile without contempt at the headstrong passions of Benvenuto Cellini, and the gay follies of Colley Cibber. The confessions of St. Austin and Rousseau disclose the secrets of the human heart; the commentaries of the learned Huet[1] have survived his evangelical demonstration; and the memoirs of Goldoni are more truly dramatic than his Italian comedies. The heretic and the churchman are strongly marked in the characters and fortunes of Whiston and Bishop Newton; and even the dulness of Michael de Marolles and Anthony Wood acquires some value from the faithful representation of men and manners. That I am equal or superior to some of these, the effects of modesty or affectation cannot force me to dissemble.

My family is originally derived from the county of Kent. The southern district, which borders on Sussex and the sea, was formerly overspread with the great forest Anderida, and even now retains the denomination of the *Weald*, or Woodland. In this district, and in the hundred and parish of Rolvenden, the Gibbons were possessed of lands in the year one thousand three hundred and twenty-six; and the elder branch of the family, with-

---

[1] The " Confessions " of Augustine and Rousseau may easily be secured, but the " Commentaries " of Huet, Bishop of Avranches, are scarce.

out much increase or diminution of property, still adheres
to its native soil.   Fourteen years after the first appearance of his name, John Gibbon is recorded as the Mar-
morarius or architect of King Edward the Third: the
strong and stately castle of Queensborough, which guarded
the entrance of the Medway, was a monument of his skill;
and the grant of an hereditary toll on the passage from
Sandwich to Stonar, in the Isle of Thanet, is the reward
of no vulgar artist.   In the visitations of the heralds the
Gibbons are frequently mentioned: they held the rank
of Esquire in an age when that title was less promiscuously
assumed: one of them, in the reign of Queen Elizabeth,
was captain of the militia of Kent; and a free school, in
the neighbouring town of Benenden, proclaims the charity
and opulence of its founder.   But time, or their own
obscurity, has cast a veil of oblivion over the virtues and
vices of my Kentish ancestors; their character or station
confined them to the labours and pleasures of a rural
life: nor is it in my power to follow the advice of the
poet, in an inquiry after a name—

> " Go! search it there, where to be born, and die,
>   Of rich and poor makes all the history "—[1]

so recent is the institution of our parish registers.   In the
beginning of the seventeenth century a younger branch
of the Gibbons of Rolvenden migrated from the country
to the city; and from this branch I do not blush to
descend.   The law requires some abilities; the church
imposes some restraints; and before our army and navy,
our civil establishments, and India empire, had opened
so many paths of fortune, the mercantile profession was
more frequently chosen by youths of a liberal race and
education, who aspired to create their own independence.

[1] Pope, *Moral Essays*, iii. 287.

Our most respectable families have not disdained the counting-house, or even the shop; their names are inrolled in the Livery and Companies of London; and in England, as well as in the Italian commonwealths, heralds have been compelled to declare that gentility is not degraded by the exercise of trade.

The armorial ensigns which, in the times of chivalry, adorned the crest and shield of the soldier, are now become an empty decoration, which every man who has money to build a carriage may paint according to his fancy on the panels. My family arms are the same which were borne by the Gibbons of Kent in an age when the College of Heralds religiously guarded the distinctions of blood and name: a lion rampant gardant, between three schallop-shells argent, on a field azure.[1] I should not however have been tempted to blazon my coat of arms, were it not connected with a whimsical anecdote.—About the reign of James the First, the three harmless schallop-shells were changed by Edmund Gibbon, Esq., into three *ogresses*, or female cannibals, with a design of stigmatising three ladies, his kinswomen, who had provoked him by an unjust lawsuit. But this singular mode of revenge, for which he obtained the sanction of Sir William Seagar, king-at-arms, soon expired with its author; and, on his own monument in the Temple church, the monsters vanish, and three schallop-shells resume their proper and hereditary place.

Our alliances by marriage it is not disgraceful to mention. The chief honour of my ancestry is James Fiens, Baron Say and Seale, and Lord High Treasurer of England in the reign of Henry the Sixth; from whom by

[1] The father of Lord Chancellor Hardwicke married an heiress of this family of Gibbon. The chancellor's escutcheon in the Temple Hall quarters the arms of Gibbon, as does also that, in Lincoln's Inn Hall, of Charles Yorke, chancellor in 1770.—SHEFFIELD.

the Phelips, the Whetnalls, and the Cromers, I am lineally
descended in the eleventh degree. His dismission and
imprisonment in the Tower were insufficient to appease
the popular clamour; and the treasurer, with his son-in-
law Cromer, was beheaded (1450), after a mock trial, by
the Kentish insurgents. The black list of his offences,
as it is exhibited in Shakspeare, displays the ignorance
and envy of a plebeian tyrant. Besides the vague re-
proaches of selling Maine and Normandy to the dauphin,
the treasurer is specially accused of luxury, for riding
on a foot-cloth, and of treason, for speaking French, the
language of our enemies: " Thou hast most traiterously
corrupted the youth of the realm," says Jack Cade to
the unfortunate lord, " in erecting a grammar-school;
and whereas before, our forefathers had no other books
than the score and the tally, thou hast caused printing to
be used; and, contrary to the king, his crown, and dignity,
thou hast built a paper-mill. It will be proved to thy
face, that thou hast men about thee who usually talk of
a noun and a verb, and such abominable words as no
christian ear can endure to hear." [1] Our dramatic poet is
generally more attentive to character than to history;
and I much fear that the art of printing was not introduced
into England till several years after Lord Say's death:
but of some of these meritorious crimes I should hope to
find my ancestor guilty; and a man of letters may be
proud of his descent from a patron and martyr of learning.

In the beginning of the last century, Robert Gibbon,
Esq., of Rolvenden in Kent [2] (who died in 1618), had a
son of the same name of Robert, who settled in London

[1] 2 *Henry VI.*, IV. vii. 32.

[2] Robert Gibbon, my lineal ancestor in the fifth degree, was captain of the Kentish militia, and, as he died in the year 1618, it may
be presumed that he had appeared in arms at the time of the
Spanish invasion. His wife was Margaret Phillips, daughter of

and became a member of the Clothworkers' Company. His wife was a daughter of the Edgars, who flourished about four hundred years in the county of Suffolk, and produced an eminent and wealthy serjeant-at-law, Sir Gregory Edgar, in the reign of Henry the Seventh. Of the sons of Robert Gibbon (who died in 1643), Matthew did not aspire above the station of a linen-draper in Leadenhall Street; but John has given to the public some curious memorials of his existence, his character, and his family. He was born on the 3rd of November, in the year 1629; his education was liberal, at a grammar-school, and afterwards in Jesus College at Cambridge; and he celebrates the retired content which he enjoyed at Allesborough in Worcestershire, in the house of Thomas Lord Coventry, where he was employed as a domestic tutor. But the spirit of my kinsman soon immerged into more active life; he visited foreign countries as a soldier and a traveller; acquired the knowledge of the French and Spanish languages; passed some time in the isle of Jersey; crossed the Atlantic, and resided upwards of a twelvemonth (1659) in the rising colony of Virginia. In this remote province his taste, or rather passion, for heraldry found a singular gratification at a war-dance of the native Indians. As they moved in measured steps, brandishing their tomahawks, his curious eye contemplated their little shields of bark, and their naked bodies, which were painted with the colours and symbols of his favourite science. " At which (says he) I exceedingly wondered; and concluded that heraldry was ingrafted *naturally* into the sense

Edward Phillips de la Weld in Tenterden, and of Rose, his wife, daughter of George Whitnell, of East Peckham, Esquire. Peckham, the seat of the Whitnells of Kent, is mentioned, not indeed much to its honour, in the *Mémoires du Comte de Grammont*, a classic work, the delight of every man and woman of taste to whom the French language is familiar.

of human race. If so, it deserves a greater esteem than nowadays is put upon it." His return to England after the restoration was soon followed by his marriage—his settlement in a house in St. Catherine's Cloyster, near the Tower, which devolved to my grandfather—and his introduction into the Heralds' College (in 1671) by the style and title of Blue-mantle Pursuivant at Arms. In this office he enjoyed near fifty years the rare felicity of uniting, in the same pursuit, his duty and inclination: his name is remembered in the college, and many of his letters are still preserved. Several of the most respectable characters of the age, Sir William Dugdale, Mr. Ashmole, Dr. John Betts, and Dr. Nehemiah Grew, were his friends; and in the society of such men, John Gibbon may be recorded without disgrace as the member of an astrological club. The study of hereditary honours is favourable to the royal prerogative; and my kinsman, like most of his family, was a high Tory both in church and state. In the latter end of the reign of Charles the Second his pen was exercised in the cause of the Duke of York: the Republican faction he most cordially detested; and as each animal is conscious of its proper arms, the herald's revenge was emblazoned on a most diabolical escutcheon. But the triumph of the Whig government checked the preferment of Blue-mantle; and he was even suspended from his office till his tongue could learn to pronounce the oath of abjuration. His life was prolonged to the age of ninety; and in the expectation of the inevitable though uncertain hour, he wishes to preserve the blessings of health, competence, and virtue. In the year 1682 he published at London his *Introductio ad Latinam Blasoniam*,[1] an original attempt, which Camden had desiderated, to define, in a Roman idiom, the terms and

[1] Introduction to Heraldic Latin.

attributes of a Gothic institution. It is not two years
since I acquired, in a foreign land, some domestic intelligence of my own family; and this intelligence was
conveyed to Switzerland from the heart of Germany. I
had formed an acquaintance with Mr. *Langer,* a lively
and ingenious scholar, while he resided at Lausanne as
preceptor to the Hereditary Prince of *Brunswick.* On
his return to his proper station of Librarian to the Ducal
Library of Wolfenbuttel, he accidentally found among
some literary rubbish a small old English volume of
heraldry, inscribed with the name of *John Gibbon.* From
the title only Mr. *Langer* judged that it might be an
acceptable present to his friend; and he judged rightly.
His manner is quaint and affected; his order is confused:
but he displays some wit, more reading, and still more
enthusiasm; and if an enthusiast be often absurd, he is
never languid. An English text is perpetually interspersed with Latin sentences in prose and verse; but in
his own poetry he claims an exemption from the laws of
prosody. Amidst a profusion of genealogical knowledge,
my kinsman could not be forgetful of his own name; and
to him I am indebted for almost the whole information
concerning the Gibbon family.[1] From this small work
(a duodecimo of one hundred and sixty-five pages) the
author expected immortal fame; and, at the conclusion
of his labour, he sings, in a strain of self-exultation—

> " Usque huc corrigitur Romana Blasonia per me;
>   Verborumque dehinc barbara forma cadat.
> Hic liber, in meritum si forsitan incidet usum,
>   Testis ritè meæ sedulitatis erit.
> Quicquid agat Zoilus, ventura fatebitur ætas
>   Artis quòd fueram non Clypearis inops." [2]

[1] Mr. Gibbon seems, after this was written, to have collected much
additional information respecting his family; as appears from a
number of manuscripts in my possession.—SHEFFIELD.

[2] Henceforward heraldic Latin is to be corrected by my rules:

Such are the hopes of authors! In the failure of those hopes John Gibbon has not been the first of his profession, and very possibly may not be the last of his name. His brother, Matthew Gibbon, the draper, had one daughter and two sons—my grandfather Edward, who was born in the year 1666, and Thomas, afterwards Dean of Carlisle. According to the mercantile creed, that the best book is a profitable ledger, the writings of John the herald would be much less precious than those of his nephew Edward: but an author professes at least to write for the public benefit; and the slow balance of trade can be pleasing to those persons only to whom it is advantageous. The successful industry of my grandfather raised him above the level of his immediate ancestors; he appears to have launched into various and extensive dealings: even his opinions were subordinate to his interest; and I find him in Flanders clothing King William's troops, while he would have contracted with more pleasure, though not perhaps at a cheaper rate, for the service of King James. During his residence abroad, his concerns at home were managed by his mother Hester, an active and notable woman. Her second husband was a widower of the name of Acton: they united the children of their first nuptials. After his marriage with the daughter of Richard Acton, goldsmith in Leadenhall Street, he gave his own sister to Sir Whitmore Acton, of Aldenham; and I am thus connected, by a triple alliance, with that ancient and loyal family of Shropshire baronets. It consisted about that time of seven brothers, all of gigantic stature; one of whom, a pigmy of six feet two inches, confessed himself

from this time debased forms of words will cease to be. This book, if perchance it come into the authority it merits, will be duly an evidence of my diligence. Whatever Zoilus, the bitter critic, may urge, the coming age will confess that I was not destitute of the art of defence.

the last and the least of the seven; adding, in the true spirit of party, that such men were not born since the Revolution.   Under the Tory administration of the four last years of Queen Anne (1710-1714), Mr. Edward Gibbon was appointed one of the Commissioners of the Customs; he sat at that board with Prior: but the merchant was better qualified for his station than the poet; since Lord Bolingbroke has been heard to declare that he had never conversed with a man who more clearly understood the commerce and finances of England.   In the year 1716 he was elected one of the directors of the South Sea Company; and his books exhibited the proof that, before his acceptance of this fatal office, he had acquired an independent fortune of sixty thousand pounds.

But his fortune was overwhelmed in the shipwreck of the year twenty, and the labours of thirty years were blasted in a single day.   Of the use or abuse of the South Sea scheme, of the guilt or innocence of my grandfather and his brother directors, I am neither a competent nor a disinterested judge.   Yet the equity of modern times must condemn the violent and arbitrary proceedings, which would have disgraced the cause of justice, and would render injustice still more odious.   No sooner had the nation awakened from its golden dream than a popular and even a parliamentary clamour demanded their victims: but it was acknowledged on all sides that the South Sea Directors, however guilty, could not be touched by any known laws of the land.   The speech of Lord Molesworth, the author of *The State of Denmark*, may show the temper, or rather the intemperance, of the House of Commons.   "Extraordinary crimes (exclaimed that ardent Whig) call aloud for extraordinary remedies.   The Roman lawgivers had not foreseen the possible existence of a parricide: but as soon as the first monster appeared,

he was sown in a sack, and cast headlong into the river;
and I shall be content to inflict the same treatment on the
authors of our present ruin." His motion was not literally
adopted; but a bill of pains and penalties was introduced,
a retroactive statute, to punish the offences, which did not
exist at the time they were committed. Such a pernicious
violation of liberty and law can be excused only by the
most imperious necessity; nor could it be defended on
this occasion by the plea of impending danger or useful
example. The legislature restrained the persons of the
directors, imposed an exorbitant security for their appearance, and marked their characters with a previous note of
ignominy: they were compelled to deliver, upon oath, the
strict value of their estates; and were disabled from making any transfer or alienation of any part of their property.
Against a bill of pains and penalties it is the common right
of every subject to be heard by his counsel at the bar:
they prayed to be heard; their prayer was refused; and
their oppressors, who required no evidence, would listen
to no defence. It had been at first proposed that one-
eighth of their respective estates should be allowed for the
future support of the directors; but it was speciously
urged, that, in the various shades of opulence and guilt,
such an unequal proportion would be too light for many,
and for some might possibly be too heavy. The character
and conduct of each man were separately weighed; but,
instead of the calm solemnity of a judicial inquiry, the
fortune and honour of three and thirty Englishmen were
made the topic of hasty conversation, the sport of a law-
less majority; and the basest member of the committee,
by a malicious word or a silent vote, might indulge
his general spleen or personal animosity. Injury was
aggravated by insult, and insult was embittered by
pleasantry. Allowances of twenty pounds, or one shilling,

were facetiously moved. A vague report that a director had formerly been concerned in *another* project, by which some unknown persons had lost their money, was admitted as a proof of his actual guilt. One man was ruined because he had dropped a foolish speech, that his horses should feed upon gold; another because he was grown so proud, that, one day at the Treasury, he had refused a civil answer to persons much above him. All were condemned, absent and unheard, in arbitrary fines and forfeitures, which swept away the greatest part of their substance. Such bold oppression can scarcely be shielded by the omnipotence of parliament: and yet it may be seriously questioned whether the judges of the South Sea Directors were the true and legal representatives of their country. The first parliament of George the First had been chosen (1715) for three years: the term had elapsed, their trust was expired; and the four additional years (1718-1722), during which they continued to sit, were derived not from the people, but from themselves; from the strong measure of the Septennial Bill, which can only be paralleled by *il serrar di consiglio* of the Venetian history.[1] Yet candour will own that to the same parliament every Englishman is deeply indebted: the Septennial Act, so vicious in its origin, has been sanctioned by time, experience, and the national consent. Its first operation secured the House of Hanover on the throne, and its permanent influence maintains the peace and stability of government. As often as a repeal has been moved in the House of Commons, I have given in its defence a clear and conscientious vote.

My grandfather could not expect to be treated with more lenity than his companions. His Tory principles

---

[1] Compare Daru, *Histoire de Venise*, liv. vi., tom. i., p 515, 520. *Il serrar di consiglio*=the shutting up of the council.

and connections rendered him obnoxious to the ruling powers: his name is reported in a suspicious secret; and his well-known abilities could not plead the excuse of ignorance or error.   In the first proceedings against the South Sea Directors, Mr. Gibbon is one of the few who were taken into custody; and, in the final sentence, the measure of his fine proclaims him eminently guilty.   The total estimate which he delivered on oath to the House of Commons amounted to one hundred and six thousand five hundred and forty-three pounds, five shillings, and sixpence, exclusive of antecedent settlements.   Two different allowances of fifteen and of ten thousand pounds were moved for Mr. Gibbon; but, on the question being put, it was carried without a division for the smaller sum. On these ruins, with the skill and credit of which parliament had not been able to despoil him, my grandfather, at a mature age, erected the edifice of a new fortune: the labours of sixteen years were amply rewarded; and I have reason to believe that the second structure was not much inferior to the first.   He had realised a very considerable property in Sussex, Hampshire, Buckinghamshire, and the New River Company; and had acquired a spacious house,[1] with gardens and lands, at Putney, in Surrey, where he resided in decent hospitality.   He died in December 1736, at the age of seventy; and by his last will, at the expense of Edward, his only son (with whose marriage he was not perfectly reconciled), enriched his two daughters, Catherine and Hester.   The former became the wife of Mr. Edward Elliston: their daughter and heiress, Catherine, was married in the year 1756 to Edward Eliot, Esq. (now Lord Eliot), of Port Eliot, in the county of Cornwall; and their three sons are my nearest male relations on the father's

---

[1] Since inhabited by Mr. Wood, Sir John Shelley, the Duke of Norfolk, etc.—SHEFFIELD.

side.   A life of devotion and celibacy was the choice of my
aunt, Mrs. Hester Gibbon, who, at the age of eighty-five,
still resides in a hermitage at Cliffe, in Northamptonshire,
having long survived her spiritual guide and faithful companion, Mr. William Law, who, at an advanced age, about
the year 1761, died in her house.   In our family he had
left the reputation of a worthy and pious man, who believed
all that he professed, and practised all that he enjoined.
The character of a nonjuror, which he maintained to the
last, is a sufficient evidence of his principles in church and
state; and the sacrifice of interest to conscience will be
always respectable.   His theological writings, which our
domestic connection has tempted me to peruse, preserve
an imperfect sort of life, and I can pronounce with more
confidence and knowledge on the merits of the author.
His last compositions are darkly tinctured by the incomprehensible visions of Jacob Behmen; and his discourse
on the absolute unlawfulness of stage-entertainments is
sometimes quoted for a ridiculous intemperance of sentiment and language—" The actors and spectators must
all be damned: the playhouse is the porch of Hell, the
place of the Devil's abode, where he holds his filthy court
of evil spirits: a play is the Devil's triumph, a sacrifice
performed to his glory, as much as in the heathen temples
of Bacchus or Venus," etc., etc.   But these sallies of
religious frenzy must not extinguish the praise which is
due to Mr. William Law as a wit and a scholar.   His argument on topics of less absurdity is specious and acute, his
manner is lively, his style forcible and clear; and, had not
his vigorous mind been clouded by enthusiasm, he might
be ranked with the most agreeable and ingenious writers
of the times.   While the Bangorian controversy was a
fashionable theme, he entered the lists on the subject of
Christ's kingdom, and the authority of the priesthood:

against the plain account of the sacrament of the Lord's Supper he resumed the combat with Bishop Hoadley, the object of Whig idolatry and Tory abhorrence; and at every weapon of attack and defence, the nonjuror, on the ground which is common to both, approves himself at least equal to the prelate. On the appearance of the *Fable of the Bees*, he drew his pen against the licentious doctrine that private vices are public benefits, and morality as well as religion must join in his applause. Mr. Law's master-work, the *Serious Call*, is still read as a popular and powerful book of devotion. His precepts are rigid, but they are founded on the gospel: his satire is sharp, but it is drawn from the knowledge of human life; and many of his portraits are not unworthy of the pen of La Bruyere. If he finds a spark of piety in his reader's mind, he will soon kindle it to a flame; and a philosopher must allow that he exposes, with equal severity and truth, the strange contradiction between the faith and practice of the Christian world. Under the names of Flavia and Miranda he has admirably described my two aunts—the heathen and the Christian sister.

My father, Edward Gibbon, was born in October 1707: at the age of thirteen he could scarcely feel that he was disinherited by Act of Parliament; and, as he advanced towards manhood, new prospects of fortune opened to his view. A parent is most attentive to supply in his children the deficiencies of which he is conscious in himself: my grandfather's knowledge was derived from a strong understanding, and the experience of the ways of men; but my father enjoyed the benefits of a liberal education as a scholar and a gentleman. At Westminster School, and afterwards at Emmanuel College in Cambridge, he passed through a regular course of academical discipline; and the care of his learning and morals was entrusted to his private tutor, the same Mr. William Law. But the mind of a saint is above or below the present world; and while the pupil proceeded on his travels, the tutor remained at Putney, the much-honoured friend and spiritual director of the whole family. My father resided some time at Paris to acquire the fashionable exercises; and as his temper was warm and social, he indulged in those pleasures for which the strictness of his former education had given him a keener relish. He afterwards visited several provinces of France; but his excursions were neither long nor remote; and the slender knowledge which he had gained of the French language was gradually obliterated. His passage through Besançon is marked by a singular consequence in the chain of human events. In a dangerous illness Mr. Gibbon was attended, at his own request, by one of his kinsmen of the name of Acton, the younger brother of a younger brother, who had applied himself to the study of physic. During the slow recovery of his patient the physician himself was attacked by the malady of love: he married his mistress, renounced his country and religion, settled at Besançon, and became the father of three sons; the eldest of whom, General Acton, is conspicuous in Europe as the principal minister of the King of the Two Sicilies. By an uncle, whom another stroke of fortune had transplanted to Leghorn, he was educated in the naval service of the emperor; and his valour and conduct in the command of the Tuscan frigates protected the retreat of the Spaniards from Algiers. On my father's return to England he was chosen, in the general election of 1734, to serve in parliament for the borough of Petersfield; a burgage tenure, of which my grandfather possessed a weighty share, till he alienated (I know not why) such important property. In the opposition to Sir Robert Walpole and the Pelhams,

prejudice and society connected his son with the Tories
—shall I say Jacobites? or, as they were pleased to style
themselves, the country gentlemen. With them he gave
many a vote; with them he drank many a bottle. Without acquiring the fame of an orator or a statesman, he
eagerly joined in the great opposition which, after a seven
years' chase, hunted down Sir Robert Walpole: and, in
the pursuit of an unpopular minister, he gratified a private
revenge against the oppressor of his family in the South
Sea persecution.

I was born at Putney, in the county of Surrey, the
27th of April, O.S., in the year one thousand seven hundred
and thirty-seven; the first child of the marriage of Edward
Gibbon, Esq., and of Judith Porten.[1] My lot might have
been that of a slave, a savage, or a peasant; nor can I
reflect without pleasure on the bounty of nature, which
cast my birth in a free and civilised country, in an age of
science and philosophy, in a family of honourable rank,
and decently endowed with the gifts of fortune. From
my birth I have enjoyed the right of primogeniture; but
I was succeeded by five brothers and one sister, all of
whom were snatched away in their infancy. My five
brothers, whose names may be found in the parish register
of Putney, I shall not pretend to lament: but from my
childhood to the present hour I have deeply and sincerely
regretted my sister, whose life was somewhat prolonged,

[1] The union to which I owe my birth was a marriage of inclination
and esteem. Mr. James Porten, a merchant of London, resided
with his family at Putney, in a house adjoining to the bridge and
churchyard, where I have passed many happy hours of my childhood. He left one son (the late Sir Stanier Porten) and three
daughters: Catherine, who preserved her maiden name, and of
whom I shall hereafter speak; another daughter married Mr.
Darrel, of Richmond, and left two sons, Edward and Robert; the
youngest of the three sisters was Judith, my mother.

and whom I remember to have seen an amiable infant. The relation of a brother and a sister, especially if they do not marry, appears to me of a very singular nature. It is a familiar and tender friendship with a female, much about our own age; an affection perhaps softened by the secret influence of sex, but pure from any mixture of sensual desire, the sole species of platonic love that can be indulged with truth, and without danger.

At the general election of 1741 Mr. Gibbon and Mr. Delmé stood an expensive and successful contest at Southampton, against Mr. Dummer and Mr. Henly, afterwards Lord Chancellor and Earl of Northington. The Whig candidates had a majority of the resident voters; but the corporation was firm in the Tory interest: a sudden creation of one hundred and seventy new freemen turned the scale; and a supply was readily obtained of respectable volunteers, who flocked from all parts of England to support the cause of their political friends. The new parliament opened with the victory of an opposition which was fortified by strong clamour and strange coalitions. From the event of the first divisions, Sir Robert Walpole perceived that he could no longer lead a majority in the House of Commons, and prudently resigned (after a dominion of one and twenty years) the guidance of the state (1742). But the fall of an unpopular minister was not succeeded, according to general expectation, by a millennium of happiness and virtue: some courtiers lost their places, some patriots lost their characters, Lord Orford's offences vanished with his power; and after a short vibration, the Pelham government was fixed on the old basis of the Whig aristocracy. In the year 1745 the throne and the constitution were attacked by a rebellion which does not reflect much honour on the national spirit; since the English friends

of the Pretender wanted courage to join his standard,
and his enemies (the bulk of the people) allowed him to
advance into the heart of the kingdom. Without daring,
perhaps without desiring, to aid the rebels, my father
invariably adhered to the Tory opposition. In the most
critical season he accepted, for the service of the party,
the office of alderman in the city of London: but the
duties were so repugnant to his inclination and habits,
that he resigned his gown at the end of a few months.
The second parliament in which he sate was prematurely
dissolved (1747): and as he was unable or unwilling to
maintain a second contest for Southampton, the life of
the senator expired in that dissolution.

The death of a new-born child before that of its parents
may seem an unnatural, but it is strictly a probable
event: since of any given number the greater part are
extinguished before their ninth year, before they possess
the faculties of the mind or body. Without accusing the
profuse waste or imperfect workmanship of nature, I
shall only observe that this unfavourable chance was
multiplied against my infant existence. So feeble was
my constitution, so precarious my life, that, in the baptism
of my brothers, my father's prudence successively repeated
my christian name of Edward, that, in case of the departure
of the eldest son, this patronymic appellation might be
still perpetuated in the family.

—— Uno avulso non deficit alter.[1]

To preserve and to rear so frail a being, the most tender
assiduity was scarcely sufficient; and my mother's
attention was somewhat diverted by her frequent preg-
nancies, by an exclusive passion for her husband, and
by the dissipation of the world, in which his taste and

[1] One torn off, a second will not be lacking.—*Æneid* vi. 143.

authority obliged her to mingle. But the maternal office was supplied by my aunt, Mrs. Catherine Porten; at whose name I feel a tear of gratitude trickling down my cheek. A life of celibacy transferred her vacant affection to her sister's first child: my weakness excited her pity; her attachment was fortified by labour and success: and if there be any, as I trust there are some, who rejoice that I live, to that dear and excellent woman they must hold themselves indebted. Many anxious and solitary days did she consume in the patient trial of every mode of relief and amusement. Many wakeful nights did she sit by my bedside in trembling expectation that each hour would be my last. Of the various and frequent disorders of my childhood my own recollection is dark; nor do I wish to expatiate on so disgusting a topic. Suffice it to say, that while every practitioner, from Sloane and Ward to the Chevalier Taylor, was successively summoned to torture or relieve me, the care of my mind was too frequently neglected for that of my health: compassion always suggested an excuse for the indulgence of the master, or the idleness of the pupil; and the chain of my education was broken as often as I was recalled from the school of learning to the bed of sickness.

As soon as the use of speech had prepared my infant reason for the admission of knowledge, I was taught the arts of reading, writing, and arithmetic. So remote is the date, so vague is the memory of their origin in myself, that, were not the error corrected by analogy, I should be tempted to conceive them as innate. In my childhood I was praised for the readiness with which I could multiply and divide, by memory alone, two sums of several figures: such praise encouraged my growing talent; and had I persevered in this line of application, I might have acquired some fame in mathematical studies.

After this previous institution at home, or at a day-school at Putney, I was delivered at the age of seven into the hands of Mr. John Kirkby, who exercised about eighteen months the office of my domestic tutor. His own words, which I shall here transcribe, inspire in his favour a sentiment of pity and esteem—" During my abode in my native county of Cumberland, in quality of an indigent curate, I used now and then in a summer, when the pleasantness of the season invited, to take a solitary walk to the sea-shore, which lies about two miles from the town where I lived. Here I would amuse myself, one while in viewing at large the agreeable prospect which surrounded me, and another while (confining my sight to nearer objects) in admiring the vast variety of beautiful shells thrown upon the beach; some of the choicest of which I always picked up, to divert my little ones upon my return. One time among the rest, taking such a journey in my head, I sat down upon the declivity of the beach with my face to the sea, which was now come up within a few yards of my feet; when immediately the sad thought of the wretched condition of my family, and the unsuccessfulness of all endeavours to amend it, came crowding into my mind, which drove me into a deep melancholy, and ever and anon forced tears from my eyes." [1]   Distress at last forced him to leave the country. His learning and virtue introduced him to my father; and at Putney he might have found at least a temporary shelter, had not an act of indiscretion again driven him into the world. One day, reading prayers in the parish church, he most unluckily forgot the name of King George: his patron, a loyal subject, dismissed him with some reluctance and a decent reward; and *how* the poor man ended his days I have never been able to learn.   Mr.

[1] From Kirkby's *Automathes.*

John Kirkby is the author of two small volumes; the *Life of Automathes* (London, 1745), and an *English and Latin Grammar* (London, 1746), which, as a testimony of gratitude, he dedicated (November 5th, 1745) to my father. The books are before me: from them the pupil may judge the preceptor; and, upon the whole, his judgment will not be unfavourable. The grammar is executed with accuracy and skill, and I know not whether any better existed at the time in our language: but the *Life of Automathes* aspires to the honours of a philosophical fiction. It is the story of a youth, the son of a shipwrecked exile, who lives alone on a desert island from infancy to the age of manhood. A hind is his nurse; he inherits a cottage, with many useful and curious instruments; some ideas remain of the education of his two first years; some arts are borrowed from the beavers of a neighbouring lake; some truths are revealed in supernatural visions. With these helps, and his own industry, Automathes becomes a self-taught though speechless philosopher, who had investigated with success his own mind, the natural world, the abstract sciences, and the great principles of morality and religion. The author is not entitled to the merit of invention, since he has blended the English story of *Robinson Crusoe* with the Arabian romance of *Hai Ebn Yokhdan*, which he might have read in the Latin version of Pocock. In the *Automathes* I cannot praise either the depth of thought or elegance of style; but the book is not devoid of entertainment or instruction; and among several interesting passages, I would select the discovery of fire, which produces by accidental mischief the discovery of conscience. A man who had thought so much on the subjects of language and education was surely no ordinary preceptor: my childish years, and his hasty departure, prevented me from enjoying the full benefit of his lessons;

but they enlarged my knowledge of arithmetic, and left me a clear impression of the English and Latin rudiments.

In my ninth year (January 1746), in a lucid interval of comparative health, my father adopted the convenient and customary mode of English education; and I was sent to Kingston-upon-Thames, to a school of about seventy boys, which was kept by Dr. Wooddeson and his assistants. Every time I have since passed over Putney Common, I have always noticed the spot where my mother, as we drove along in the coach, admonished me that I was now going into the world, and must learn to think and act for myself. The expression may appear ludicrous; yet there is not, in the course of life, a more remarkable change than the removal of a child from the luxury and freedom of a wealthy house to the frugal diet and strict subordination of a school; from the tenderness of parents, and the obsequiousness of servants, to the rude familiarity of his equals, the insolent tyranny of his seniors, and the rod, perhaps, of a cruel and capricious pedagogue. Such hardships may steel the mind and body against the injuries of fortune; but my timid reserve was astonished by the crowd and tumult of the school; the want of strength and activity disqualified me for the sports of the play-field; nor have I forgotten how often in the year forty-six I was reviled and buffeted for the sins of my Tory ancestors. By the common methods of discipline, at the expense of many tears and some blood, I purchased the knowledge of the Latin syntax: and not long since I was possessed of the dirty volumes of Phædrus and Cornelius Nepos, which I painfully construed and darkly understood. The choice of these authors is not injudicious. The *Lives* of Cornelius Nepos, the friend of Atticus and Cicero, are composed in the style of the purest age: his simplicity is elegant, his brevity copious: he exhibits a series of men and manners;

and with such illustrations as every pedant is not indeed qualified to give, this classic biographer may initiate a young student in the history of Greece and Rome. The use of fables or apologues has been approved in every age from ancient India to modern Europe. They convey in familiar images the truths of morality and prudence; and the most childish understanding (I advert to the scruples of Rousseau) will not suppose either that beasts *do* speak, or that men *may* lie. A fable represents the genuine characters of animals; and a skilful master might extract from Pliny and Buffon some pleasing lessons of natural history, a science well adapted to the taste and capacity of children. The Latinity of Phædrus is not exempt from an alloy of the silver age; but his manner is concise, terse, and sententious: the Thracian slave discreetly breathes the spirit of a freeman; and when the text is sound, the style is perspicuous. But his fables, after a long oblivion, were first published by Peter Pithou, from a corrupt manuscript. The labours of fifty editors confess the defects of the copy, as well as the value of the original; and the schoolboy may have been whipped for misapprehending a passage which Bentley could not restore, and which Burman could not explain.

My studies were too frequently interrupted by sickness; and after a real or nominal residence at Kingston school of near two years, I was finally recalled (December 1747) by my mother's death, which was occasioned, in her thirty-eighth year, by the consequences of her last labour. I was too young to feel the importance of my loss; and the image of her person and conversation is faintly imprinted in my memory. The affectionate heart of my aunt, Catherine Porten, bewailed a sister and a friend; but my poor father was inconsolable, and the transport of grief seemed to threaten his life or his reason. I can never forget the scene of our first interview, some weeks after the fatal event; the awful silence, the room hung with black, the mid-day tapers, his sighs and tears; his praises of my mother, a saint in heaven; his solemn adjuration that I would cherish her memory and imitate her virtues; and the fervour with which he kissed and blessed me as the sole surviving pledge of their loves. The storm of passion insensibly subsided into calmer melancholy. At a convivial meeting of his friends, Mr. Gibbon might affect or enjoy a gleam of cheerfulness; but his plan of happiness was for ever destroyed: and after the loss of his companion he was left alone in a world, of which the business and pleasures were to him irksome or insipid. After some unsuccessful trials he renounced the tumult of London and the hospitality of Putney, and buried himself in the rural or rather rustic solitude of Buriton; from which, during several years, he seldom emerged.

As far back as I can remember, the house, near Putney Bridge and churchyard, of my maternal grandfather, appears in the light of my proper and native home. It was there that I was allowed to spend the greatest part of my time, in sickness or in health, during my school vacations and my parents' residence in London, and finally after my mother's death. Three months after that event, in the spring of 1748, the commercial ruin of her father, Mr. James Porten, was accomplished and declared. As his effects were not sold, nor the house evacuated, till the Christmas following, I enjoyed during the whole year the society of my aunt, without much consciousness of her impending fate. I feel a melancholy pleasure in repeating my obligations to that excellent woman, Mrs. Catherine Porten, the true mother of my mind as well as of my health. Her natural good sense was improved by the perusal of the best books in the English language; and if her reason was sometimes clouded by prejudice, her sentiments were never disguised by hypocrisy or affectation. Her indulgent tenderness, the frankness of her temper, and my innate rising curiosity, soon removed all distance between us: like friends of an equal age, we freely conversed on every topic, familiar or abstruse; and it was her delight and reward to observe the first shoots of my young ideas.[1] Pain and languor were often soothed by the voice of instruction and amusement; and to her kind lessons I ascribe my early and invincible love of reading, which I would not exchange for the treasures of India. I should perhaps be astonished, were it possible to ascertain the date at which a favourite tale was engraved, by frequent repetition, in my memory: the Cavern of the Winds; the Palace of Felicity; and the fatal moment, at the end of three months or centuries, when Prince Adolphus is overtaken by Time, who had worn out so many pair of wings in the pursuit. Before I left Kingston school I was well acquainted with Pope's Homer and the *Arabian Nights' Entertainments*, two books which will always please by the moving picture of human manners and specious miracles: nor was I then capable of discerning that Pope's translation is a portrait endowed with every merit excepting that of likeness to the original. The verses of Pope accustomed my ear to the sound of poetic harmony: in the death of Hector, and the shipwreck of Ulysses, I tasted the new emotions of terror and pity; and seriously disputed with my aunt on the vices and virtues of the heroes of the Trojan war. From Pope's Homer to Dryden's Virgil was an easy

---

[1] Gibbon evidently has in his mind the well-known lines in Thomson's *Seasons* (" Spring," l. 1149)—

" Delightful task to rear the tender thoughts
To teach the young idea how to shoot."

transition; but I know not how, from some fault in the
author, the translator, or the reader, the pious Æneas
did not so forcibly seize on my imagination; and I derived
more pleasure from Ovid's *Metamorphoses*, especially in
the fall of Phaeton, and the speeches of Ajax and Ulysses.
My grandfather's flight unlocked the door of a tolerable
library; and I turned over many English pages of poetry
and romance, of history and travels. Where a title
attracted my eye, without fear or awe I snatched the
volume from the shelf; and Mrs. Porten, who indulged
herself in moral and religious speculations, was more prone
to encourage than to check a curiosity above the strength
of a boy. This year (1748), the twelfth of my age, I shall
note as the most propitious to the growth of my intellectual stature.

The relics of my grandfather's fortune afforded a bare
annuity for his own maintenance; and his daughter, my
worthy aunt, who had already passed her fortieth year,
was left destitute. Her noble spirit scorned a life of
obligation and dependence; and after revolving several
schemes, she preferred the humble industry of keeping
a boarding-house for Westminster School,[1] where she
laboriously earned a competence for her old age. This
singular opportunity of blending the advantages of private
and public education decided my father. After the
Christmas holidays, in January 1749, I accompanied
Mrs. Porten to her new house in College Street; and was
immediately entered in the school, of which Dr. John
Nicoll was at that time head-master. At first I was alone:
but my aunt's resolution was praised; her character was

---

[1] It is said in the family that she was principally induced to
this undertaking by her affection for her nephew, whose weak
constitution required her constant and unremitted attention.—
SHEFFIELD.

esteemed; her friends were numerous and active: in the
course of some years she became the mother of forty or
fifty boys, for the most part of family and fortune; and
as her primitive habitation was too narrow, she built and
occupied a spacious mansion in Dean's Yard. I shall
always be ready to join in the common opinion, that our
public schools, which have produced so many eminent
characters, are the best adapted to the genius and constitution of the English people. A boy of spirit may
acquire a previous and practical experience of the world;
and his playfellows may be the future friends of his heart
or his interest. In a free intercourse with his equals, the
habits of truth, fortitude, and prudence will insensibly
be matured. Birth and riches are measured by the standard
of personal merit; and the mimic scene of a rebellion has
displayed in their true colours the ministers and patriots
of the rising generation. Our seminaries of learning do
not exactly correspond with the precept of a Spartan king,[1]
"that the child should be instructed in the arts which
will be useful to the man;" since a finished scholar may
emerge from the head of Westminster or Eton in total
ignorance of the business and conversation of English
gentlemen in the latter end of the eighteenth century.
But these schools may assume the merit of teaching all
that they pretend to teach, the Latin and Greek languages:
they deposit in the hands of a disciple the keys of two
valuable chests; nor can he complain if they are afterwards lost or neglected by his own fault. The necessity
of leading in equal ranks so many unequal powers of
capacity and application will prolong to eight or ten years
the juvenile studies which might be dispatched in half
that time by the skilful master of a single pupil. Yet even
the repetition of exercise and discipline contributes to fix

[1] Agesilaus.

in a vacant mind the verbal science of grammar and
prosody; and the private or voluntary student, who
possesses the sense and spirit of the classics, may offend,
by a false quantity, the scrupulous ear of a well-flogged
critic.   For myself, I must be content with a very small
share of the civil and literary fruits of a public school.
In the space of two years (1749, 1750), interrupted by
danger and debility, I painfully climbed into the third
form: and my riper age was left to acquire the beauties
of the Latin, and the rudiments of the Greek tongue.
Instead of audaciously mingling in the sports, the quarrels,
and the connections of our little world, I was still cherished
at home under the maternal wing of my aunt; and my
removal from Westminster long preceded the approach
of manhood.

The violence and variety of my complaints, which
had excused my frequent absence from Westminster
School, at length engaged Mrs. Porten, with the advice
of physicians, to conduct me to Bath: at the end of
the Michaelmas vacation (1750) she quitted me with
reluctance, and I remained several months under the
care of a trusty maid-servant.   A strange nervous
affection, which alternately contracted my legs, and
produced, without any visible symptoms, the most
excruciating pain, was ineffectually opposed by the
various methods of bathing and pumping.   From Bath
I was transported to Winchester, to the house of a
physician; and after the failure of his medical skill, we
had again recourse to the virtues of the Bath waters.
During the intervals of these fits I moved with my father
to Buriton and Putney; and a short unsuccessful trial
was attempted to renew my attendance at Westminster
School.   But my infirmities could not be reconciled with
the hours and discipline of a public seminary; and instead

of a domestic tutor, who might have watched the favourable moments, and gently advanced the progress of my learning, my father was too easily content with such occasional teachers as the different places of my residence could supply. I was never forced, and seldom was I persuaded, to admit these lessons: yet I read with a clergyman at Bath some odes of Horace, and several episodes of Virgil, which gave me an imperfect and transient enjoyment of the Latin poets. It might now be apprehended that I should continue for life an illiterate cripple: but, as I approached my sixteenth year, nature displayed in my favour her mysterious energies: my constitution was fortified and fixed; and my disorders, instead of growing with my growth and strengthening with my strength, most wonderfully vanished. I have never possessed or abused the insolence of health: but since that time few persons have been more exempt from real or imaginary ills; and, till I am admonished by the gout, the reader will no more be troubled with the history of my bodily complaints. My unexpected recovery again encouraged the hope of my education; and I was placed at Esher, in Surrey, in the house of the Reverend Mr. Philip Francis, in a pleasant spot, which promised to unite the various benefits of air, exercise, and study (January 1752). The translator of Horace might have taught me to relish the Latin poets, had not my friends discovered in a few weeks that he preferred the pleasures of London to the instruction of his pupils. My father's perplexity at this time, rather than his prudence, was urged to embrace a singular and desperate measure. Without preparation or delay he carried me to Oxford; and I was matriculated in the university as a gentleman-commoner of Magdalen College before I had accomplished the fifteenth year of my age (April 3, 1752).

The curiosity which had been implanted in my infant mind was still alive and active; but my reason was not sufficiently informed to understand the value, or to lament the loss, of three precious years from my entrance at Westminster to my admission at Oxford. Instead of repining at my long and frequent confinement to the chamber or the couch, I secretly rejoiced in those infirmities, which delivered me from the exercises of the school and the society of my equals. As often as I was tolerably exempt from danger and pain, reading, free desultory reading, was the employment and comfort of my solitary hours. At Westminster, my aunt sought only to amuse and indulge me; in my stations at Bath and Winchester, at Buriton and Putney, a false compassion respected my sufferings; and I was allowed, without control or advice, to gratify the wanderings of an unripe taste. My indiscriminate appetite subsided by degrees in the *historic* line: and since philosophy has exploded all innate ideas and natural propensities, I must ascribe this choice to the assiduous perusal of the *Universal History*, as the octavo volumes successively appeared. This unequal work, and a treatise of Hearne, the *Ductor Historicus*,[1] referred and introduced me to the Greek and Roman historians, to as many at least as were accessible to an English reader. All that I could find were greedily devoured, from Littlebury's lame Herodotus, and Spelman's valuable Xenophon, to the pompous folios of Gordon's Tacitus, and a ragged Procopius of the beginning of the last century. The cheap acquisition of so much knowledge confirmed my dislike to the study of languages; and I argued with Mrs. Porten, that, were I master of Greek and Latin, I must interpret to myself

---

[1] *Ductor Historicus, or a Short System of Universal History*, etc., by Thomas Hearne, Oxford, 1704, 8vo. 2 vols.

in English the thoughts of the original, and that such extemporary versions must be inferior to the elaborate translations of professed scholars; a silly sophism, which could not easily be confuted by a person ignorant of any other language than her own. From the ancient I leaped to the modern world: many crude lumps of Speed, Rapin, Mezeray, Davila, Machiavel, Father Paul, Bower, etc., I devoured like so many novels; and I swallowed with the same voracious appetite the descriptions of India and China, of Mexico and Peru.

My first introduction to the historic scenes which have since engaged so many years of my life must be ascribed to an accident. In the summer of 1751 I accompanied my father on a visit to Mr. Hoare's, in Wiltshire; but I was less delighted with the beauties of Stourhead than with discovering in the library a common book, the *Continuation of Echard's Roman History*, which is indeed executed with more skill and taste than the previous work. To me the reigns of the successors of Constantine were absolutely new; and I was immersed in the passage of the Goths over the Danube, when the summons of the dinner-bell reluctantly dragged me from my intellectual feast. This transient glance served rather to irritate than to appease my curiosity; and as soon as I returned to Bath I procured the second and third volumes of Howell's *History of the World*, which exhibit the Byzantine period on a larger scale. Mahomet and his Saracens soon fixed my attention; and some instinct of criticism directed me to the genuine sources. Simon Ockley, an original in every sense, first opened my eyes; and I was led from one book to another, till I had ranged round the circle of Oriental history. Before I was sixteen I had exhausted all that could be learned in English of the Arabs and Persians, the Tartars and Turks; and the same ardour urged me to guess at the French of d'Herbelot, and to construe the barbarous Latin of Pocock's Abulfaragius. Such vague and multifarious reading could not teach me to think, to write, or to act; and the only principle that darted a ray of light into the indigested chaos was an early and rational application to the order of time and place. The maps of Cellarius and Wells imprinted in my mind the picture of ancient geography: from Strauchius [1] I imbibed the elements of chronology: the Tables of Helvicus and Anderson, the Annals of Usher and Prideaux, distinguished the connection of events, and engraved the multitude of names and dates in a clear and indelible series. But in the discussion of the first ages I over-leaped the bounds of modesty and use. In my childish balance I presumed to weigh the systems of Scaliger and Petavius, of Marsham and Newton, which I could seldom study in the originals; and my sleep has been disturbed by the difficulty of reconciling the Septuagint with the Hebrew computation. I arrived at Oxford with a stock of erudition that might have puzzled a doctor, and a degree of ignorance of which a schoolboy would have been ashamed.

At the conclusion of this first period of my life I am tempted to enter a protest against the trite and lavish praise of the happiness of our boyish years, which is echoed with so much affectation in the world. That happiness I have never known, that time I have never regretted; and were my poor aunt still alive, she would bear testimony to the early and constant uniformity of my sentiments. It will indeed be replied that *I* am not a competent judge; that pleasure is incompatible with pain; that joy is excluded from sickness; and that the felicity of a schoolboy consists in the perpetual motion of

[1] Egidius Strauchius, not Stranchius as in some editions.

thoughtless and playful agility, in which I was never qualified to excel. My name, it is most true, could never be enrolled among the sprightly race, the idle progeny of Eton or Westminster,

> " Who foremost might delight to cleave,
> With pliant arm, the glassy wave,
> Or urge the flying ball." [1]

The poet may gaily describe the short hours of recreation; but he forgets the daily tedious labours of the school, which is approached each morning with anxious and reluctant steps.

A traveller who visits Oxford or Cambridge is surprised and edified by the apparent order and tranquillity that prevail in the seats of the English muses. In the most celebrated universities of Holland, Germany, and Italy, the students, who swarm from different countries, are loosely dispersed in private lodgings at the houses of the burghers: they dress according to their fancy and fortune; and in the intemperate quarrels of youth and wine, their *swords*, though less frequently than of old, are sometimes stained with each other's blood. The use of arms is banished from our English universities; the uniform habit of the academics, the square cap and black gown, is adapted to the civil and even clerical profession; and from the doctor in divinity to the undergraduate, the degrees of learning and age are externally distinguished. Instead of being scattered in a town, the students of Oxford and Cambridge are united in colleges; their maintenance is provided at their own expense, or that of the founders; and the stated hours of the hall and chapel represent the discipline of a regular, and, as it were,

[1] Gray's *Eton College*, l. 25.

a religious community. The eyes of the traveller are attracted by the size or beauty of the public edifices: and the principal colleges appear to be so many palaces, which a liberal nation has erected and endowed for the habitation of science. My own introduction to the university of Oxford forms a new æra in my life; and at the distance of forty years I still remember my first emotions of surprise and satisfaction. In my fifteenth year I felt myself suddenly raised from a boy to a man: the persons whom I respected as my superiors in age and academical rank entertained me with every mark of attention and civility; and my vanity was flattered by the velvet cap and silk gown which distinguish a gentleman-commoner from a plebeian student. A decent allowance, more money than a schoolboy had ever seen, was at my own disposal; and I might command, among the tradesmen of Oxford, an indefinite and dangerous latitude of credit. A key was delivered into my hands, which gave me the free use of a numerous and learned library: my apartment consisted of three elegant and well-furnished rooms in the new building, a stately pile, of Magdalen College; and the adjacent walks, had they been frequented by Plato's disciples, might have been compared to the Attic shade on the banks of the Ilissus. Such was the fair prospect of my entrance (April 3, 1752) into the university of Oxford.

A venerable prelate, whose taste and erudition must reflect honour on the society in which they were formed, has drawn a very interesting picture of his academical life. "I was educated (says Bishop Lowth) in the UNIVERSITY OF OXFORD. I enjoyed all the advantages, both public and private, which that famous seat of learning so largely affords. I spent many years in that illustrious society, in a well-regulated course of useful discipline and studies, and in the agreeable and improving commerce of gentlemen and of scholars; in a society where emulation without envy, ambition without jealousy, contention without animosity, incited industry, and awakened genius; where a liberal pursuit of knowledge, and a genuine freedom of thought, was raised, encouraged, and pushed forward by example, by commendation, and by authority. I breathed the same atmosphere that the HOOKERS, the CHILLINGWORTHS, and the LOCKES had breathed before; whose benevolence and humanity were as extensive as their vast genius and comprehensive knowledge; who always treated their adversaries with civility and respect; who made candour, moderation, and liberal judgment as much the rule and law as the subject of their discourse. And do you reproach me with my education in this place, and with my relation to this most respectable body, which I shall always esteem my greatest advantage and my highest honour?" I transcribe with pleasure this eloquent passage, without examining what benefits or what rewards were derived by Hooker, or Chillingworth, or Locke, from their academical institution; without inquiring whether in this angry controversy the spirit of Lowth himself is purified from the intolerant zeal which Warburton had ascribed to the genius of the place. It may indeed be observed that the atmosphere of Oxford did not agree with Mr. Locke's constitution, and that the philosopher justly despised the academical bigots who expelled his person and condemned his principles. The expression of gratitude is a virtue and a pleasure: a liberal mind will delight to cherish and celebrate the memory of its parents; and the teachers of science are the parents of the mind. I applaud the filial piety which it is impossible for me to imitate; since I must not confess an imaginary debt, to assume the merit of a just or generous

retribution.   To the university of Oxford I acknowledge
no obligation; and she will as cheerfully renounce me for
a son, as I am willing to disclaim her for a mother.   I
spent fourteen months at Magdalen College; they proved
the fourteen months the most idle and unprofitable of my
whole life: the reader will pronounce between the school
and the scholar, but I cannot affect to believe that nature
had disqualified me for all literary pursuits.   The specious
and ready excuse of my tender age, imperfect preparation,
and hasty departure, may doubtless be alleged; nor do
I wish to defraud such excuses of their proper weight.
Yet in my sixteenth year I was not devoid of capacity or
application; even my childish reading had displayed an
early though blind propensity for books; and the shallow
flood might have been taught to flow in a deep channel
and a clear stream.   In the discipline of a well-constituted
academy, under the guidance of skilful and vigilant
professors, I should gradually have risen from translations
to originals, from the Latin to the Greek classics, from
dead languages to living science: my hours would have
been occupied by useful and agreeable studies, the wanderings of fancy would have been restrained, and I should
have escaped the temptations of idleness, which finally
precipitated my departure from Oxford.

Perhaps in a separate annotation I may coolly examine
the fabulous and real antiquities of our sister universities,
a question which has kindled such fierce and foolish
disputes among their fanatic sons.   In the meanwhile it
will be acknowledged that these venerable bodies are
sufficiently old to partake of all the prejudices and
infirmities of age.   The schools of Oxford and Cambridge
were founded in a dark age of false and barbarous science;
and they are still tainted with the vices of their origin.
Their primitive discipline was adapted to the education

of priests and monks; and the government still remains in the hands of the clergy, an order of men whose manners are remote from the present world, and whose eyes are dazzled by the light of philosophy. The legal incorporation of these societies by the charters of popes and kings had given them a monopoly of the public instruction; and the spirit of monopolists is narrow, lazy, and oppressive; their work is more costly and less productive than that of independent artists; and the new improvements so eagerly grasped by the competition of freedom are admitted with slow and sullen reluctance in those proud corporations, above the fear of a rival, and below the confession of an error. We may scarcely hope that any reformation will be a voluntary act; and so deeply are they rooted in law and prejudice, that even the omnipotence of parliament would shrink from an inquiry into the state and abuses of the two universities.

The use of academical degrees, as old as the thirteenth century, is visibly borrowed from the mechanic corporations; in which an apprentice, after serving his time, obtains a testimonial of his skill, and a licence to practise his trade and mystery. It is not my design to depreciate those honours, which could never gratify or disappoint my ambition; and I should applaud the institution, if the degrees of bachelor or licentiate were bestowed as the reward of manly and successful study: if the name and rank of doctor or master were strictly reserved for the professors of science who have approved their title to the public esteem.

In all the universities of Europe, excepting our own, the languages and sciences are distributed among a numerous list of effective professors; the students, according to their taste, their calling, and their diligence, apply themselves to the proper masters; and in the annual repetition of public and private lectures, these masters are assiduously employed. Our curiosity may inquire what number of professors has been instituted at Oxford? (for I shall now confine myself to my own university); by whom are they appointed, and what may be the probable chances of merit or incapacity? how many are stationed to the three faculties, and how many are left for the liberal arts? what is the form, and what the substance, of their lessons? But all these questions are silenced by one short and singular answer, " That in the university of Oxford the greater part of the public professors have for these many years given up altogether even the pretence of teaching." Incredible as the fact may appear, I must rest my belief on the positive and impartial evidence of a master of moral and political wisdom, who had himself resided at Oxford. Dr. Adam Smith assigns as the cause of their indolence, that, instead of being paid by voluntary contributions, which would urge them to increase the number, and to deserve the gratitude of their pupils, the Oxford professors are secure in the enjoyment of a fixed stipend, without the necessity of labour, or the apprehension of control. It has indeed been observed, nor is the observation absurd, that, excepting in experimental sciences, which demand a costly apparatus and a dexterous hand, the many valuable treatises that have been published on every subject of learning may now supersede the ancient mode of oral instruction. Were this principle true in its utmost latitude, I should only infer that the offices and salaries which are become useless ought without delay to be abolished. But there still remains a material difference between a book and a professor; the hour of the lecture enforces attendance; attention is fixed by the presence, the voice, and the occasional questions of the teacher; the most idle will carry something away; and the more diligent will compare the instructions which they have heard in the school with the volumes which they peruse in their chamber. The advice of a skilful professor will adapt a course of reading to every mind and every situation; his authority will discover, admonish, and at last chastise the negligence of his disciples; and his vigilant inquiries will ascertain the steps of their literary progress. Whatever science he professes he may illustrate in a series of discourses, composed in the leisure of his closet, pronounced on public occasions, and finally delivered to the press. I observe with pleasure, that in the university of Oxford Dr. Lowth, with equal eloquence and erudition, has executed this task in his incomparable *Prælectiones* on the Poetry of the Hebrews.

The college of St. Mary Magdalen was founded in the fifteenth century by Wainfleet, Bishop of Winchester; and now consists of a president, forty fellows, and a number of inferior students. It is esteemed one of the largest and most wealthy of our academical corporations, which may be compared to the Benedictine abbeys of catholic countries; and I have loosely heard that the estates belonging to Magdalen College, which are leased by those indulgent landlords at small quit-rents and occasional fines, might be raised, in the hands of private avarice, to an annual revenue of nearly thirty thousand pounds. Our colleges are supposed to be schools of science, as well as of education; nor is it unreasonable to expect that a body of literary men, devoted to a life of celibacy, exempt from the care of their own subsistence, and amply provided with books, should devote their leisure to the prosecution of study, and that some effects of their studies should be manifested to the world. The shelves of their library groan under the weight of the Benedictine folios, of the editions of the fathers, and the collections of the middle ages, which have issued from the single abbey of St. Germain de Préz at Paris. A composition of genius must be the offspring of one mind; but such works of industry as may be divided among many hands, and must be continued during many years, are the peculiar province of a laborious community. If I inquire into the manufactures of the monks of Magdalen, if I extend the inquiry to the other colleges of Oxford and Cambridge, a silent blush, or a scornful frown, will be the only reply. The fellows or monks of my time were decent easy men, who supinely enjoyed the gifts of the founder: their days were filled by a series of uniform employments; the chapel and the hall, the coffee-house and the common room, till they retired, weary and well satisfied, to a long slumber. From the toil of reading, or thinking, or writing, they had absolved their conscience; and the first shoots of learning and ingenuity withered on the ground, without yielding any fruits to the owners or the public. As a gentleman-commoner, I was admitted to the society of the fellows, and fondly expected that some questions of literature would be the amusing and instructive topics of their discourse. Their conversation stagnated in a round of college business, Tory politics, personal anecdotes, and private scandal: their dull and deep potations excused the brisk intemperance of youth: and their constitutional toasts were not expressive of the most lively loyalty for the house of Hanover. A general election was now approaching: the great Oxfordshire contest already blazed with all the malevolence of party zeal. Magdalen College was devoutly attached to the old interest! and the names of Wenman and Dashwood were more frequently pronounced than those of Cicero and Chrysostom. The example of the senior fellows could not inspire the undergraduates with a liberal spirit or studious emulation; and I cannot describe, as I never knew, the discipline of college. Some duties may possibly have been imposed on the poor scholars, whose ambition aspired to the peaceful honours of a fellowship (*ascribi quietis ordinibus . . . Deorum*);[1] but no independent members were admitted below the rank of a gentleman-commoner, and our velvet cap was the cap of liberty. A tradition prevailed that some of our predecessors had spoken Latin declamations in the hall; but of this ancient custom no vestige remained: the obvious methods of public exercises and examinations were totally unknown; and I have never heard that either the president or the society interfered in the private economy of the tutors and their pupils.

The silence of the Oxford professors, which deprives the youth of public instruction, is imperfectly supplied by the tutors, as they are styled, of the several colleges. Instead of confining themselves to a single science, which had satisfied the ambition of Burman or Bernouilli, they teach, or promise to teach, either history, or mathematics, or ancient literature, or moral philosophy; and as it is possible that they may be defective in all, it is highly probable that of some they will be ignorant. They are paid, indeed, by private contributions; but their appointment depends on the head of the house: their diligence is voluntary, and will consequently be languid, while the pupils themselves, or their parents, are not indulged in the liberty of choice or change. The first tutor into whose hands I was resigned appears to have been one of the best of the tribe: Dr. Waldegrave was a learned and pious man, of a mild disposition, strict morals, and abstemious life, who seldom mingled in the politics or

[1] To be admitted into the dignified assembly of the Gods.—Horace, *Odes*, III. iii. 1. 35.

the jollity of the college. But his knowledge of the world was confined to the university; his learning was of the last, rather than of the present age; his temper was indolent; his faculties, which were not of the first rate, had been relaxed by the climate, and he was satisfied, like his fellows, with the slight and superficial discharge of an important trust. As soon as my tutor had sounded the insufficiency of his disciple in school-learning, he proposed that we should read every morning, from ten to eleven, the comedies of Terence. The sum of my improvement in the university of Oxford is confined to three or four Latin plays; and even the study of an elegant classic, which might have been illustrated by a comparison of ancient and modern theatres, was reduced to a dry and literal interpretation of the author's text. During the first weeks I constantly attended these lessons in my tutor's room; but as they appeared equally devoid of profit and pleasure, I was once tempted to try the experiment of a formal apology. The apology was accepted with a smile. I repeated the offence with less ceremony; the excuse was admitted with the same indulgence: the slightest motive of laziness or indisposition, the most trifling avocation at home or abroad, was allowed as a worthy impediment; nor did my tutor appear conscious of my absence or neglect. Had the hour of lecture been constantly filled, a single hour was a small portion of my academic leisure. No plan of study was recommended for my use; no exercises were prescribed for his inspection; and, at the most precious season of youth, whole days and weeks were suffered to elapse without labour or amusement, without advice or account. I should have listened to the voice of reason and of my tutor; his mild behaviour had gained my confidence. I preferred his society to that of the younger students;

and in our evening walks to the top of Heddington Hill we freely conversed on a variety of subjects. Since the days of Pocock and Hyde, Oriental learning has always been the pride of Oxford, and I once expressed an inclination to study Arabic. His prudence discouraged this childish fancy; but he neglected the fair occasion of directing the ardour of a curious mind. During my absence in the summer vacation Dr. Waldegrave accepted a college living at Washington in Sussex, and on my return I no longer found him at Oxford. From that time I have lost sight of my first tutor; but at the end of thirty years (1781) he was still alive; and the practice of exercise and temperance had entitled him to a healthy old age.

The long recess between the Trinity and Michaelmas terms empties the colleges of Oxford, as well as the courts of Westminster. I spent at my father's house at Buriton in Hampshire the two months of August and September. It is whimsical enough, that as soon as I left Magdalen College my taste for books began to revive; but it was the same blind and boyish taste for the pursuit of exotic history. Unprovided with original learning, unformed in the habits of thinking, unskilled in the arts of composition, I resolved—to write a book. The title of this first essay, *The Age of Sesostris*, was perhaps suggested by Voltaire's *Age of Louis XIV.*, which was new and popular; but my sole object was to investigate the probable date of the life and reign of the conqueror of Asia. I was then enamoured of Sir John Marsham's *Canon Chronicus;* an elaborate work, of whose merits and defects I was not yet qualified to judge. According to his specious though narrow plan, I settled my hero about the time of Solomon, in the tenth century before the Christian era. It was therefore incumbent on me, unless I would adopt Sir Isaac Newton's shorter chronology, to remove a formidable objection; and my solution, for a youth of fifteen, is not devoid of ingenuity. In his version of the Sacred Books, Manetho the high priest has identified Sethosis, or Sesostris, with the elder brother of Danaus, who landed in Greece, according to the Parian Marble, fifteen hundred and ten years before Christ. But in my supposition the high priest is guilty of a voluntary error: flattery is the prolific parent of falsehood. Manetho's history of Egypt is dedicated to Ptolemy Philadelphus, who derived a fabulous or illegitimate pedigree from the Macedonian kings of the race of Hercules. Danaus is the ancestor of Hercules; and after the failure of the elder branch, his descendants, the Ptolemies, are the sole representatives of the royal family, and may claim by inheritance the kingdom which they hold by conquest. Such were my juvenile discoveries; at a riper age I no longer presume to connect the Greek, the Jewish, and the Egyptian antiquities, which are lost in a distant cloud. Nor is this the only instance in which the belief and knowledge of the child are superseded by the more rational ignorance of the man. During my stay at Buriton my infant labour was diligently prosecuted, without much interruption from company or country diversions; and I already heard the music of public applause. The discovery of my own weakness was the first symptom of taste. On my return to Oxford the *Age of Sesostris* was wisely relinquished; but the imperfect sheets remained twenty years at the bottom of a drawer, till, in a general clearance of papers (November 1772), they were committed to the flames.

After the departure of Dr. Waldegrave I was transferred, with his other pupils, to his academical heir, whose literary character did not command the respect of the college. Dr. —— well remembered that he had a salary to receive, and only forgot that he had a duty to perform.

Instead of guiding the studies, and watching over the behaviour of his disciple, I was never summoned to attend even the ceremony of a lecture; and, excepting one voluntary visit to his rooms, during the eight months of his titular office the tutor and pupil lived in the same college as strangers to each other. The want of experience, of advice, and of occupation soon betrayed me into some improprieties of conduct, ill-chosen company, late hours, and inconsiderate expense. My growing debts might be secret; but my frequent absence was visible and scandalous: and a tour to Bath, a visit into Buckingham-shire, and four excursions to London in the same winter, were costly and dangerous frolics. They were indeed without a meaning, as without an excuse. The irksome-ness of a cloistered life repeatedly tempted me to wander; but my chief pleasure was that of travelling; and I was too young and bashful to enjoy, like a Manly Oxonian in Town, the pleasures of London. In all these excursions I eloped from Oxford; I returned to college; in a few days I eloped again, as if I had been an independent stranger in a hired lodging, without once hearing the voice of admonition, without once feeling the hand of control. Yet my time was lost, my expenses were multiplied, my behaviour abroad was unknown; folly as well as vice should have awakened the attention of my superiors, and my tender years would have justified a more than ordinary degree of restraint and discipline.

It might at least be expected that an ecclesiastical school should inculcate the orthodox principles of religion. But our venerable mother had contrived to unite the opposite extremes of bigotry and indifference; an heretic, or un-believer, was a monster in her eyes; but she was always, or often, or sometimes, remiss in the spiritual education of her own children. According to the statutes of the university, every student, before he is matriculated, must subscribe his assent to the Thirty-nine Articles of the Church of England, which are signed by more than read, and read by more than believe them. My insufficient age excused me, however, from the immediate performance of this legal ceremony; and the vice-chancellor directed me to return as soon as I should have accomplished my fifteenth year; recommending me, in the meanwhile, to the instruction of my college. My college forgot to instruct; I forgot to return, and was myself forgotten by the first magistrate of the university. Without a single lecture, either public or private, either Christian or Protestant, without any academical subscription, without any episcopal confirmation, I was left by the dim light of my catechism to grope my way to the chapel and communion-table, where I was admitted, without a question how far, or by what means, I might be qualified to receive the sacrament. Such almost incredible neglect was productive of the worst mischiefs. From my childhood I had been fond of religious disputation: my poor aunt has been often puzzled by the mysteries which she strove to believe; nor had the elastic spring been totally broken by the weight of the atmosphere of Oxford. The blind activity of idleness urged me to advance without armour into the dangerous mazes of controversy; and, at the age of sixteen, I bewildered myself in the errors of the Church of Rome.

The progress of my conversion may tend to illustrate at least the history of my own mind. It was not long since Dr. Middleton's free inquiry had sounded an alarm in the theological world: much ink and much gall had been spilt in the defence of the primitive miracles; and the two dullest of their champions were crowned with academic honours by the university of Oxford. The

name of Middleton was unpopular; and his proscription
very naturally led me to peruse his writings, and those of
his antagonists. His bold criticism, which approaches
the precipice of infidelity, produced on my mind a singular
effect; and had I persevered in the communion of Rome,
I should now apply to my own fortune the prediction of
the Sibyl,

—— Via prima salutis,
Quod minimè reris, Graiâ pandetur ab urbe.[1]

The elegance of style and freedom of argument were
repelled by a shield of prejudice. I still revered the
character, or rather the names, of the saints and fathers
whom Dr. Middleton exposes; nor could he destroy my
implicit belief that the gift of miraculous powers was
continued in the church during the first four or five
centuries of Christianity. But I was unable to resist the
weight of historical evidence, that within the same period
most of the leading doctrines of popery were already
introduced in theory and practice: nor was my conclusion
absurd, that miracles are the test of truth, and that the
church must be orthodox and pure which was so often
approved by the visible interposition of the Deity. The
marvellous tales which are so boldly attested by the Basils
and Chrysostoms, the Austins and Jeroms, compelled me
to embrace the superior merits of celibacy, the institution
of the monastic life, the use of the sign of the cross, of holy
oil, and even of images, the invocation of saints, the
worship of relics, the rudiments of purgatory in prayers
for the dead, and the tremendous mystery of the sacrifice
of the body and blood of Christ, which insensibly swelled

---

[1] " Hope, where unlooked for, comes thy toils to crown
Thy road to safety from a Grecian town."
Æneid B. vi. l. 96 (Fairfax Taylor).

into the prodigy of transubstantiation. In these dispositions, and already more than half a convert, I formed an unlucky intimacy with a young gentleman of our college. With a character less resolute, Mr. Molesworth had imbibed the same religious opinions; and some popish books, I know not through what channel, were conveyed into his possession. I read, I applauded, I believed: the English translations of two famous works of Bossuet, Bishop of Meaux, the *Exposition of the Catholic Doctrine*, and the *History of the Protestant Variations*, achieved my conversion, and I surely fell by a noble hand.[1] I have since examined the originals with a more discerning eye, and shall not hesitate to pronounce that Bossuet is indeed a master of all the weapons of controversy. In the *Exposition*, a specious apology, the orator assumes, with consummate art, the tone of candour and simplicity; and the ten-horned monster is transformed, at his magic touch, into the milk-white hind, who must be loved as soon as she is seen. In the *History*, a bold and well-aimed attack, he displays, with a happy mixture of narrative and argument, the faults and follies, the changes and contradictions of our first reformers; whose variations (as he dexterously contends) are the mark of historical error, while the perpetual unity of the Catholic Church is the sign and test of infallible truth. To my present feelings it seems incredible that I should ever believe that I believed in transubstantiation. But my conqueror oppressed me with the sacramental words, " Hoc est corpus meum," [2] and dashed

[1] Mr. Gibbon never talked with me on the subject of his conversion to popery but once: and then he imputed his change to the works of Parsons the Jesuit, who lived in the reign of Elizabeth, and who, he said, had urged all the best arguments in favour of the Roman Catholic religion.—SHEFFIELD.

[2] This is my body.

against each other the figurative half-meanings of the Protestant sects: every objection was resolved into omnipotence; and after repeating at St. Mary's the Athanasian Creed, I humbly acquiesced in the mystery of the real presence.

> " To take up half on trust, and half to try,
>   Name it not faith, but bungling bigotry.
>   Both knave and fool the merchant we may call,
>   To pay great sums, and to compound the small,
> For who would break with Heaven, and would not break for all? " [1]

No sooner had I settled my new religion than I resolved to profess myself a Catholic. Youth is sincere and impetuous; and a momentary glow of enthusiasm had raised me above all temporal considerations.[2]

By the keen Protestants, who would gladly retaliate the example of persecution, a clamour is raised of the increase of popery: and they are always loud to declaim against the toleration of priests and Jesuits who pervert so many of his majesty's subjects from their religion and allegiance. On the present occasion, the fall of one or more of her sons directed this clamour against the university; and it was confidently affirmed that popish missionaries were suffered, under various disguises, to introduce themselves into the colleges of Oxford. But justice obliges me to declare that, as far as relates to myself, this assertion is false; and that I never conversed with a priest, or even with a Papist, till my resolution from books was absolutely fixed. In my last excursion to London I addressed myself to Mr. Lewis, a Roman Catholic bookseller in Russell Street, Covent Garden, who recommended me to a priest,

---

[1] Dryden's *The Hind and the Panther*, l. 141.

[2] He described the letter to his father, announcing his conversion, as written with all the pomp, the dignity, and self-satisfaction of a martyr.—SHEFFIELD.

of whose name and order I am at present ignorant.[1]   In our first interview he soon discovered that persuasion was needless.   After sounding the motives and merits of my conversion, he consented to admit me into the pale of the church; and at his feet on the 8th of June 1753, I solemnly, though privately, abjured the errors of heresy. The seduction of an English youth of family and fortune was an act of as much danger as glory; but he bravely overlooked the danger, of which I was not then sufficiently informed.   " Where a person is reconciled to the see of Rome, or procures others to be reconciled, the offence (says Blackstone) amounts to high treason."   And if the humanity of the age would prevent the execution of this sanguinary statute, there were other laws of a less odious cast, which condemned the priest to perpetual imprisonment, and transferred the proselyte's estate to his nearest relation.   An elaborate controversial epistle, approved by my director, and addressed to my father, announced and justified the step which I had taken.   My father was neither a bigot nor a philosopher; but his affection deplored the loss of an only son; and his good sense was astonished at my strange departure from the religion of my country.   In the first sally of passion he divulged a secret which prudence might have suppressed, and the gates of Magdalen College were for ever shut against my return.   Many years afterwards, when the name of Gibbon was become as notorious as that of Middleton, it was industriously whispered at Oxford that the historian had formerly "turned Papist;" my character stood

---

[1] His name was Baker, a Jesuit, and one of the chaplains of the Sardinian ambassador.   Mr. Gibbon's conversion made some noise; and Mr. Lewis, the Roman Catholic bookseller of Russell Street, Covent Garden, was summoned before the Privy Council, and interrogated on the subject.   This was communicated by Mr. Lewis's son, 1814.—SHEFFIELD.

exposed to the reproach of inconstancy; and this invidious topic would have been handled without mercy by my opponents, could they have separated my cause from that of the university. For my own part, I am proud of an honest sacrifice of interest to conscience. I can never blush if my tender mind was entangled in the sophistry that seduced the acute and manly understandings of CHILLINGWORTH and BAYLE, who afterwards emerged from superstition to scepticism.

While Charles the First governed England, and was himself governed by a Catholic queen, it cannot be denied that the missionaries of Rome laboured with impunity and success in the court, the country, and even the universities. One of the sheep,

———— Whom the grim wolf with privy paw
Daily devours apace, and nothing said,[1]

is Mr. William Chillingworth, Master of Arts, and Fellow of Trinity College, Oxford; who, at the ripe age of twenty-eight years, was persuaded to elope from Oxford, to the English seminary at Douay in Flanders. Some disputes with Fisher, a subtle Jesuit, might first awaken him from the prejudices of education; but he yielded to his own victorious argument, " that there must be somewhere an infallible judge; and that the Church of Rome is the only Christian society which either does or can pretend to that character." After a short trial of a few months Mr. Chillingworth was again tormented by religious scruples: he returned home, resumed his studies, unravelled his mistakes, and delivered his mind from the yoke of authority and superstition. His new creed was built on the principle that the Bible is our sole judge, and private reason our sole interpreter: and he ably maintains this

[1] Milton's *Lycidas*, l. 128.

principle in the *Religion of a Protestant,* a book which, after startling the doctors of Oxford, is still esteemed the most solid defence of the Reformation. The learning, the virtue, the recent merits of the author, entitled him to fair preferment: but the slave had now broken his fetters; and the more he weighed, the less was he disposed to subscribe to the Thirty-nine Articles of the Church of England. In a private letter he declares, with all the energy of language, that he could not subscribe to them without subscribing to his own damnation; and that, if ever he should depart from this immovable resolution, he would allow his friends to think him a madman, or an atheist. As the letter is without a date, we cannot ascertain the number of weeks or months that elapsed between this passionate abhorrence and the Salisbury Register, which is still extant. " Ego Gulielmus Chillingworth, . . . omnibus hisce articulis, . . . et singulis in iisdem contentis, volens et ex animo subscribo, et consensum meum iisdem præbeo. 20 die Julii 1638."[1] But, alas, the chancellor and prebendary of Sarum soon deviated from his own subscription: as he more deeply scrutinised the article of the Trinity, neither scripture nor the primitive fathers could long uphold his orthodox belief; and he could not but confess " that the doctrine of Arius is either a truth, or at least no damnable heresy." From this middle region of the air, the descent of his reason would naturally rest on the firmer ground of the Socinians: and if we may credit a doubtful story, and the popular opinion, his anxious inquiries at last subsided in philosophic indifference. So conspicuous, however,

---

[1] " I, William Chillingworth, to all these articles and to the contents of each among them, hereby willingly subscribe my assent, and intimate my agreement with them—this 20 day of July 1638."

were the candour of his nature and the innocence of his heart, that this apparent levity did not affect the reputation of Chillingworth. His frequent changes proceeded from too nice an inquisition into truth. His doubts grew out of himself; he assisted them with all the strength of his reason: he was then too hard for himself; but finding as little quiet and repose in those victories, he quickly recovered, by a new appeal to his own judgment: so that in all his sallies and retreats he was in fact his own convert.

Bayle was the son of a Calvinist minister in a remote province in France, at the foot of the Pyrenees. For the benefit of education, the Protestants were tempted to risk their children in the Catholic universities; and in the twenty-second year of his age young Bayle was seduced by the arts and arguments of the Jesuits of Thoulouse. He remained about seventeen months (19th March 1699 —19th August 1670) in their hands, a voluntary captive; and a letter to his parents, which the new convert composed or subscribed (15th April 1670), is darkly tinged with the spirit of popery. But nature had designed him to think as he pleased, and to speak as he thought: his piety was offended by the excessive worship of creatures; and the study of physics convinced him of the impossibility of transubstantiation, which is abundantly refuted by the testimony of our senses. His return to the communion of a falling sect was a bold and disinterested step, that exposed him to the rigour of the laws; and a speedy flight to Geneva protected him from the resentment of his spiritual tyrants, unconscious, as they were, of the full value of the prize which they had lost. Had Bayle adhered to the Catholic Church, had he embraced the ecclesiastical profession, the genius and favour of such a proselyte might have aspired to wealth and honours in his native country: but the hypocrite would have found less happiness in the comforts of a benefice, or the dignity of a mitre, than he enjoyed at Rotterdam in a private state of exile, indigence and freedom. Without a country, or a patron, or a prejudice, he claimed the liberty, and subsisted by the labours, of his pen: the inequality of his voluminous works is explained and excused by his alternately writing for himself, for the booksellers, and for posterity; and if a severe critic would reduce him to a single folio, that relic, like the books of the Sibyl, would become still more valuable. A calm and lofty spectator of the religious tempest, the philosopher of Rotterdam condemned with equal firmness the persecution of Louis the Fourteenth, and the republican maxims of the Calvinists; their vain prophecies, and the intolerant bigotry which sometimes vexed his solitary retreat. In reviewing the controversies of the times, he turned against each other the arguments of the disputants; successively wielding the arms of the Catholics and Protestants, he proves that neither the way of authority nor the way of examination can afford the multitude any test of religious truth; and dexterously concludes that custom and education must be the sole grounds of popular belief. The ancient paradox of Plutarch, that atheism is less pernicious than superstition, acquires a tenfold vigour when it is adorned with the colours of his wit, and pointed with the acuteness of his logic. His critical dictionary is a vast repository of facts and opinions; and he balances the *false* religions in his sceptical scales, till the opposite quantities (if I may use the language of algebra) annihilate each other. The wonderful power which he so boldly exercised, of assembling doubts and objections, had tempted him jocosely to assume the title of the " νεφεληγερέτα Ζεύς—the cloud-compelling Jove;" and in a conversation with the ingenious Abbé (afterwards Cardinal de Polignac, he freely disclosed his universal Pyrrhonism. " I am most truly (said Bayle) a protestant; for I protest indifferently against all systems and all sects."

The academical resentment which I may possibly have provoked will prudently spare this plain narrative of my studies, or rather of my idleness; and of the unfortunate event which shortened the term of my residence at Oxford. But it may be suggested that my father was unlucky in the choice of a society, and the chance of a tutor. It will perhaps be asserted, that in the lapse of forty years many improvements have taken place in the college and in the university. I am not unwilling to believe that some tutors might have been found more active than Dr. Waldegrave and less contemptible than Dr. ——. At a more recent period many students have been attracted by the merit and reputation of Sir William Scott, then a tutor in University College, and now conspicuous in the profession of the civil law: my personal acquaintance with that gentleman has inspired me with a just esteem for his abilities and knowledge; and I am assured that his lectures on history would compose, were they given to the public, a most valuable treatise. Under the auspices of the late deans, a more regular discipline has been introduced, as I am told, at Christ Church; a course of classical and philosophical studies is proposed, and even pursued, in that numerous seminary: learning has been made a duty, a pleasure, and even a fashion; and several young gentlemen do honour to the college in which they have been educated. According to the will of the donor, the profit of the second part of Lord Clarendon's History has been applied to the establishment of a riding-school, that the polite exercises might be taught, I know not with what success, in the university. The Vinerian professor-ship is of far more serious importance; the laws of his country are the first science of an Englishman of rank and fortune, who is called to be a magistrate, and may hope to be a legislator. This judicious institution was coldly entertained by the graver doctors, who complained (I have heard the complaint) that it would take the young people from their books; but Mr. Viner's benefaction is not unprofitable, since it has at least produced the excellent commentaries of Sir William Blackstone.

After carrying me to Putney, to the house of his friend Mr. Mallet,[1] by whose philosophy I was rather scandalised than reclaimed, it was necessary for my father to form a new plan of education, and to devise some method which, if possible, might effect the cure of my spiritual malady. After much debate it was determined, from the advice and personal experience of Mr. Eliot (now Lord Eliot), to fix me, during some years, at Lausanne in Switzerland. Mr. Frey, a Swiss gentleman of Basil, undertook the conduct of the journey: we left London the 19th of June, crossed the sea from Dover to Calais, travelled post through several provinces of France, by the direct road of St. Quentin, Rheims, Langres, and Besançon, and arrived the 30th of June at Lausanne, where I was immediately settled under the roof and tuition of Mr. Pavilliard, a Calvinist minister.

The first marks of my father's displeasure rather astonished than afflicted me: when he threatened to banish, and disown, and disinherit a rebellious son, I cherished a secret hope that he would not be able or willing to effect his menaces; and the pride of conscience

[1] The author of a *Life of Bacon*, which has been rated above its value; of some forgotten poems and plays; and of the pathetic ballad of " William and Margaret." His tenets were deistical; perhaps a stronger term might have been used.—SHEFFIELD.

encouraged me to sustain the honourable and important
part which I was now acting. My spirits were raised and
kept alive by the rapid motion of my journey, the new
and various scenes of the Continent, and the civility of
Mr. Frey, a man of sense, who was not ignorant of books
or the world. But after he had resigned me into Pavilliard's hands, and I was fixed in my new habitation, I
had leisure to contemplate the strange and melancholy
prospect before me. My first complaint arose from my
ignorance of the language. In my childhood I had once
studied the French grammar, and I could imperfectly
understand the easy prose of a familiar subject. But
when I was thus suddenly cast on a foreign land, I found
myself deprived of the use of speech and of hearing; and,
during some weeks, incapable not only of enjoying the
pleasures of conversation, but even of asking or answer-
ing a question in the common intercourse of life. To a
home-bred Englishman every object, every custom was
offensive; but the native of any country might have been
disgusted with the general aspect of his lodging and
entertainment. I had now exchanged my elegant apartment in Magdalen College, for a narrow, gloomy street,
the most unfrequented of an unhandsome town, for an
old inconvenient house, and for a small chamber ill
contrived and ill furnished, which on the approach of
winter, instead of a companionable fire, must be warmed
by the dull invisible heat of a stove. From a man I was
again degraded to the dependence of a schoolboy. Mr.
Pavilliard managed my expenses, which had been reduced
to a diminutive state: I received a small monthly allowance for my pocket-money; and, helpless and awkward
as I have ever been, I no longer enjoyed the indispensable
comfort of a servant. My condition seemed as destitute
of hope as it was devoid of pleasure: I was separated for

an indefinite, which appeared an infinite term, from my native country; and I had lost all connection with my Catholic friends. I have since reflected with surprise, that, as the Romish clergy of every part of Europe maintain a close correspondence with each other, they never attempted, by letters or messages, to rescue me from the hands of the heretics, or at least to confirm my zeal and constancy in the profession of the faith. Such was my first introduction to Lausanne; a place where I spent nearly five years with pleasure and profit, which I afterwards revisited without compulsion, and which I have finally selected as the most grateful retreat for the decline of my life.

But it is the peculiar felicity of youth that the most unpleasing objects and events seldom make a deep or lasting impression; it forgets the past, enjoys the present, and anticipates the future. At the flexible age of sixteen I soon learned to endure, and gradually to adopt, the new forms of arbitrary manners: the real hardships of my situation were alienated by time. Had I been sent abroad in a more splendid style, such as the fortune and bounty of my father might have supplied, I might have returned home with the same stock of language and science which our countrymen usually import from the Continent. An exile and a prisoner as I was, their example betrayed me into some irregularities of wine, of play, and of idle excursions: but I soon felt the impossibility of associating with them on equal terms; and after the departure of my first acquaintance, I held a cold and civil correspondence with their successors. This seclusion from English society was attended with the most solid benefits. In the Pays de Vaud the French language is used with less imperfection than in most of the distant provinces of France: in Pavilliard's family necessity compelled me

to listen and to speak; and if I was at first disheartened
by the apparent slowness, in a few months I was astonished
by the rapidity of my progress. My pronunciation was
formed by the constant repetition of the same sounds;
the variety of words and idioms, the rules of grammar, and
distinctions of genders, were impressed in my memory:
ease and freedom were obtained by practice; correctness
and elegance by labour; and before I was recalled home,
French, in which I spontaneously thought, was more
familiar than English to my ear, my tongue, and my pen.
The first effect of this opening knowledge was the revival
of my love of reading, which had been chilled at Oxford;
and I soon turned over, without much choice, almost
all the French books in my tutor's library. Even these
amusements were productive of real advantage: my taste
and judgment were now somewhat riper. I was introduced
to a new mode of style and literature; by the comparison
of manners and opinions, my views were enlarged, my
prejudices were corrected, and a copious voluntary
abstract of the *Histoire de l'Eglise et de l'Empire*,[1] by le
Sueur, may be placed in a middle line between my childish
and my manly studies. As soon as I was able to converse with the natives, I began to feel some satisfaction
in their company: my awkward timidity was polished and
emboldened; and I frequented for the first time assemblies
of men and women. The acquaintance of the Pavilliards
prepared me by degrees for more elegant society. I was
received with kindness and indulgence in the best families
of Lausanne; and it was in one of these that I formed
an intimate and lasting connection with Mr. Deyverdun,
a young man of an amiable temper and excellent understanding. In the arts of fencing and dancing, small
indeed was my proficiency; and some months were idly

[1] *History of the Church and Empire*, by Jean le Sueur.

wasted in the riding-school.   My unfitness to bodily exercise reconciled me to a sedentary life, and the horse, the
favourite of my countrymen, never contributed to the
pleasures of my youth.

My obligations to the lessons of Mr. Pavilliard gratitude
will not suffer me to forget: he was endowed with a clear
head and a warm heart; his innate benevolence had
assuaged the spirit of the church; he was rational, because
he was moderate: in the course of his studies he had
acquired a just though superficial knowledge of most
branches of literature; by long practice he was skilled
in the arts of teaching; and he laboured with assiduous
patience to know the character, gain the affection, and
open the mind of his English pupil.   As soon as we began
to understand each other, he gently led me, from a blind
and undistinguishing love of reading, into the path of
instruction.   I consented with pleasure that a portion of
the morning hours should be consecrated to a plan of
modern history and geography, and to the critical perusal
of the French and Latin classics: and at each step I felt
myself invigorated by the habits of application and
method.   His prudence repressed and dissembled some
youthful sallies; and as soon as I was confirmed in the
habits of industry and temperance, he gave the reins into
my own hands.   His favourable report of my behaviour
and progress gradually obtained some latitude of action
and expense; and he wished to alleviate the hardships of
my lodging and entertainment.   The principles of philosophy were associated with the examples of taste; and
by a singular chance, the book, as well as the man, which
contributed the most effectually to my education, has a
stronger claim on my gratitude than on my admiration.
Mr. De Crousaz, the adversary of Bayle and Pope, is not
distinguished by lively fancy or profound reflection; and

even in his own country, at the end of a few years, his name and writings are almost obliterated. But his philosophy had been formed in the school of Locke, his divinity in that of Limborch and Le Clerc; in a long and laborious life, several generations of pupils were taught to think, and even to write; his lessons rescued the academy of Lausanne from Calvinistic prejudice; and he had the rare merit of diffusing a more liberal spirit among the clergy and people of the Pays de Vaud. His system of logic, which in the last editions has swelled to six tedious and prolix volumes, may be praised as a clear and methodical abridgment of the art of reasoning, from our simple ideas to the most complex operations of the human understanding. This system I studied, and meditated, and abstracted, till I obtained the free command of a universal instrument, which I soon presumed to exercise on my catholic opinions. Pavilliard was not unmindful that his first task, his most important duty, was to reclaim me from the errors of popery. The inter-mixture of sects has rendered the Swiss clergy acute and learned on the topics of controversy; and I have some of his letters in which he celebrates the dexterity of his attack, and my gradual concessions, after a firm and well-managed defence.[1] I was willing, and I am now willing, to allow him a handsome share of the honour of my conversion: yet I must observe that it was principally effected by my private reflections; and I still remember my solitary transport at the discovery of a philosophical

---

[1] M. Pavilliard has described to me the astonishment with which he gazed on Mr. Gibbon standing before him: a thin little figure, with a large head, disputing and urging, with the greatest ability, all the best arguments that had ever been used in favour of popery. Mr. Gibbon many years ago became very fat and corpulent, but he had uncommonly small bones, and was very slightly made.—SHEFFIELD.

argument against the doctrine of transubstantiation: *that* the text of scripture, which seems to inculcate the real presence, is attested only by a single sense—our sight; while the real presence itself is disproved by three of our senses—the sight, the touch, and the taste. The various articles of the Romish creed disappeared like a dream; and after a full conviction, on Christmas Day 1754, I received the sacrament in the church of Lausanne. It was here that I suspended my religious inquiries, acquiescing with implicit belief in the tenets and mysteries which are adopted by the general consent of Catholics and Protestants.

Such, from my arrival at Lausanne, during the first eighteen or twenty months (July 1753—March 1755), were my useful studies, the foundation of all my future improvements. But every man who rises above the common level has received two educations: the first from his teachers; the second, more personal and important, from himself. He will not, like the fanatics of the last age, define the moment of grace; but he cannot forget the era of his life in which his mind has expanded to its proper form and dimensions. My worthy tutor had the good sense and modesty to discern how far he could be useful: as soon as he felt that I advanced beyond his speed and measure, he wisely left me to my genius; and the hours of lesson were soon lost in the voluntary labour of the whole morning, and sometimes of the whole day. The desire of prolonging my time gradually confirmed the salutary habit of early rising, to which I have always adhered, with some regard to seasons and situations: but it is happy for my eyes and my health that my temperate ardour has never been seduced to trespass on the hours of the night. During the last three years of my residence at Lausanne I may assume the merit of serious and solid application; but I am tempted to distinguish the last eight months of the year 1755 as the period of the most extraordinary diligence and rapid progress.[1] In my French and Latin translations I adopted an excellent method, which, from my own success, I would recommend to the imitation of students. I chose some classic writer, such as Cicero and Vertot, the most approved for purity and elegance of style. I translated, for instance, an epistle of Cicero into French; and, after throwing it aside till the words and phrases were obliterated from my memory, I re-translated my French into such Latin as I could find; and then compared each sentence of my imperfect version with the ease, the grace, the propriety of the Roman orator. A similar experiment was made on several pages of the Revolutions of Vertot; I turned them into Latin, returned them after a sufficient interval into my own French, and again scrutinised the resemblance or dissimilitude of the copy and the original. By degrees I was less ashamed, by degrees I was more satisfied with myself; and I persevered in the practice of these double translations, which filled several books, till I had acquired

---

[1] JOURNAL, December 1755.—In finishing this year, I must remark how favourable it was to my studies. In the space of eight months, from the beginning of April, I learnt the principles of drawing; made myself complete master of the French and Latin languages, with which I was very superficially acquainted before, and wrote and translated a great deal in both; read Cicero's *Epistles ad Familiares*, his *Brutus*, all his *Orations*, his *Dialogues de Amicitiâ* and *de Senectute*; Terence, twice; and Pliny's *Epistles*. In French, Giannone's *History of Naples*, and l'Abbé Bannier's *Mythology*, and M. de Boehat's *Mémoires sur la Suisse*, and wrote a very ample relation of my tour. I likewise began to study Greek, and went through the grammar. I began to make very large collections of what I read. But what I esteem most of all, from the perusal and meditation of De Crousaz's *Logic*, I not only understood the principles of that science, but formed my mind to a habit of thinking and reasoning I had no idea of before.

the knowledge of both idioms, and the command at least
of a correct style. This useful exercise of writing was
accompanied and succeeded by the more pleasing occupation of reading the best authors. The perusal of the
Roman classics was at once my exercise and reward.
Dr. Middleton's History, which I then appreciated above
its true value, naturally directed me to the writings of
Cicero. The most perfect editions, that of Olivet, which
may adorn the shelves of the rich, that of Ernesti, which
should lie on the table of the learned, were not within my
reach. For the familiar epistles I used the text and
English commentary of Bishop Ross; but my general
edition was that of Verburgius, published at Amsterdam
in two large volumes in folio, with an indifferent choice of
various notes. I read, with application and pleasure, *all*
the epistles, *all* the orations, and the most important
treatises of rhetoric and philosophy; and as I read, I
applauded the observation of Quintilian, that every
student may judge of his own proficiency by the satisfaction which he receives from the Roman orator. I
tasted the beauties of language, I breathed the spirit of
freedom, and I imbibed from his precepts and examples
the public and private sense of a man. Cicero in Latin,
and Xenophon in Greek, are indeed the two ancients
whom I would first propose to a liberal scholar; not only
for the merit of their style and sentiments, but for the
admirable lessons, which may be applied almost to every
situation of public and private life. Cicero's *Epistles* may
in particular afford the models of every form of correspondence, from the careless effusions of tenderness and
friendship, to the well-guarded declaration of discreet
and dignified resentment. After finishing this great
author, a library of eloquence and reason, I formed a

more extensive plan of reviewing the Latin classics,[1]
under the four divisions of, 1, historians; 2, poets; 3,
orators; and 4, philosophers, in a chronological series,
from the days of Plautus and Sallust to the decline of
the language and empire of Rome: and this plan, in the
last twenty-seven months of my residence at Lausanne
(January 1756—April 1758), I *nearly* accomplished. Nor
was this review, however rapid, either hasty or superficial.
I indulged myself in a second and even a third perusal
of Terence, Virgil, Horace, Tacitus, etc., and studied to
imbibe the sense and spirit most congenial to my own.
I never suffered a difficult or corrupt passage to escape,
till I had viewed it in every light of which it was
susceptible: though often disappointed, I always consulted
the most learned or ingenious commentators, Torrentius
and Dacier on Horace, Catrou and Servius on Virgil,
Lipsius on Tacitus, Meziriac on Ovid, etc.; and in the
ardour of my inquiries I embraced a large circle of
historical and critical erudition. My abstracts of each
book were made in the French language: my observations
often branched into particular essays; and I can still
read, without contempt, a dissertation of eight folio pages
on eight lines (287-294) of the fourth *Georgic* of Virgil.
Mr. Deyverdun, my friend, whose name will be frequently
repeated, had joined with equal zeal, though not with
equal perseverance, in the same undertaking. To him
every thought, every composition, was instantly communicated; with him I enjoyed the benefits of a free
conversation on the topics of our common studies.

---

[1] JOURNAL, January 1756.—I determined to read over the Latin
authors in order; and read this year, Virgil, Sallust, Livy, Velleius
Paterculus, Valerius Maximus, Tacitus, Suetonius, Quintus Curtius,
Justin, Florus, Plautus, Terence, and Lucretius. I also read and
meditated Locke upon the Understanding.

But it is scarcely possible for a mind endowed with any active curiosity to be long conversant with the Latin classics without aspiring to know the Greek originals, whom they celebrate as their masters, and of whom they so warmly recommend the study and imitation;

—— Vos exemplaria Græca
Nocturnâ versate manu, versate diurnâ.[1]

It was now that I regretted the early years which had been wasted in sickness or idleness, or mere idle reading; that I condemned the perverse method of our schoolmasters, who, by first teaching the mother language, might descend with so much ease and perspicuity to the origin and etymology of a derivative idiom. In the nineteenth year of my age I determined to supply this defect; and the lessons of Pavilliard again contributed to smooth the entrance of the way, the Greek alphabet, the grammar, and the pronunciation according to the French accent. At my earnest request we presumed to open the *Iliad ;* and I had the pleasure of beholding, though darkly and through a glass,[2] the true image of Homer, whom I had long since admired in an English dress. After my tutor had left me to myself, I worked my way through about half the *Iliad,* and afterwards interpreted alone a large portion of Xenophon and Herodotus. But my ardour, destitute of aid and emulation, was gradually cooled, and, from the barren task of searching words in a lexicon, I withdrew to the free and familiar conversation of Virgil and Tacitus. Yet in my residence at Lausanne I had laid a solid foundation, which enabled me, in a more propitious season, to prosecute the study of Grecian literature.

[1] Study your examples of Greek literature alike by night and by day.—Horace, *De Arte Poetica,* l. 268.
[2] Cf. I Cor. xiii. 12.

From a blind idea of the usefulness of such abstract science, my father had been desirous, and even pressing, that I should devote some time to the mathematics; nor could I refuse to comply with so reasonable a wish. During two winters I attended the private lectures of Monsieur de Traytorrens, who explained the elements of algebra and geometry, as far as the conic sections of the Marquis de l'Hôpital, and appeared satisfied with my diligence and improvement.[1] But as my childish propensity for numbers and calculations was totally extinct, I was content to receive the passive impression of my professor's lectures, without any active exercise of my own powers. As soon as I understood the principles I relinquished for ever the pursuit of the mathematics; nor can I lament that I desisted before my mind was hardened by the habit of rigid demonstration, so destructive of the finer feelings of moral evidence, which must, however, determine the actions and opinions of our lives. I listened with more pleasure to the proposal of studying the law of nature and nations, which was taught in the academy of Lausanne by Mr. Vicat, a professor of some learning and reputation. But, instead of attending his public or private course, I preferred in my closet the lessons of his

---

[1] JOURNAL, January 1757.—I began to study algebra under M. de Traytorrens, went through the elements of algebra and geometry and the three first books of the Marquis de l'Hôpital's *Conic Sections*. I also read Tibullus, Catullus, Propertius, Horace (with Dacier's and Torrentius's notes), Virgil, Ovid's *Epistles*, with Meziriac's *Commentary*, the *Ars Amandi*, and the *Elegies*; likewise the *Augustus* and *Tiberius* of Suetonius, and a Latin translation of Dion Cassius, from the death of Julius Cæsar to the death of Augustus. I also continued my correspondence, begun last year, with M. Allamand of Bex, and the Professor Breitinger of Zurich; and opened a new one with the Professor Gesner of Gottingen.

N.B.—Last year and this I read St. John's Gospel, with part of Xenophon's *Cyropædia*; the *Iliad*, and Herodotus: but, upon the whole, I rather neglected my Greek.

masters, and my own reason. Without being disgusted
by Grotius or Puffendorf, I studied in their writings the
duties of a man, the rights of a citizen, the theory of
justice (it is, alas! a theory), and the laws of peace and
war, which have had some influence on the practice of
modern Europe. My fatigues were alleviated by the
good sense of their commentator Barbeyrac. Locke's
Treatise of Government instructed me in the knowledge of
Whig principles, which are rather founded in reason than
experience; but my delight was in the frequent perusal
of Montesquieu, whose energy of style, and boldness of
hypothesis, were powerful to awaken and stimulate the
genius of the age. The logic of De Crousaz had prepared
me to engage with his master Locke, and his antagonist
Bayle; of whom the former may be used as a bridle, and
the latter as a spur, to the curiosity of a young philosopher.
According to the nature of their respective works, the
schools of argument and objection, I carefully went
through the *Essay on Human Understanding*, and occasionally consulted the most interesting articles of the
Philosophic Dictionary. In the infancy of my reason I
turned over, as an idle amusement, the most serious and
important treatise: in its maturity the most trifling
performance could exercise my taste or judgment; and
more than once I have been led by a novel into a deep
and instructive train of thinking. But I cannot forbear
to mention three particular books, since they may have
remotely contributed to form the historian of the Roman
empire. 1. From the *Provincial Letters of Pascal*, which
almost every year I have perused with new pleasure, I
learned to manage the weapon of grave and temperate
irony, even on subjects of ecclesiastical solemnity. 2.
The Life of Julian, by the Abbé de la Bleterie, first
introduced me to the man and the times; and I should

be glad to recover my first essay on the truth of the miracle which stopped the rebuilding of the Temple of Jerusalem.   3. In Giannone's *Civil History of Naples* I observed with a critical eye the progress and abuse of sacerdotal power, and the revolutions of Italy in the darker ages.   This various reading, which I now conducted with discretion, was digested, according to the precept and model of Mr. Locke, into a large commonplace-book; a practice, however, which I do not strenuously recommend.   The action of the pen will doubtless imprint an idea on the mind as well as on the paper; but I much question whether the benefits of this laborious method are adequate to the waste of time; and I must agree with Dr. Johnson (*Idler*, No. 74), " that what is twice read is commonly better remembered than what is transcribed."

During two years, if I forget some boyish excursions of a day or a week, I was fixed at Lausanne; but at the end of the third summer my father consented that I should make the tour of Switzerland with Pavilliard: and our short absence of one month (September 21—October 20, 1755) was a reward and relaxation of my assiduous studies.   The fashion of climbing the mountains and reviewing the *glaciers* had not yet been introduced by foreign travellers, who seek the sublime beauties of nature. But the political face of the country is not less diversified by the forms and spirit of so many various republics, from the jealous government of the *few* to the licentious freedom of the *many*.   I contemplated with pleasure the new prospects of men and manners; though my conversation with the natives would have been more free and instructive had I possessed the German as well as the French language. We passed through most of the principal towns in Switzerland; Neufchâtel, Bienne, Soleurre, Arau, Baden, Zurich,

Basil, and Bern. In every place we visited the churches, arsenals, libraries, and all the most eminent persons; and after my return I digested my notes in fourteen or fifteen sheets of a French journal, which I despatched to my father, as a proof that my time and his money had not been misspent. Had I found this journal among his papers I might be tempted to select some passages; but I will not transcribe the printed accounts, and it may be sufficient to notice a remarkable spot, which left a deep and lasting impression on my memory. From Zurich we proceeded to the Benedictine Abbey of Einsiedlen, more commonly styled Our Lady of the Hermits. I was astonished by the profuse ostentation of riches in the poorest corner of Europe; amidst a savage scene of woods and mountains, a palace appears to have been erected by magic; and it was erected by the potent magic of religion. A crowd of palmers and votaries was prostrate before the altar. The title and worship of the Mother of God provoked my indignation; and the lively naked image of superstition suggested to me, as in the same place it had done to Zuinglius, the most pressing argument for the reformation of the church. About two years after this tour I passed at Geneva a useful and agreeable month; but this excursion and some short visits in the Pays de Vaud did not materially interrupt my studious and sedentary life at Lausanne.

My thirst of improvement, and the languid state of science at Lausanne, soon prompted me to solicit a literary correspondence with several men of learning, whom I had not an opportunity of personally consulting. 1. In the perusal of Livy (xxx. 44) I had been stopped by a sentence in a speech of Hannibal, which cannot be reconciled by any torture with his character or argument. The commentators dissemble or confess their perplexity.

It occurred to me that the change of a single letter, by substituting *otio* instead of *odio*, might restore a clear and consistent sense; but I wished to weigh my emendation in scales less partial than my own. I addressed myself to M. Crevier, the successor of Rollin, and a professor in the University of Paris, who had published a large and valuable edition of Livy. His answer was speedy and polite; he praised my ingenuity, and adopted my conjecture. 2. I maintained a Latin correspondence, at first anonymous, and afterwards in my own name, with Professor Breitinger of Zurich, the learned editor of a Septuagint Bible. In our frequent letters we discussed many questions of antiquity, many passages of the Latin classics. I proposed my interpretations and amendments. His censures, for he did not spare my boldness of conjecture, were sharp and strong; and I was encouraged by the consciousness of my strength, when I could stand in free debate against a critic of such eminence and erudition. 3. I corresponded on similar topics with the celebrated Professor Matthew Gesner, of the University of Gottingen; and he accepted as courteously as the two former the invitation of an unknown youth. But his abilities might possibly be decayed; his elaborate letters were feeble and prolix; and when I asked his proper direction, the vain old man covered half a sheet of paper with the foolish enumeration of his titles and offices. 4. These professors of Paris, Zurich, and Gottingen were strangers whom I presumed to address on the credit of their name; but Mr. Allamand, minister at Bex, was my personal friend, with whom I maintained a more free and interesting correspondence. He was a master of language, of science, and, above all, of dispute; and his acute and flexible logic could support, with equal address, and perhaps with equal indifference, the adverse sides of every possible question.

His spirit was active, but his pen had been indolent. Mr. Allamand had exposed himself to much scandal and reproach by an anonymous letter (1745) to the Protestants of France, in which he labours to persuade them that *public* worship is the exclusive right and duty of the state, and that their numerous assemblies of dissenters and rebels were not authorised by the law or the gospel. His style is animated, his arguments specious; and if the Papist may seem to lurk under the mask of a Protestant, the philosopher is concealed under the disguise of a Papist. After some trials in France and Holland, which were defeated by his fortune or his character, a genius that might have enlightened or deluded the world was buried in a country living, unknown to fame, and discontented with mankind. *Est sacrificulus in pago, et rusticos decipit.*[1] As often as private or ecclesiastical business called him to Lausanne I enjoyed the pleasure and benefit of his conversation, and we were mutually flattered by our attention to each other. Our correspondence in his absence chiefly turned on Locke's metaphysics, which he attacked, and I defended; the origin of ideas, the principles of evidence, and the doctrine of liberty;

And found no end, in wandering mazes lost.[2]

By fencing with so skilful a master I acquired some dexterity in the use of my philosophic weapons; but I was still the slave of education and prejudice. He had some measures to keep; and I much suspect that he never showed me the true colours of his secret scepticism.

Before I was recalled from Switzerland I had the satis-

---

[1] He is a humble priest in some rural district and deceives the rustics.

[2] Milton, *Paradise Lost*, ii. l. 561.

faction of seeing the most extraordinary man of the age;
a poet, an historian, a philosopher, who has filled thirty
quartos, of prose and verse, with his various productions,
often excellent, and always entertaining. Need I add
the name of Voltaire? After forfeiting, by his own mis-
conduct, the friendship of the first of kings, he retired, at
the age of sixty, with a plentiful fortune, to a free and
beautiful country, and resided two winters (1757 and 1758)
in the town or neighbourhood of Lausanne. My desire
of beholding Voltaire, whom I then rated above his
real magnitude, was easily gratified. He received me
with civility as an English youth; but I cannot boast
of any peculiar notice or distinction, *Virgilium vidi
tantum.*[1]

The ode which he composed on his first arrival on the
banks of the Leman Lake, *O Maison d'Aristippe! O Jardin
d'Epicure,*[2] etc., had been imparted as a secret to the gentleman by whom I was introduced. He allowed me to read
it twice; I knew it by heart; and, as my discretion was
not equal to my memory, the author was soon displeased
by the circulation of a copy. In writing this trivial
anecdote, I wished to observe whether my memory was
impaired, and I have the comfort of finding that every
line of the poem is still engraved in fresh and indelible
characters. The highest gratification which I derived
from Voltaire's residence at Lausanne was the uncommon
circumstance of hearing a great poet declaim his own
productions on the stage. He had formed a company of
gentlemen and ladies, some of whom were not destitute
of talents. A decent theatre was framed at Monrepos, a
country-house at the end of a suburb; dresses and scenes

[1] I saw Virgil only.—Ovid, *Tristia*, IV. x. 51.
[2] " O House of Aristippus,
O Garden of Epicurus."
Œuvres de Voltaire, vol. xi. 174.

were provided at the expense of the actors; and the
author directed the rehearsals with the zeal and attention
of paternal love. In two successive winters his tragedies
of *Zayre, Alzire, Zulime,* and his sentimental comedy of
the *Enfant Prodigue,* were played at the theatre of Monrepos. Voltaire represented the characters best adapted
to his years, Lusignan, Alvaréz, Benassar, Euphemon.
His declamation was fashioned to the pomp and cadence
of the old stage; and he expressed the enthusiasm of
poetry rather than the feelings of nature. My ardour,
which soon became conspicuous, seldom failed of procuring
me a ticket. The habits of pleasure fortified my taste
for the French theatre, and that taste has perhaps abated
my idolatry for the gigantic genius of Shakspeare, which is
inculcated from our infancy as the first duty of an Englishman. The wit and philosophy of Voltaire, his table and
theatre, refined, in a visible degree, the manners of
Lausanne; and, however addicted to study, I enjoyed
my share of the amusements of society. After the
representation of Monrepos I sometimes supped with
the actors. I was now familiar in some, and acquainted
in many, houses; and my evenings were generally devoted
to cards and conversation, either in private parties or
numerous assemblies.

I hesitate, from the apprehension of ridicule, when I
approach the delicate subject of my early love. By this
word I do not mean the polite attention, the gallantry,
without hope or design, which has originated in the spirit
of chivalry, and is interwoven with the texture of French
manners. I understand by this passion the union of
desire, friendship, and tenderness, which is inflamed by a
single female, which prefers her to the rest of her sex,
and which seeks her possession as the supreme or the sole
happiness of our being. I need not blush at recollecting

the object of my choice; and though my love was disappointed of success, I am rather proud that I was once
capable of feeling such a pure and exalted sentiment.
The personal attractions of Mademoiselle Susán Curchod
were embellished by the virtues and talents of the mind.
Her fortune was humble, but her family was respectable.
Her mother, a native of France, had preferred her religion
to her country. The profession of her father did not
extinguish the moderation and philosophy of his temper,
and he lived content with a small salary and laborious
duty in the obscure lot of minister of Crassy, in the
mountains that separate the Pays de Vaud from the
county of Burgundy. In the solitude of a sequestered
village he bestowed a liberal, and even learned, education
on his only daughter. She surpassed his hopes by her
proficiency in the sciences and languages; and in her
short visits to some relations at Lausanne, the wit, the
beauty, and erudition of Mademoiselle Curchod were the
theme of universal applause. The report of such a prodigy
awakened my curiosity; I saw and loved. I found her
learned without pedantry, lively in conversation, pure in
sentiment, and elegant in manners; and the first sudden
emotion was fortified by the habits and knowledge of a
more familiar acquaintance. She permitted me to make
her two or three visits at her father's house. I passed
some happy days there, in the mountains of Burgundy,
and her parents honourably encouraged the connection.
In a calm retirement the gay vanity of youth no longer
fluttered in her bosom; she listened to the voice of truth
and passion, and I might presume to hope that I had made
some impression on a virtuous heart. At Crassy and
Lausanne I indulged my dream of felicity: but on my
return to England, I soon discovered that my father would
not hear of this strange alliance, and that, without his

consent, I was myself destitute and helpless. After a painful struggle I yielded to my fate; I sighed as a lover, I obeyed as a son;[1] my wound was insensibly healed by time, absence, and the habits of a new life. My cure was accelerated by a faithful report of the tranquillity and cheerfulness of the lady herself, and my love subsided in friendship and esteem. The minister of Crassy soon afterwards died; his stipend died with him: his daughter retired to Geneva, where, by teaching young ladies, she earned a hard subsistence for herself and her mother; but in her lowest distress she maintained a spotless reputation and a dignified behaviour. A rich banker of Paris, a citizen of Geneva, had the good fortune and good sense to discover and possess this inestimable treasure; and in the capital of taste and luxury she resisted the temptations of wealth, as she had sustained the hardships of indigence. The genius of her husband has exalted him to the most conspicuous station in Europe. In every change of prosperity and disgrace he has reclined on the bosom of a faithful friend; and Mademoiselle Curchod is now the wife of M. Necker, the minister, and perhaps the legislator, of the French monarchy.

Whatsoever have been the fruits of my education, they must be ascribed to the fortunate banishment which placed me at Lausanne. I have sometimes applied to my own fate the verses of Pindar, which remind an Olympic champion that his victory was the consequence of his exile; and that at home, like a domestic fowl, his days might have rolled away inactive or inglorious.

---

[1] See Œuvres de Rousseau, tom. xxxiii. p. 88, 89, octavo edition. As an author, I shall not appeal from the judgment, or taste, or caprice of Jean Jacques; but that extraordinary man, whom I admire and pity, should have been less precipitate in condemning the moral character and conduct of a stranger.

. . . . ἤτοι καὶ τεά κεν,
'Ενδομάχας ἅτ' ἀλέκτωρ,
Συγγόνῳ παρ' ἑστίᾳ
'Ακλεὴς τιμὰ κατεφυλλορόησεν ποδῶν·
Εἰ μὴ στάσις ἀντιάνειρα
Κνωσίας σ'ἄμερσε πάτρας.[1]   *Olymp.* xii.

If my childish revolt against the religion of my country
had not stripped me in time of my academic gown, the
five important years, so liberally improved in the studies
and conversation of Lausanne, would have been steeped
in port and prejudice among the monks of Oxford. Had
the fatigue of idleness compelled me to read, the path
of learning would not have been enlightened by a ray of
philosophic freedom. I should have grown to manhood
ignorant of the life and language of Europe, and my
knowledge of the world would have been confined to an
English cloister. But my religious error fixed me at
Lausanne, in a state of banishment and disgrace. The
rigid course of discipline and abstinence to which I was
condemned invigorated the constitution of my mind and
body; poverty and pride estranged me from my countrymen. One mischief, however, and in their eyes a serious
and irreparable mischief, was derived from the success of
my Swiss education: I had ceased to be an Englishman.
At the flexible period of youth, from the age of sixteen to
twenty-one, my opinions, habits, and sentiments were
cast in a foreign mould; the faint and distant remem-

[1] Thus, like the crested bird of Mars, at home
        Engaged in foul domestic jars,
        And wasted with intestine wars,
    Inglorious hadst thou spent thy vig'rous bloom;
        Had not sedition's civil broils
        Expell'd thee from thy native *Crete*,
        And driv'n thee with more glorious toils
    Th' *Olympic* crown in *Pisa's* plain to meet.
                              WEST's *Pind.*

brance of England was almost obliterated; my native
language was grown less familiar; and I should have
cheerfully accepted the offer of a moderate independence
on the terms of perpetual exile. By the good sense and
temper of Pavilliard my yoke was insensibly lightened:
he left me master of my time and actions; but he could
neither change my situation nor increase my allowance,
and with the progress of my years and reason I im-
patiently sighed for the moment of my deliverance. At
length, in the spring of the year one thousand seven
hundred and fifty-eight, my father signified his permission
and his pleasure that I should immediately return home.
We were then in the midst of a war: the resentment of
the French at our taking their ships without a declaration
had rendered that polite nation somewhat peevish and
difficult. They denied a passage to English travellers,
and the road through Germany was circuitous, toilsome,
and perhaps, in the neighbourhood of the armies, exposed
to some danger. In this perplexity, two Swiss officers
of my acquaintance in the Dutch service, who were
returning to their garrisons, offered to conduct me through
France as one of their companions; nor did we sufficiently
reflect that my borrowed name and regimentals might
have been considered, in case of a discovery, in a very
serious light. I took my leave of Lausanne on the 11th
of April 1758, with a mixture of joy and regret, in the
firm resolution of revisiting, as a man, the persons and
places which had been so dear to my youth. We travelled
slowly, but pleasantly, in a hired coach, over the hills of
Franche-compté and the fertile province of Lorraine, and
passed, without accident or inquiry, through several
fortified towns of the French frontier: from thence we
entered the wild Ardennes of the Austrian duchy of
Luxemburg; and after crossing the Meuse at Liége, we

traversed the heaths of Brabant, and reached, on the fifteenth day, our Dutch garrison of Bois le Duc. In our passage through Nancy my eye was gratified by the aspect of a regular and beautiful city, the work of Stanislaus, who, after the storms of Polish royalty, reposed in the love and gratitude of his new subjects of Lorraine. In our halt at Maestricht I visited Mr. De Beaufort, a learned critic, who was known to me by his specious arguments against the five first centuries of the Roman History. After dropping my regimental companions I stepped aside to visit Rotterdam and the Hague. I wished to have observed a country, the monument of freedom and industry; but my days were numbered, and a longer delay would have been ungraceful. I hastened to embark at the Brill, landed the next day at Harwich, and proceeded to London, where my father awaited my arrival. The whole term of my first absence from England was four years, ten months, and fifteen days.

In the prayers of the church our personal concerns are judiciously reduced to the threefold distinction of *mind*, *body*, and *estate*. The sentiments of the mind excite and exercise our social sympathy. The review of my moral and literary character is the most interesting to myself and to the public; and I may expatiate, without reproach, on my private studies, since they have produced the public writings which can alone entitle me to the esteem and friendship of my readers. The experience of the world inculcates a discreet reserve on the subject of our person and estate, and we soon learn that a free disclosure of our riches or poverty would provoke the malice of envy, or encourage the insolence of contempt.

The only person in England whom I was impatient to see was my aunt Porten, the affectionate guardian of my tender years.   I hastened to her house in College Street, Westminster; and the evening was spent in the effusions of joy and confidence.   It was not without some awe and apprehension that I approached the presence of my father. My infancy, to speak the truth, had been neglected at home; the severity of his look and language at our last parting still dwelt on my memory; nor could I form any notion of his character, or my probable reception.   They were both more agreeable than I could expect.   The domestic discipline of our ancestors has been relaxed by the philosophy and softness of the age; and if my father remembered that he had trembled before a stern parent, it was only to adopt with his own son an opposite mode of behaviour.   He received me as a man and a friend; all constraint was banished at our first interview, and we ever afterwards continued on the same terms of easy and equal politeness.   He applauded the success of my education; every word and action was expressive of the most cordial affection; and our lives would have passed without a cloud, if his economy had been equal to his fortune, or if his fortune had been equal to his desires. During my absence he had married his second wife, Miss Dorothea Patton, who was introduced to me with the most unfavourable prejudice.   I considered his second marriage as an act of displeasure, and I was disposed to hate the rival of my mother.   But the injustice was in my own fancy, and the imaginary monster was an amiable and deserving woman.   I could not be mistaken in the first view of her understanding, her knowledge, and the elegant spirit of her conversation: her polite welcome, and her assiduous care to study and gratify my wishes, announced at least that the surface would be smooth; and my suspicions of art and falsehood were gradually dispelled by the full discovery of her warm and exquisite

sensibility. After some reserve on my side, our minds
associated in confidence and friendship; and as Mrs.
Gibbon had neither children nor the hopes of children,
we more easily adopted the tender names and genuine
characters of mother and of son. By the indulgence of
these parents, I was left at liberty to consult my taste or
reason in the choice of place, of company, and of amusements; and my excursions were bounded only by the
limits of the island and the measure of my income. Some
faint efforts were made to procure me the employment of
secretary to a foreign embassy; and I listened to a scheme
which would again have transported me to the Continent.
Mrs. Gibbon, with seeming wisdom, exhorted me to take
chambers in the Temple, and devote my leisure to the
study of the law. I cannot repent of having neglected
her advice. Few men, without the spur of necessity,
have resolution to force their way through the thorns
and thickets of that gloomy labyrinth. Nature had not
endowed me with the bold and ready eloquence which
makes itself heard amidst the tumult of the bar; and I
should probably have been diverted from the labours of
literature, without acquiring the fame or fortune of a
successful pleader. I had no need to call to my aid the
regular duties of a profession; every day, every hour,
was agreeably filled; nor have I known, like so many of
my countrymen, the tediousness of an idle life.

Of the two years (May 1758—May 1760) between my
return to England and the embodying of the Hampshire
militia, I passed about nine months in London, and the
remainder in the country. The metropolis affords many
amusements, which are open to all. It is itself an astonish-
ing and perpetual spectacle to the curious eye; and each
taste, each sense may be gratified by the variety of objects
which will occur in the long circuit of a morning walk. I

assiduously frequented the theatres at a very propitious era of the stage, when a constellation of excellent actors, both in tragedy and comedy, was eclipsed by the meridian brightness of Garrick in the maturity of his judgment and vigour of his performance. The pleasures of a town-life are within the reach of every man who is regardless of his health, his money, and his company. By the contagion of example I was sometimes seduced; but the better habits which I had formed at Lausanne induced me to seek a more elegant and rational society; and if my search was less easy and successful than I might have hoped, I shall at present impute the failure to the disadvantages of my situation and character. Had the rank and fortune of my parents given them an annual establishment in London, their own house would have introduced me to a numerous and polite circle of acquaintance. But my father's taste had always preferred the highest and the lowest company, for which he was equally qualified; and after a twelve years' retirement he was no longer in the memory of the great with whom he had associated. I found myself a stranger in the midst of a vast and unknown city; and at my entrance into life I was reduced to some dull family parties, and some scattered connections, which were not such as I should have chosen for myself. The most useful friends of my father were the Mallets: they received me with civility and kindness, at first on his account, and afterwards on my own; and (if I may use Lord Chesterfield's words) I was soon *domesticated* in their house. Mr. Mallet, a name among the English poets, is praised by an unforgiving enemy for the ease and elegance of his conversation, and his wife was not destitute of wit or learning. By his assistance I was introduced to Lady Hervey, the mother of the present Earl of Bristol. Her age and infirmities confined her at home; her dinners were select; in the evening her house was open to the best company of both sexes and all nations; nor was I displeased at her preference and affectation of the manners, the language, and the literature of France. But my progress in the English world was in general left to my own efforts, and those efforts were languid and slow. I had not been endowed by art or nature with those happy gifts of confidence and address which unlock every door and every bosom; nor would it be reasonable to complain of the just consequences of my sickly childhood, foreign education, and reserved temper. While coaches were rattling through Bond Street, I have passed many a solitary evening in my lodging with my books. My studies were sometimes interrupted by a sigh, which I breathed towards Lausanne; and on the approach of spring I withdrew without reluctance from the noisy and extensive scene of crowds without company, and dissipation without pleasure. In each of the twenty-five years of my acquaintance with London (1758-1783) the prospect gradually brightened; and this unfavourable picture most properly belongs to the first period after my return from Switzerland.

My father's residence in Hampshire, where I have passed many light, and some heavy hours, was at Buriton, near Petersfield, one mile from the Portsmouth road, and at the easy distance of fifty-eight miles from London.[1] An old mansion, in a state of decay, had been converted into the fashion and convenience of a modern house; and if strangers had nothing to see, the inhabitants had little to desire. The spot was not happily chosen, at the end of the village and the bottom of the hill: but the aspect

[1] The estate and manor of Beriton, otherwise Buriton, were considerable, and were sold a few years ago to Lord Stawell.— SHEFFIELD.

of the adjacent grounds was various and cheerful; the downs commanded a noble prospect, and the long hanging woods in sight of the house could not perhaps have been improved by art or expense. My father kept in his own hands the whole of the estate, and even rented some additional land; and whatsoever might be the balance of profit and loss, the farm supplied him with amusement and plenty. The produce maintained a number of men and horses, which were multiplied by the intermixture of domestic and rural servants; and in the intervals of labour the favourite team, a handsome set of bays or greys, was harnessed to the coach. The economy of the house was regulated by the taste and prudence of Mrs. Gibbon. She prided herself in the elegance of her occasional dinners; and from the uncleanly avarice of Madame Pavilliard, I was suddenly transported to the daily neatness and luxury of an English table. Our immediate neighbourhood was rare and rustic; but from the verge of our hills, as far as Chichester and Goodwood, the western district of Sussex was interspersed with noble seats and hospitable families, with whom we cultivated a friendly, and might have enjoyed a very frequent, intercourse. As my stay at Buriton was always voluntary, I was received and dismissed with smiles; but the comforts of my retirement did not depend on the ordinary pleasures of the country. My father could never inspire me with his love and knowledge of farming. I never handled a gun, I seldom mounted a horse; and my philosophic walks were soon terminated by a shady bench, where I was long detained by the sedentary amusement of reading or meditation. At home I occupied a pleasant and spacious apartment; the library on the same floor was soon considered as my peculiar domain; and I might say with truth that I was never less alone than when by myself.

My sole complaint, which I piously suppressed, arose from
the kind restraint imposed on the freedom of my time.
By the habit of early rising I always secured a sacred
portion of the day, and many scattered moments were
stolen and employed by my studious industry.   But the
family hours of breakfast, of dinner, of tea, and of supper,
were regular and long: after breakfast Mrs. Gibbon
expected my company in her dressing-room; after tea
my father claimed my conversation and the perusal of
the newspapers; and in the midst of an interesting work
I was often called down to receive the visit of some idle
neighbours.   Their dinners and visits required, in due
season, a similar return; and I dreaded the period of the
full moon, which was usually reserved for our more distant
excursions.   I could not refuse attending my father, in
the summer of 1759, to the races at Stockbridge, Reading,
and Odiham, where he had entered a horse for the hunters'
plate; and I was not displeased with the sight of our
Olympic games, the beauty of the spot, the fleetness of
the horses, and the gay tumult of the numerous spectators.
As soon as the militia business was agitated, many days
were tediously consumed in meetings of deputy-lieutenants
at Petersfield, Alton, and Winchester.   In the close of the
same year, 1759, Sir Simeon (then Mr.) Stewart attempted
an unsuccessful contest for the county of Southampton,
against Mr. Legge, Chancellor of the Exchequer: a well-
known contest, in which Lord Bute's influence was first
exerted and censured.   Our canvass at Portsmouth and
Gosport lasted several days; but the interruption of my
studies was compensated in some degree by the spectacle
of English manners, and the acquisition of some practical
knowledge.

If in a more domestic or more dissipated scene my
application was somewhat relaxed, the love of knowledge

was inflamed and gratified by the command of books; and I compared the poverty of Lausanne with the plenty of London. My father's study at Buriton was stuffed with much trash of the last age, with much high church divinity and politics, which have long since gone to their proper place: yet it contained some valuable editions of the classics and the fathers, the choice, as it should seem, of Mr. Law; and many English publications of the times had been occasionally added. From this slender beginning I have gradually formed a numerous and select library, the foundation of my works, and the best comfort of my life, both at home and abroad. On the receipt of the first quarter, a large share of my allowance was appropriated to my literary wants. I cannot forget the joy with which I exchanged a bank-note of twenty pounds for the twenty volumes of the *Memoirs of the Academy of Inscriptions;* nor would it have been easy, by any other expenditure of the same sum, to have procured so large and lasting a fund of rational amusement. At a time when I most assiduously frequented this school of ancient literature, I thus expressed my opinion of a learned and various collection, which since the year 1759 has been doubled in magnitude, though not in merit—"Une de ces sociétés, qui ont mieux immortalisé Louis XIV. qu'une ambition souvent pernicieuse aux hommes, commençoit déjà ces recherches qui réunissent la justesse de l'esprit, l'aménité, et l'érudition: où l'on voit tant de découvertes, et quelquefois, ce qui ne cède qu'à peine aux découvertes, une *ignorance* modeste et *savante*." [1] The review of my library must be reserved for the period of its maturity;

---

[1] One of those Societies, which have rather immortalised Louis XIV. than an ambition often pernicious to men, already had commenced those researches which combined justness of insight, amenity, and erudition; where one notes so many discoveries, and at times that which only yields to discoveries—a modest and wholesome ignorance.

but in this place I may allow myself to observe that I
am not conscious of having ever bought a book from a
motive of ostentation, that every volume, before it was
deposited on the shelf, was either read or sufficiently
examined, and that I soon adopted the tolerating maxim
of the elder Pliny, "nullum esse librum tam malum ut
non ex aliquâ parte prodesset." [1]   I could not yet find
leisure or courage to renew the pursuit of the Greek
language, excepting by reading the lessons of the Old and
New Testament every Sunday, when I attended the family
to church.   The series of my Latin authors was less strenuously completed; but the acquisition, by inheritance or
purchase, of the best editions of Cicero, Quintilian, Livy,
Tacitus, Ovid, etc., afforded a fair prospect, which I
seldom neglected.   I persevered in the useful method of
abstracts and observations; and a single example may
suffice, of a note which had almost swelled into a work.
The solution of a passage of Livy (xxxviii. 38) involved
me in the dry and dark treatises of Greaves, Arbuthnot,
Hooper, Bernard, Eisenschmidt, Gronovius, La Barré,
Freret, etc.; and in my French essay (chap. 20) I ridicu-
lously send the reader to my own *manuscript* remarks on
the weights, coins, and measures of the ancients, which
were abruptly terminated by the militia drum.

As I am now entering on a more ample field of society
and study, I can only hope to avoid a vain and prolix
garrulity by overlooking the vulgar crowd of my acquaintance, and confining myself to such intimate friends
among books and men as are best entitled to my notice
by their own merit and reputation, or by the deep impression which they have left on my mind.   Yet I will
embrace this occasion of recommending to the young

---

[1] There is no book so bad that one cannot benefit from some
part of it."— *Pliny the Younger: Epist.* iii. 5-10.

student a practice which about this time I myself adopted.
After glancing my eye over the design and order of a new
book, I suspended the perusal till I had finished the task
of self-examination, till I had revolved, in a solitary walk,
all that I knew or believed or had thought on the subject
of the whole work, or of some particular chapter: I was
then qualified to discern how much the author added to
my original stock; and if I was sometimes satisfied by
the agreement, I was sometimes armed by the opposition,
of our ideas.   The favourite companions of my leisure
were our English writers since the Revolution: they
breathe the spirit of reason and liberty; and they most
seasonably contributed to restore the purity of my own
language, which had been corrupted by the long use of a
foreign idiom.   By the judicious advice of Mr. Mallet,
I was directed to the writings of Swift and Addison; wit
and simplicity are their common attributes; but the style
of Swift is supported by manly original vigour; that of
Addison is adorned by the female graces of elegance and
mildness.   The old reproach, that no British altars had
been raised to the Muse of History, was recently disproved
by the first performances of Robertson and Hume, the
histories of Scotland and of the Stuarts.   I will assume
the presumption of saying that I was not unworthy to
read them: nor will I disguise my different feelings in the
repeated perusals.   The perfect composition, the nervous
language, the well-turned periods of Dr. Robertson,
inflamed me to the ambitious hope that I might one day
tread in his footsteps: the calm philosophy, the careless
inimitable beauties of his friend and rival, often forced me
to close the volume with a mixed sensation of delight
and despair.

The design of my first work, the *Essay on the Study of
Literature*, was suggested by a refinement of vanity, the
desire of justifying and praising the object of a favourite

pursuit. In France, to which my ideas were confined, the learning and language of Greece and Rome were neglected by a philosophic age. The guardian of those studies, the Academy of Inscriptions, was degraded to the lowest rank among the three royal societies of Paris: the new appellation of Erudits was contemptuously applied to the successors of Lipsius and Casaubon; and I was provoked to hear (see M. d'Alembert, *Discours Préliminaire à l'Encyclopédie*) that the exercise of the memory, their sole merit, had been superseded by the nobler faculties of the imagination and the judgment. I was ambitious of proving, by my own example, as well as by my precepts, that all the faculties of the mind may be exercised and displayed by the study of ancient literature; I began to select and adorn the various proofs and illustrations which had offered themselves in reading the classics; and the first pages or chapters of my *Essay* were composed before my departure from Lausanne. The hurry of the journey, and of the first weeks of my English life, suspended all thoughts of serious application: but my object was ever before my eyes; and no more than ten days, from the first to the eleventh of July, were suffered to elapse after my summer establishment at Buriton. My *Essay* was finished in about six weeks; and as soon as a fair copy had been transcribed by one of the French prisoners at Petersfield, I looked round for a critic and judge of my first performance. A writer can seldom be content with the doubtful recompense of solitary approbation; but a youth ignorant of the world, and of himself, must desire to weigh his talents in some scales less partial than his own: my conduct was natural, my motive laudable, my choice of Dr. Maty judicious and fortunate. By descent and education Dr. Maty, though born in Holland, might be considered as a Frenchman; but he was fixed in London by the practice of physic and an office in the British Museum. His reputation was justly founded on the eighteen volumes of the *Journal Britannique,* which he had supported, almost alone, with perseverance and success. This humble though useful labour, which had once been dignified by the genius of Bayle and the learning of Le Clerc, was not disgraced by the taste, the knowledge, and the judgment of Maty: he exhibits a candid and pleasing view of the state of literature in England during a period of six years (January 1750—December 1755); and, far different from his angry son, he handles the rod of criticism with the tenderness and reluctance of a parent. The author of the *Journal Britannique* sometimes aspires to the character of a poet and philosopher: his style is pure and elegant; and in his virtues, or even in his defects, he may be ranked as one of the last disciples of the school of Fontenelle. His answer to my first letter was prompt and polite: after a careful examination he returned my manuscript, with some animadversion and much applause; and when I visited London in the ensuing winter, we discussed the design and execution in several free and familiar conversations. In a short excursion to Buriton I reviewed my *Essay,* according to his friendly advice; and after suppressing a third, adding a third, and altering a third, I consummated my first labour by a short preface, which is dated February 3rd, 1759. Yet I still shrunk from the press with the terrors of virgin modesty: the manuscript was safely deposited in my desk; and as my attention was engaged by new objects, the delay might have been prolonged till I had fulfilled the precept of Horace, "nonumque prematur in annum." [1]   Father

---

[1] "Let it be kept in the desk for nine years."—Horace, *De Arte Poetica,* l. 388.

Sirmond, a learned Jesuit, was still more rigid, since he advised a young friend to expect the mature age of fifty before he gave himself or his writings to the public (Olivet, *Histoire de l'Académie Françoise*, tom. ii. p. 143). The counsel was singular; but it is still more singular that it should have been approved by the example of the author. Sirmond was himself fifty-five years of age when he published (in 1614) his first work, an edition of Sidonius Apollinaris, with many valuable annotations. (See his Life, before the great edition of his works in five volumes folio, Paris, 1696, è Typographiâ Regiâ.)

Two years elapsed in silence: but in the spring of 1761 I yielded to the authority of a parent, and complied, like a pious son, with the wish of my own heart. My private resolves were influenced by the state of Europe. About this time the belligerent powers had made and accepted overtures of peace; our English plenipotentiaries were named to assist at the Congress of Augsburg, which never met: I wished to attend them as a gentleman or as secretary; and my father fondly believed that the proof of some literary talents might introduce me to public notice and second the recommendations of my friends. After a last revisal I consulted with Mr. Mallet and Dr. Maty, who approved the design and promoted the execution. Mr. Mallet, after hearing me read my manuscript, received it from my hands, and delivered it into those of Becket, with whom he made an agreement in my name; an easy agreement: I required only a certain number of copies; and, without transferring my property, I devolved on the bookseller the charges and profits of the edition. Dr. Maty undertook, in my absence, to correct the sheets: he inserted, without my knowledge, an elegant and flattering epistle to the author; which is composed, however, with so much art, that, in case of a defeat, his favourable report might have been ascribed to the indulgence of a friend for the rash attempt of a *young English* gentleman. The work was printed and published, under the title of " Essai sur l'Etude de la Littérature, à Londres, chez T. Becket et P. A. de Hondt, 1761," in a small volume in duodecimo: my dedication to my father, a proper and pious address, was composed the 28th of May: Dr. Maty's letter is dated the 16th of June; and I received the first copy (June 23rd) at Alresford, two days before I marched with the Hampshire militia. Some weeks afterwards, on the same ground, I presented my book to the late Duke of York, who breakfasted in Colonel Pitt's tent. By my father's direction, and Mallet's advice, many literary gifts were distributed to several eminent characters in England and France; two books were sent to the Count de Caylus, and the Duchesse d'Aiguillon, at Paris: I had reserved twenty copies for my friends at Lausanne, as the first fruits of my education, and a grateful token of my remembrance: and on all these persons I levied an unavoidable tax of civility and compliment. It is not surprising that a work, of which the style and sentiments were so totally foreign, should have been more successful abroad than at home. I was delighted by the copious extracts, the warm commendations, and the flattering predictions of the journals of France and Holland: and the next year (1762) a new edition (I believe at Geneva) extended the fame, or at least the circulation, of the work. In England it was received with cold indifference, little read, and speedily forgotten: a small impression was slowly dispersed; the bookseller murmured, and the author (had his feelings been more exquisite) might have wept over the blunders and baldness of the English translation. The publication of my *History* fifteen years afterwards revived the memory

of my first performance, and the *Essay* was eagerly sought
in the shops. But I refused the permission which Becket
solicited of reprinting it: the public curiosity was imperfectly satisfied by a pirated copy of the booksellers of
Dublin; and when a copy of the original edition has been
discovered in a sale, the primitive value of half-a-crown
has risen to the fanciful price of a guinea or thirty shillings.

I have expatiated on the petty circumstances and
period of my first publication, a memorable era in the
life of a student when he ventures to reveal the measure
of his mind: his hopes and fears are multiplied by the
idea of self-importance, and he believes for a while that
the eyes of mankind are fixed on his person and performance. Whatever may be my present reputation, it no
longer rests on the merit of this first essay; and at the
end of twenty-eight years I may appreciate my juvenile
work with the impartiality, and almost with the indifference, of a stranger. In his answer to Lady Hervey,
the Count de Caylus admires, or affects to admire, " les
livres sans nombre que Mr. Gibbon a lus et très bien lus." [1]
But, alas! my stock of erudition at that time was scanty
and superficial; and if I allow myself the liberty of naming
the Greek masters, my genuine and personal acquaintance
was confined to the Latin classics. The most serious
defect of my *Essay* is a kind of obscurity and abruptness,
which always fatigues, and may often elude, the attention
of the reader. Instead of a precise and proper definition
of the title itself, the sense of the word *Littérature* is loosely
and variously applied: a number of remarks and examples,
historical, critical, philosophical, are heaped on each other
without method or connection; and, if we except some
introductory pages, all the remaining chapters might

[1] The volumes, so numerous which Mr. Gibbon has not only
read but read to such advantage.— *Miscel. Works*, II. 43.

indifferently be reversed or transposed. The obscurity of many passages is often affected, *brevis esse laboro, obscurus fio ;* [1] the desire of expressing perhaps a common idea with sententious and oracular brevity; alas! how fatal has been the imitation of Montesquieu! But this obscurity sometimes proceeds from a mixture of light and darkness in the author's mind; from a partial ray which strikes upon an angle, instead of spreading itself over the surface of an object. After this fair confession I shall presume to say that the *Essay* does credit to a young writer of two-and-twenty years of age, who had read with taste, who thinks with freedom, and who writes in a foreign language with spirit and elegance. The defence of the early *History of Rome* and the new *Chronology* of Sir Isaac Newton form a specious argument. The patriotic and political design of the *Georgics* is happily conceived; and any probable conjecture, which tends to raise the dignity of the poet and the poem, deserves to be adopted without a rigid scrutiny. Some dawnings of a philosophic spirit enlighten the general remarks on the study of history and of man. I am not displeased with the inquiry into the origin and nature of the gods of polytheism, which might deserve the illustration of a riper judgment. Upon the whole, I may apply to the first labour of my pen the speech of a far superior artist, when he surveyed the first productions of his pencil. After viewing some portraits which he had painted in his youth, my friend Sir Joshua Reynolds acknowledged to me that he was rather humbled than flattered by the comparison with his present works; and that, after so much time and study, he had conceived his improvement to be much greater than he found it to have been.

---

[1] Labouring to be concise I become obscure.
Horace, *De Arte Poetica*, l. 25.

At Lausanne I composed the first chapters of my *Essay* in French, the familiar language of my conversation and studies, in which it was easier for me to write than in my mother-tongue. After my return to England I continued the same practice, without any affectation, or design of repudiating (as Dr. Bentley would say) my vernacular idiom. But I should have escaped some anti-Gallican clamour had I been content with the more natural character of an English author. I should have been more consistent had I rejected Mallet's advice of prefixing an English dedication to a French book; a confusion of tongues that seemed to accuse the ignorance of my patron. The use of a foreign dialect might be excused by the hope of being employed as a negotiator, by the desire of being generally understood on the Continent; but my true motive was doubtless the ambition of new and singular fame, an Englishman claiming a place among the writers of France. The Latin tongue had been consecrated by the service of the church, it was refined by the imitation of the ancients; and in the fifteenth and sixteenth centuries the scholars of Europe enjoyed the advantage, which they have gradually resigned, of conversing and writing in a common and learned idiom. As that idiom was no longer in any country the vulgar speech, they all stood on a level with each other; yet a citizen of old Rome might have smiled at the best Latinity of the Germans and Britons; and we may learn from the *Ciceronianus* of Erasmus how difficult it was found to steer a middle course between pedantry and barbarism. The Romans themselves had sometimes attempted a more perilous task, of writing in a living language, and appealing to the taste and judgment of the natives. The vanity of Tully was doubly interested in the Greek memoirs of his own consulship; and if he modestly

supposes that some Latinisms m'ght be detected in his
style, he is confident of his own skill n the art of Isocrates
and Aristotle; and he requests his friend Atticus to
disperse the copies of his work at Athens, and in the other
cities of Greece (*ad Atticum*, i. 19, ii. 1). But it must not
be forgotten that, from infancy to manhood, Cicero and
his contemporaries had read, and declaimed, and composed, with equal diligence in both languages; and that
he was not allowed to frequent a Latin school till he
had imbibed the lessons of the Greek grammarians and
rhetoricians. In modern times the language of France
has been diffused by the merit of her writers, the social
manners of the natives, the influence of the monarchy,
and the exile of the Protestants. Several foreigners have
seized the opportunity of speaking to Europe in this
common dialect, and Germany may plead the authority
of Leibnitz and Frederic, of the first of her philosophers
and the greatest of her kings. The just pride and laudable
prejudice of England has restrained this communication
of idioms; and, of all the nations on this side of the Alps,
my countrymen are the least practised and least perfect
in the exercise of the French tongue. By Sir William
Temple and Lord Chesterfield it was only used on occasions
of civility and business, and their printed letters will not
be quoted as models of composition. Lord Bolingbroke
may have published in French a sketch of his *Reflections
on Exile ;* but his reputation now reposes on the address
of Voltaire, " Docte sermones utriusque linguæ; "[1] and,
by his English dedication to Queen Caroline and his
Essay on Epic Poetry, it should seem that Voltaire himself wished to deserve a return of the same compliment.
The exception of Count Hamilton cannot fairly be urged;
though an Irishman by birth, he was educated in France

[1] His learned addresses in both languages.

from his childhood. Yet I am surprised that a long residence in England, and the habits of domestic conversation, did not affect the ease and purity of his inimitable style; and I regret the omission of his English verses, which might have afforded an amusing object of comparison. I might therefore assume the *primus ego in patriam, etc. ;* [1] but with what success I have explored this untrodden path must be left to the decision of my French readers. Dr. Maty, who might himself be questioned as a foreigner, has secured his retreat at my expense. " Je ne crois pas que vous vous piquiez d'être moins facile à reconnoître pour un Anglois que Lucullus pour un Romain." [2] My friends at Paris have been more indulgent: they received me as a countryman, or at least as a provincial; but they were friends and Parisians. [3] The defects which Maty insinuates, " Ces traits saillants, ces figures hardies, ce sacrifice de la règle au sentiment, et de la cadence à la force," [4] are the faults of the youth rather than of the stranger: and after the long and laborious exercise of my own language I am conscious that my French style has been ripened and improved.

I have already hinted that the publication of my *Essay* was delayed till I had embraced the military profession. I shall now amuse myself with the recollection of an active

[1] " I first into my fatherland shall come," from Virgil, *Georgics*, III. 10—rendered by Dryden, " I first of Romans, shall in triumph come from conquered Greece and bring her trophies home."

[2] I do not believe that you plumed yourself on being less easy to understand as an Englishman than Lucullus as a Roman."

[3] The copious extracts which were given in the *Journal Etranger* by Mr. Suard, a judicious critic, must satisfy both the author and the public. I may here observe, that I have never seen in any literary review a tolerable account of my *History*. The manufacture of journals, at least on the Continent, is miserably debased.

[4] Those virile traits, those bold figures, that sacrifice of rules to sentiment and of assonance to strength."—*Miscel. Works*, IV. 13.

scene, which bears no affinity to any other period of my studious and social life.

In the outset of a glorious war the English people had been defended by the aid of German mercenaries. A national militia has been the cry of every patriot since the Revolution; and this measure, both in parliament and in the field, was supported by the country gentlemen or Tories, who insensibly transferred their loyalty to the House of Hanover: in the language of Mr. Burke, they have changed the idol, but they have preserved the idolatry. In the act of offering our names and receiving our commissions as major and captain in the Hampshire regiment (June 12, 1759), we had not supposed that we should be dragged away, my father from his farm, myself from my books, and condemned, during two years and a half (May 10, 1760—December 23, 1762), to a wandering life of military servitude. But a weekly or monthly exercise of thirty thousand provincials would have left them useless and ridiculous; and after the pretence of an invasion had vanished, the popularity of Mr. Pitt gave a sanction to the illegal step of keeping them till the end of the war under arms, in constant pay and duty, and at a distance from their respective homes. When the king's order for our embodying came down, it was too late to retreat, and too soon to repent. The South battalion of the Hampshire militia was a small independent corps of four hundred and seventy-six officers and men, commanded by Lieutenant-Colonel Sir Thomas Worsley, who, after a prolix and passionate contest, delivered us from the tyranny of the Lord Lieutenant, the Duke of Bolton. My proper station, as first captain, was at the head of my own, and afterwards of the grenadier company; but in the absence, or even in the presence, of the two field officers, I was entrusted by my friend and my father with the effective labour of dictating the orders, and exercising the battalion. With the help of an original journal, I could write the history of my bloodless and inglorious campaigns; but as these events have lost much of their importance in my own eyes, they shall be despatched in a few words. From Winchester, the first place of assembly (June 4, 1760), we were removed, at our own request, for the benefit of a foreign education. By the arbitrary, and often capricious, orders of the War Office, the battalion successively marched to the pleasant and hospitable Blandford (June 17); to Hilsea barracks, a seat of disease and discord (September 1); to Cranbrook in the Weald of Kent (December 11); to the sea-coast of Dover (December 27); to Winchester camp (June 25, 1761); to the populous and disorderly town of Devizes (October 23); to Salisbury (February 28, 1762); to our beloved Blandford a second time (March 9); and finally, to the fashionable resort of Southampton (June 2), where the colours were fixed till our final dissolution (December 23). On the beach at Dover we had exercised in sight of the Gallic shores. But the most splendid and useful scene of our life was a four months' encampment on Winchester Down, under the command of the Earl of Effingham. Our army consisted of the Thirty-fourth Regiment of Foot and six militia corps. The consciousness of defects was stimulated by friendly emulation. We improved our time and opportunities in morning and evening field-days; and in the general reviews the South Hampshire were rather a credit than a disgrace to the line. In our subsequent quarters of the Devizes and Blandford we advanced with a quick step in our military studies; the ballot of the ensuing summer renewed our vigour and youth; and had the militia subsisted another year, we might have contested the prize with the most perfect of our brethren.

The loss of so many busy and idle hours was not compensated by any elegant pleasure; and my temper was insensibly soured by the society of our rustic officers. In every state there exists, however, a balance of good and evil. The habits of a sedentary life were usefully broken by the duties of an active profession: in the healthful exercise of the field I hunted with a battalion, instead of a pack; and at that time I was ready, at any hour of the day or night, to fly from quarters to London, from London to quarters, on the slightest call of private or regimental business. But my principal obligation to the militia was the making me an Englishman and a soldier. After my foreign education, with my reserved temper, I should long have continued a stranger to my native country, had I not been shaken in this various scene of new faces and new friends; had not experience forced me to feel the characters of our leading men, the state of parties, the forms of office, and the operation of our civil and military system. In this peaceful service I imbibed the rudiments of the language and science of tactics, which opened a new field of study and observation. I diligently read and meditated the *Mémoires Militaires* of Quintus Icilius (Mr. Guichardt), the only writer who has united the merits of a professor and a veteran. The discipline and evolutions of a modern battalion gave me a clearer notion of the phalanx and the legion; and the captain of the Hampshire grenadiers (the reader may smile) has not been useless to the historian of the Roman Empire.

A youth of any spirit is fired even by the play of arms, and in the first sallies of my enthusiasm I had seriously attempted to embrace the regular profession of a soldier. But this military fever was cooled by the enjoyment of our mimic Bellona, who soon unveiled to my eyes her naked deformity. How often did I sigh for my proper station in society and letters! How often (a proud comparison) did I repeat the complaint of Cicero in the command of a provincial army! " Clitellæ bovi sunt impositæ. Est incredibile quàm me negotii tædeat. Non habet satis magnum campum ille tibi non ignotus cursus animi; et industriæ meæ præclara opera cessat. Lucem, *libros*, urbem, domum, vos desidero. Sed feram, ut potero; sit modo annuum. Si prorogatur, actum est." [1] From a service without danger I might indeed have retired without disgrace; but as often as I hinted a wish of resigning, my fetters were riveted by the friendly entreaties of the colonel, the parental authority of the major, and my own regard for the honour and welfare of the battalion. When I felt that my personal escape was impracticable, I bowed my neck to the yoke: my servitude was protracted far beyond the annual patience of Cicero; and it was not till after the preliminaries of peace that I received my discharge, from the act of government which disembodied the militia.

When I complain of the loss of time, justice to myself and to the militia must throw the greatest part of that reproach on the first seven or eight months, while I was obliged to learn as well as to teach. The dissipation of Blandford, and the disputes of Portsmouth, consumed the hours which were not employed in the field; and amid the perpetual hurry of an inn, a barrack, or a guard-room, all literary ideas were banished from my mind. After this long fast, the longest which I have ever known, I

---

[1] " The paniers of the ass have been put on the ox; it is incredible how tired I am of the whole business. The activity of my mind, wherewith you are not unacquainted, has not sufficient scope wherein to exert itself, and the notable results of my industry go for nothing. I long for fame, books, city life, and my home. If I can, I shall endure it, provided the limit be only one year; if it is prolonged all is at an end."—*Epist. ad Atticum*, lib. v. 15.

once more tasted at Dover the pleasures of reading and thinking; and the hungry appetite with which I opened a volume of Tully's philosophical works is still present to my memory. The last review of my *Essay* before its publication had prompted me to investigate the *nature of the gods;* my inquiries led me to the *Histoire Critique du Manichéisme* of Beausobre, who discusses many deep questions of Pagan and Christian theology: and from this rich treasury of facts and opinions I deduced my own consequences, beyond the holy circle of the author. After this recovery I never relapsed into indolence; and my example might prove that in the life most averse to study some hours may be stolen, some minutes may be snatched. Amidst the tumult of Winchester camp I sometimes thought and read in my tent; in the more settled quarters of the Devizes, Blandford, and Southampton, I always secured a separate lodging and the necessary books; and in the summer of 1762, while the new militia was raising, I enjoyed at Beriton two or three months of literary repose. In forming a new plan of study, I hesitated between the mathematics and the Greek language; both of which I had neglected since my return from Lausanne. I consulted a learned and friendly mathematician, Mr. George Scott, a pupil of de Moivre; and his map of a country which I have never explored may perhaps be more serviceable to others. As soon as I had given the preference to Greek, the example of Scaliger and my own reason determined me on the choice of Homer, the father of poetry, and the Bible of the ancients: but Scaliger ran through the *Iliad* in one-and-twenty days; and I was not dissatisfied with my own diligence for performing the same labour in an equal number of weeks. After the first difficulties were surmounted, the language of nature and harmony soon became easy and familiar, and each day

I sailed upon the ocean with a brisker gale and a more
steady course.

'Εν δ' ἄνεμος πρῆσεν μέσον ἱστίον, ἀμφὶ δὲ κῦμα
Στείρῃ πορφύρεον μεγάλ' ἴαχε, νηὸς ἰούσης·
'Η δ' ἔθεεν κατὰ κῦμα διαπρήσσουσα κέλευθαν.   *Ilias*, A. 481.[1]

In the study of a poet who has since become the most
intimate of my friends, I successively applied many
passages and fragments of Greek writers; and among
these I shall notice a Life of Homer, in the *Opuscula
Mythologica* of Gale, several books of the *Geography* of
Strabo, and the entire treatise of Longinus, which, from
the title and the style, is equally worthy of the epithet
of *sublime*.   My grammatical skill was improved, my
vocabulary was enlarged; and in the militia I acquired
a just and indelible knowledge of the first of languages.
On every march, in every journey, Horace was always in
my pocket, and often in my hand; but I should not
mention his two critical epistles, the amusement of a
morning, had they not been accompanied by the elaborate
commentary of Dr. Hurd, now Bishop of Worcester.   On
the interesting subjects of composition and imitation of
epic and dramatic poetry I presumed to think for myself;
and thirty close-written pages in folio could scarcely
comprise my full and free discussion of the sense of the
master and the pedantry of the servant.

After his oracle Dr. Johnson, my friend Sir Joshua
Reynolds denies all original genius, any natural propensity
of the mind to one art or science rather than another.

---

[1] " ——Fair wind and blowing fresh,
Apollo sent them; quick they reared the mast,
Then spread the unsullied canvas to the gale,
And the wind filled it.   Roared the sable flood
Around the bark that ever as she went
Dashed wide the brine, and scudded swift away."

Without engaging in a metaphysical or rather verbal dispute, I *know*, by experience, that from my early youth I aspired to the character of an historian.   While I served in the militia, before and after the publication of my *Essay*, this idea ripened in my mind; nor can I paint in more lively colours the feelings of the moment than by transcribing some passages, under their respective dates, from a journal which I kept at that time.

BERITON, APRIL 14, 1761.

(*In a short excursion from Dover.*)

" Having thought of several subjects for an historical composition, I chose the expedition of Charles VIII. of France into Italy.   I read two memoirs of Mr. de Fonce-magne in the *Academy of Inscriptions* (tom. xvii. p. 539-607), and abstracted them.   I likewise finished this day a dissertation, in which I examined the right of Charles VIII. to the crown of Naples, and the rival claims of the House of Anjou and Arragon: it consists of ten folio pages, besides large notes."

BERITON, AUGUST 4, 1761.

(*In a week's excursion from Winchester camp.*)

" After having long revolved subjects for my intended historical essay, I renounced my first thought of the expedition of Charles VIII. as too remote from us, and rather an introduction to great events than great and important in itself.   I successively chose and rejected the crusade of Richard I., the barons' wars against John and Henry III., the history of Edward the Black Prince, the lives and comparisons of Henry V. and the Emperor Titus, the life of Sir Philip Sidney, and that of the Marquis of

Montrose. At length I have fixed on Sir Walter Raleigh
for my hero. His eventful story is varied by the characters
of the soldier and sailor, the courtier and historian; and
it may afford such a fund of materials as I desire, which
have not yet been properly manufactured. At present
I cannot attempt the execution of this work. Free
leisure, and the opportunity of consulting many books,
both printed and manuscript, are as necessary as they are
impossible to be attained in my present way of life. However, to acquire a general insight into my subject and
resources, I read the *Life of Sir Walter Raleigh* by Dr.
Birch, his copious article in the *General Dictionary* by
the same hand, and the reigns of Queen Elizabeth and
James I. in Hume's *History of England*."

BERITON, JANUARY 1762.
(In a month's absence from the Devizes.)

" During this interval of repose I again turned my
thoughts to Sir Walter Raleigh, and looked more closely
into my materials. I read the two volumes in quarto of
the *Bacon Papers*, published by Dr. Birch; the *Fragmenta
Regalia* of Sir Robert Naunton; Mallet's *Life of Lord
Bacon*, and the political treatises of that great man in the
first volume of his works, with many of his letters in the
second; Sir William Monson's *Naval Tracts ;* and the
elaborate *Life of Sir Walter Raleigh*, which Mr. Oldys has
prefixed to the best edition of his *History of the World*.
My subject opens upon me, and in general improves upon
a nearer prospect."

BERITON, JULY 26, 1762.
(During my summer residence.)

" I am afraid of being reduced to drop my hero; but
my time has not, however, been lost in the research of

his story, and of a memorable era of our English annals. The *Life of Sir Walter Raleigh*, by Oldys, is a very poor performance; a servile panegyric, or flat apology, tediously minute, and composed in a dull and affected style. Yet the author was a man of diligence and learning, who had read everything relative to his subject, and whose ample collections are arranged with perspicuity and method. Excepting some anecdotes lately revealed in the *Sidney* and *Bacon Papers*, I know not what I should be able to add. My ambition (exclusive of the uncertain merit of style and sentiment) must be confined to the hope of giving a good abridgment of Oldys. I have even the disappointment of finding some parts of this copious work very dry and barren; and these parts are unluckily some of the most characteristic; Raleigh's colony of Virginia, his quarrels with Essex, the true secret of his conspiracy, and, above all, the detail of his private life, the most essential and important to a biographer. My best resource would be in the circumjacent history of the times, and perhaps in some digressions artfully introduced, like the fortunes of the Peripatetic philosophy in the portrait of Lord Bacon. But the reigns of Elizabeth and James I. are the periods of English history which have been the most variously illustrated; and what new lights could I reflect on a subject which has exercised the accurate industry of *Birch*, the lively and curious acuteness of *Walpole*, the critical spirit of *Hurd*, the vigorous sense of *Mallet* and *Robertson*, and the impartial philosophy of *Hume* ? Could I even surmount these obstacles, I should shrink with terror from the modern history of England, where every character is a problem, and every reader a friend or an enemy; where a writer is supposed to hoist a flag of party, and is devoted to damnation by the adverse faction. Such would be *my* reception at home:

and abroad, the historian of Raleigh must encounter an indifference far more bitter than censure or reproach. The events of his life are interesting; but his character is ambiguous, his actions are obscure, his writings are English, and his fame is confined to the narrow limits of our language and our island. I must embrace a safer and more extensive theme.

"There is one which I should prefer to all others, *The History of the Liberty of the Swiss*, of that independence which a brave people rescued from the House of Austria, defended against a dauphin of France, and finally sealed with the blood of Charles of Burgundy. From such a theme, so full of public spirit, of military glory, of examples of virtue, of lessons of government, the dullest stranger would catch fire: what might not *I* hope, whose talents, whatsoever they may be, would be inflamed with the zeal of patriotism! But the materials of this history are inaccessible to me, fast locked in the obscurity of an old barbarous German dialect, of which I am totally ignorant, and which I cannot resolve to learn for this sole and peculiar purpose.

"I have another subject in view, which is the contrast of the former history: the one a poor, warlike, virtuous republic, which emerges into glory and freedom; the other a commonwealth, soft, opulent, and corrupt; which, by just degrees, is precipitated from the abuse to the loss of her liberty: both lessons are, perhaps, equally instructive. This second subject is, *The History of the Republic of Florence, under the House of Medicis :* a period of one hundred and fifty years, which rises or descends from the dregs of the Florentine democracy to the title and dominion of Cosmo de Medicis in the Grand Duchy of Tuscany. I might deduce a chain of revolutions not un-worthy of the pen of Vertot; singular men, and singular events; the Medicis four times expelled, and as often recalled; and the Genius of Freedom reluctantly yielding to the arms of Charles V. and the policy of Cosmo. The character and fate of Savonarola, and the revival of arts and letters in Italy, will be essentially connected with the elevation of the family and the fall of the republic. The Medicis, *stirps quasi fataliter nata ad instauranda vel fovenda studia* (*Lipsius ad Germanos et Gallos*, Epist. viii.), were illustrated by the patronage of learning; and enthusiasm was the most formidable weapon of their adversaries. On this splendid subject I shall most probably fix; but *when*, or *where*, or *how* will it be executed? I behold in a dark and doubtful perspective

Res altâ terrâ, et caligine mersas." [1]

The youthful habits of the language and manners of France had left in my mind an ardent desire of revisiting the Continent on a larger and more liberal plan. According to the law of custom, and perhaps of reason, foreign travel completes the education of an English gentleman: my father had consented to my wish, but I was detained above four years by my rash engagement in the militia. I eagerly grasped the first moments of freedom: three or four weeks in Hampshire and London were employed in the preparations of my journey, and the farewell visits of friendship and civility: my last act in town was to applaud Mallet's new tragedy of *Elvira*; a post-chaise conveyed me to Dover, the packet to Boulogne, and such was my diligence that I reached Paris on the 28th of January 1763, only thirty-six days after the disbanding of the militia. Two or three years were loosely defined for the term of my absence; and I was left at liberty to

[1] " Things plunged in the depths of the earth and in darkness." —*Æneid*, vi. 267.

spend that time in such places and in such a manner as
was most agreeable to my taste and judgment.

In this first visit I passed three months and a half
(January 28—May 9), and a much longer space might
have been agreeably filled without any intercourse with
the natives. At home we are content to move in the daily
round of pleasure and business; and a scene which is
always present is supposed to be within our knowledge,
or at least within our power. But in a foreign country,
curiosity is our business and our pleasure; and the
traveller, conscious of his ignorance, and covetous of his
time, is diligent in the search and the view of every object
than can deserve his attention. I devoted many hours
of the morning to the circuit of Paris and the neighbourhood, to the visit of churches and palaces conspicuous by
their architecture, to the royal manufactures, collections
of books and pictures, and all the various treasures of art,
of learning, and of luxury. An Englishman may hear
without reluctance that in these curious and costly
articles Paris is superior to London; since the opulence
of the French capital arises from the defects of its government and religion. In the absence of Louis XIV. and
his successors, the Louvre has been left unfinished: but
the millions which have been lavished on the sands of
Versailles, and the morass of Marli, could not be supplied
by the legal allowance of a British king. The splendour
of the French nobles is confined to their town residence;
that of the English is more usefully distributed in their
country seats; and we should be astonished at our own
riches, if the labours of architecture, the spoils of Italy
and Greece, which are now scattered from Inverary to
Wilton, were accumulated in a few streets between
Marylebone and Westminster. All superfluous ornament
is rejected by the cold frugality of the Protestants; but

the Catholic superstition, which is always the enemy of reason, is often the parent of the arts. The wealthy communities of priests and monks expend their revenues in stately edifices; and the parish church of St. Sulpice, one of the noblest structures in Paris, was built and adorned by the private industry of a late curé. In this outset, and still more in the sequel of my tour, my eye was amused; but the pleasing vision cannot be fixed by the pen; the particular images are darkly seen through the medium of five-and-twenty years, and the narrative of my life must not degenerate into a book of travels.

But the principal end of my journey was to enjoy the society of a polished and amiable people, in whose favour I was strongly prejudiced, and to converse with some authors, whose conversation, as I fondly imagined, must be far more pleasing and instructive than their writings. The moment was happily chosen. At the close of a successful war the British name was respected on the Continent:

——— Clarum et venerabile nomen
Gentibus.[1]

Our opinions, our fashions, even our games, were adopted in France; a ray of national glory illuminated each individual, and every Englishman was supposed to be born a patriot and a philosopher. For myself, I carried a personal recommendation; my name and my *Essay* were already known; the compliment of having written in the French language entitled me to some returns of civility and gratitude. I was considered as a man of letters, who wrote for amusement. Before my departure I had obtained from the Duke de Nivernois, Lady Hervey, the Mallets, Mr. Walpole, etc., many letters of recom-

---

[1] "A name illustrious and venerable among the nations."—Lucan, ix. 202.

mendation to their private or literary friends. Of these
epistles the reception and success were determined by the
character and situation of the persons by whom and to
whom they were addressed: the seed was sometimes cast
on a barren rock, and it sometimes multiplied a hundred
fold in the production of new shoots, spreading branches,
and exquisite fruit. But upon the whole, I had reason to
praise the national urbanity, which from the court has
diffused its gentle influence to the shop, the cottage, and
the schools. Of the men of genius of the age, Montesquieu
and Fontenelle were no more; Voltaire resided on his own
estate near Geneva; Rousseau in the preceding year had
been driven from his hermitage of Montmorency; and I
blush at my having neglected to seek, in this journey, the
acquaintance of Buffon. Among the men of letters whom
I saw, d'Alembert and Diderot held the foremost rank in
merit, or at least in fame. I shall content myself with
enumerating the well-known names of the Count de Caylus,
of the Abbé de la Bleterie, Barthelemy, Reynal, Arnaud,
of Messieurs de la Condamine, du Clos, de Ste. Palayé,
de Bougainville, Caperonnier, de Guignes, Suard, etc.,
without attempting to discriminate the shades of their
characters, or the degrees of our connection. Alone, in
a morning visit, I commonly found the artists and authors
of Paris less vain, and more reasonable, than in the circles
of their equals, with whom they mingle in the houses of
the rich. Four days in a week I had a place, without
invitation, at the hospitable tables of Mesdames Geoffrin
and du Bocage, of the celebrated Helvetius, and of the
Baron d'Olbach. In these symposia the pleasures of the
table were improved by lively and liberal conversation;
the company was select, though various and voluntary.

The society of Madame du Bocage was more soft and
moderate than that of her rivals, and the evening con-

versations of M. de Foncemagne were supported by the good sense and learning of the principal members of the Academy of Inscriptions. The opera and the Italians I occasionally visited; but the French theatre, both in tragedy and comedy, was my daily and favourite amusement. Two famous actresses then divided the public applause. For my own part, I preferred the consummate art of the Clairon to the intemperate sallies of the Dumesnil, which were extolled by her admirers as the genuine voice of nature and passion. Fourteen weeks insensibly stole away; but had I been rich and independent, I should have prolonged, and perhaps have fixed, my residence at Paris.

Between the expensive style of Paris and of Italy it was prudent to interpose some months of tranquil simplicity, and at the thoughts of Lausanne I again lived in the pleasures and studies of my early youth. Shaping my course through Dijon and Besançon, in the last of which places I was kindly entertained by my cousin Acton, I arrived in the month of May 1763 on the banks of the Leman Lake. It had been my intention to pass the Alps in the autumn; but such are the simple attractions of the place, that the year had almost expired before my departure from Lausanne in the ensuing spring. An absence of five years had not made much alteration in manners, or even in persons. My old friends, of both sexes, hailed my voluntary return; the most genuine proof of my attachment. They had been flattered by the present of my book, the produce of their soil; and the good Pavilliard shed tears of joy as he embraced a pupil whose literary merit he might fairly impute to his own labours. To my old list I added some new acquaintance, and among the strangers I shall distinguish Prince Lewis of Wirtemberg, the brother of the reigning duke, at whose country-house, near Lausanne, I frequently dined: a wandering meteor, and at length a falling star, his light and ambitious spirit had successively dropped from the firmament of Prussia, of France, and of Austria; and his faults, which he styled his misfortunes, had driven him into philosophic exile in the Pays de Vaud. He could now moralise on the vanity of the world, the equality of mankind, and the happiness of a private station. His address was affable and polite, and, as he had shone in courts and armies, his memory could supply, and his eloquence could adorn, a copious fund of interesting anecdotes. His first enthusiasm was that of charity and agriculture; but the sage gradually lapsed in the saint, and Prince Lewis of Wirtemberg is now buried in a hermitage near Mayence, in the last stage of mystic devotion. By some ecclesiastical quarrel, Voltaire had been provoked to withdraw himself from Lausanne, and retire to his castle at Ferney, where I again visited the poet and the actor, without seeking his more intimate acquaintance, to which I might now have pleaded a better title. But the theatre which he had founded, the actors whom he had formed, survived the loss of their master; and recent from Paris, I attended with pleasure at the representation of several tragedies and comedies. I shall not descend to specify particular names and characters; but I cannot forget a private institution which will display the innocent freedom of Swiss manners. My favourite society had assumed, from the age of its members, the proud denomination of the spring (*la société du printems*). It consisted of fifteen or twenty young unmarried ladies, of genteel though not of the very first families; the eldest perhaps about twenty; all agreeable, several handsome, and two or three of exquisite beauty. At each other's houses they assembled almost every day, without the control, or even the

presence, of a mother or an aunt; they were trusted to
their own prudence among a crowd of young men of every
nation in Europe. They laughed, they sung, they danced,
they played at cards, they acted comedies; but in the
midst of this careless gaiety they respected themselves,
and were respected by the men; the invisible line between
liberty and licentiousness was never transgressed by a
gesture, a word, or a look, and their virgin chastity was
never sullied by the breath of scandal or suspicion: a
singular institution, expressive of the innocent simplicity
of Swiss manners. After having tasted the luxury of
England and Paris, I could not have returned with satisfaction to the coarse and homely table of Madame Pavilliard; nor was her husband offended that I now entered
myself as a *pensionnaire*, or boarder, in the elegant house
of Mr. de Mesery, which may be entitled to a short remembrance, as it has stood above twenty years, perhaps,
without a parallel in Europe. The house in which we
lodged was spacious and convenient, in the best street,
and commanding from behind a noble prospect over the
country and the lake. Our table was served with neatness and plenty; the boarders were select; we had the
liberty of inviting any guests at a stated price; and in
the summer the scene was occasionally transferred to
a pleasant villa about a league from Lausanne. The
characters of master and mistress were happily suited
to each other, and to their situation. At the age of
seventy-five, Madame de Mesery, who has survived her
husband, is still a graceful, I had almost said a handsome
woman. She was alike qualified to preside in her kitchen
and her drawing-room; and such was the equal propriety
of her conduct, that, of two or three hundred foreigners,
none ever failed in respect, none could complain of her
neglect, and none could ever boast of her favour. Mesery

himself, of the noble family of De Crousaz, was a man of
the world, a jovial companion, whose easy manners and
natural sallies maintained the cheerfulness of his house.
His wit could laugh at his own ignorance: he disguised,
by an air of profusion, a strict attention to his interest;
and in this situation he appeared like a nobleman who
spent his fortune and entertained his friends. In this
agreeable society I resided nearly eleven months (May
1763—April 1764); and in this second visit to Lausanne,
among a crowd of my English companions, I knew and
esteemed Mr. Holroyd (now Lord Sheffield); and our
mutual attachment was renewed and fortified in the
subsequent stages of our Italian journey. Our lives are
in the power of chance, and a slight variation on either
side, in time or place, might have deprived me of a friend
whose activity in the ardour of youth was always prompted
by a benevolent heart, and directed by a strong understanding.

If my studies at Paris had been confined to the study
of the world, three or four months would not have been
unprofitably spent. My visits, however superficial, to
the Academy of Medals and the public libraries, opened
a new field of inquiry; and the view of so many manuscripts of different ages and characters induced me to
consult the two great Benedictine works, the *Diplomatica*
of Mabillon, and the *Palæographia* of Montfaucon. I
studied the theory without attaining the practice of the
art: nor should I complain of the intricacy of Greek
abbreviations and Gothic alphabets, since every day, in
a familiar language, I am at a loss to decipher the hieroglyphics of a female note. In a tranquil scene, which
revived the memory of my first studies, idleness would
have been less pardonable: the public libraries of Lausanne
and Geneva liberally supplied me with books; and if

many hours were lost in dissipation, many more were employed in literary labour. In the country, Horace and Virgil, Juvenal and Ovid, were my assiduous companions: but, in town, I formed and executed a plan of study for the use of my Transalpine expedition: the topography of old Rome, the ancient geography of Italy, and the science of medals. 1. I diligently read, almost always with a pen in my hand, the elaborate treatises of Nardini, Donatus, etc., which fill the fourth volume of the *Roman Antiquities* of Grævius. 2. I next undertook and finished the *Italia Antiqua* of Cluverius, a learned native of Prussia, who had measured, on foot, every spot, and has compiled and digested every passage of the ancient writers. These passages in Greek or Latin authors I perused in the text of Cluverius, in two folio volumes: but I separately read the descriptions of Italy by Strabo, Pliny, and Pomponius Mela, the Catalogues of the epic poets, the Itineraries of Wesseling's Antoninus, and the coasting voyage of Rutilius Numatianus; and I studied two kindred subjects in the *Mesures Itinéraires* of d'Anville, and the copious work of Bergier, *Histoire des grands Chemins de l'Empire Romain*. From these materials I formed a table of roads and distances reduced to our English measure; filled a folio commonplace-book with my collections and remarks on the geography of Italy; and inserted in my journal many long and learned notes on the insulæ and populousness of Rome, the social war, the passage of the Alps by Hannibal, etc. 3. After glancing my eye over Addison's agreeable dialogues, I more seriously read the great work of Ezechiel Spanheim, *de Præstantiâ et Usû Numismatum*, and applied with him the medals of the kings and emperors, the families and colonies, to the illustration of ancient history. And thus was I armed for my Italian journey.

I shall advance with rapid brevity in the narrative of

this tour, in which somewhat more than a year (April
1764—May 1765) was agreeably employed.   Content with
tracing my line of march, and slightly touching on my
personal feelings, I shall waive the minute investigation
of the scenes which have been viewed by thousands, and
described by hundreds, of our modern travellers.   ROME
is the great object of our pilgrimage; and 1st, the journey;
2nd, the residence; and 3rd, the return, will form the
most proper and perspicuous division.   1. I climbed
Mount Cenis, and descended into the plain of Piedmont,
not on the back of an elephant, but on a light osier seat,
in the hands of the dexterous and intrepid chairmen of
the Alps.   The architecture and government of Turin
presented the same aspect of tame and tiresome uniformity, but the court was regulated with decent and
splendid economy; and I was introduced to his Sardinian
majesty Charles Emanuel, who, after the incomparable
Frederic, held the second rank (*proximus longo tamen
intervallo*) among the kings of Europe.   The size and
populousness of Milan could not surprise an inhabitant
of London; but the fancy is amused by a visit to the
Boromean Islands, an enchanted palace, a work of the
fairies in the midst of a lake encompassed with mountains,
and far removed from the haunts of men.   I was less
amused by the marble palaces of Genoa than by the recent
memorials of her deliverance (in December 1746) from
the Austrian tyranny; and I took a military survey of
every scene of action within the enclosure of her double
walls.   My steps were detained at Parma and Modena by
the precious relics of the Farnese and Este collections;
but, alas! the far greater part had been already transported, by inheritance or purchase, to Naples and Dresden.
By the road of Bologna and the Apennine I at last reached
Florence, where I reposed from June to September, during

the heat of the summer months. In the Gallery, and especially in the Tribune, I first acknowledged, at the feet of the Venus of Medicis, that the chisel may dispute the pre-eminence with the pencil, a truth in the fine arts which cannot on this side of the Alps be felt or understood. At home I had taken some lessons of Italian; on the spot I read with a learned native the classics of the Tuscan idiom; but the shortness of my time, and the use of the French language, prevented my acquiring any facility of speaking; and I was a silent spectator in the conversations of our envoy, Sir Horace Mann, whose most serious business was that of entertaining the English at his hospitable table. After leaving Florence I compared the solitude of Pisa with the industry of Lucca and Leghorn, and continued my journey through Sienna to Rome, where I arrived in the beginning of October. 2. My temper is not very susceptible of enthusiasm, and the enthusiasm which I do not feel I have ever scorned to affect. But at the distance of twenty-five years I can neither forget nor express the strong emotions which agitated my mind as I first approached and entered the *eternal city*. After a sleepless night, I trod, with a lofty step, the ruins of the Forum; each memorable spot where Romulus *stood*, or Tully spoke, or Cæsar fell, was at once present to my eye; and several days of intoxication were lost or enjoyed before I could descend to a cool and minute investigation. My guide was Mr. Byers, a Scotch antiquary of experience and taste; but in the daily labour of eighteen weeks the powers of attention were sometimes fatigued, till I was myself qualified, in a last review, to select and study the capital works of ancient and modern art. Six weeks were borrowed for my tour of Naples, the most populous of cities relative to its size, whose luxurious inhabitants seem to dwell on the confines of paradise and

hell-fire. I was presented to the boy-king by our new
envoy, Sir William Hamilton; who, wisely diverting his
correspondence from the Secretary of State to the Royal
Society and British Museum, has elucidated a country
of such inestimable value to the naturalist and antiquarian.
On my return I fondly embraced, for the last time, the
miracles of Rome; but I departed without kissing the
foot of Rezzonico (Clement XIII.), who neither possessed
the wit of his predecessor Lambertini, nor the virtues of
his successor Ganganelli.   3. In my pilgrimage from Rome
to Loretto I again crossed the Apennine: from the coast
of the Adriatic I traversed a fruitful and populous country,
which could alone disprove the paradox of Montesquieu,
that modern Italy is a desert. Without adopting the
exclusive prejudice of the natives, I sincerely admire the
paintings of the Bologna school. I hastened to escape
from the sad solitude of Ferrara, which in the age of Cæsar
was still more desolate. The spectacle of Venice afforded
some hours of astonishment; the university of Padua is
a dying taper; but Verona still boasts her amphitheatre,
and his native Vicenza is adorned by the classic architecture of Palladio: the road of Lombardy and Piedmont
(did Montesquieu find them without inhabitants?) led me
back to Milan, Turin, and the passage of Mount Cenis,
where I again crossed the Alps in my way to Lyons.

The use of foreign travel has been often debated as a
general question; but the conclusion must be finally
applied to the character and circumstances of each
individual. With the education of boys, *where* or *how*
they may pass over some juvenile years with the least
mischief to themselves or others, I have no concern. But
after supposing the previous and indispensable requisites
of age, judgment, a competent knowledge of men and
books, and a freedom from domestic prejudices, I will

briefly describe the qualifications which I deem most essential to a traveller. He should be endowed with an active, indefatigable vigour of mind and body, which can seize every mode of conveyance, and support, with a careless smile, every hardship of the road, the weather, or the inn. The benefits of foreign travel will correspond with the degrees of these qualifications; but, in this sketch, those to whom I am known will not accuse me of framing my own panegyric. It was at Rome, on the 15th of October 1764, as I sat musing amidst the ruins of the Capitol, while the barefooted friars were singing vespers in the temple of Jupiter,[1] that the idea of writing the decline and fall of the city first started to my mind. But my original plan was circumscribed to the decay of the city rather than of the empire; and though my reading and reflections began to point towards that object, some years elapsed, and several avocations intervened, before I was seriously engaged in the execution of that laborious work.

I had not totally renounced the southern provinces of France, but the letters which I found at Lyons were expressive of some impatience. Rome and Italy had satiated my curious appetite, and I was now ready to return to the peaceful retreat of my family and books. After a happy fortnight I reluctantly left Paris, embarked at Calais, again landed at Dover, after an interval of two years and five months, and hastily drove through the summer dust and solitude of London.

On the 25th of June 1765, I arrived at my father's house; and the five years and a half between my travels and my father's death (1770) are the portion of my life

[1] Now the church of the Zocolants, or Franciscan Friars.— SHEFFIELD.

which I passed with the least enjoyment, and which I remember with the least satisfaction. Every spring I attended the monthly meeting and exercise of the militia at Southampton; and by the resignation of my father, and the death of Sir Thomas Worsley, I was successively promoted to the rank of major and lieutenant-colonel commandant; but I was each year more disgusted with the inn, the wine, the company, and the tiresome repetition of annual attendance and daily exercise. At home, the economy of the family and farm still maintained the same creditable appearance. My connection with Mrs. Gibbon was mellowed into a warm and solid attachment; my growing years abolished the distance that might yet remain between a parent and a son; and my behaviour satisfied my father, who was proud of the success, however imperfect in his own lifetime, of my literary talents. Our solitude was soon and often enlivened by the visit of the friend of my youth, M. Deyverdun, whose absence from Lausanne I had sincerely lamented. About three years after my first departure he had emigrated from his native lake to the banks of the Oder in Germany. The *res angusta domi*, the waste of a decent patrimony by an improvident father, obliged him, like many of his countrymen, to confide in his own industry; and he was entrusted with the education of a young prince, the grandson of the Margrave of Schavedt, of the royal family of Prussia. Our friendship was never cooled, our correspondence was sometimes interrupted; but I rather wished than hoped to obtain M. Deyverdun for the companion of my Italian tour. An unhappy though honourable passion drove him from his German court; and the attractions of hope and curiosity were fortified by the expectation of my speedy return to England. During four successive summers he passed several weeks or months at Beriton, and our free conversations, on every topic that could interest the heart or understanding, would have reconciled me to a desert or a prison. In the winter months of London my sphere of knowledge and action was somewhat enlarged by the many new acquaintance which I had contracted in the militia and abroad; and I must regret, as more than an acquaintance, Mr. Godfrey Clarke of Derbyshire, an amiable and worthy young man, who was snatched away by an untimely death. A weekly convivial meeting was established by myself and other travellers, under the name of the Roman Club.[1]

The renewal, or perhaps the improvement, of my English life was embittered by the alteration of my own feelings. At the age of twenty-one I was, in my proper station of a youth, delivered from the yoke of education, and delighted with the comparative state of liberty and affluence. My filial obedience was natural and easy; and in the gay prospect of futurity my ambition did not extend beyond the enjoyment of my books, my leisure, and my patrimonial estate, undisturbed by the cares of a family and the duties of a profession. But in the militia I was armed with power; in my travels I was exempt from control; and as I approached, as I gradually passed my thirtieth year, I began to feel the desire of being master in my own house. The most gentle authority will sometimes frown without reason, the most cheerful submission will sometimes murmur without cause; and such is the law of our imperfect nature, that we must

[1] The members were Lord Mountstuart (now Marquis of Bute), Colonel Edmonstone, William Weddal, Rev. Mr. Palgrave, Earl of Berkley, Godfrey Clarke (Member for Derbyshire), Holroyd (Lord Sheffield), Major Ridley, Thomas Charles Bigge, Sir William Guise, Sir John Aubrey, the late Earl of Abingdon, Hon. Peregrine Bertie, Rev. Mr. Cleaver, Hon. John Damer, Hon. George Damer (late Earl of Dorchester), Sir Thomas Gascoygne, Sir John Hort, E. Gibbon.

either command or obey; that our personal liberty is supported by the obsequiousness of our own dependants. While so many of my acquaintance were married or in parliament, or advancing with a rapid step in the various roads of honour and fortune, I stood alone, immovable and insignificant; for after the monthly meeting of 1770 I had even withdrawn myself from the militia, by the resignation of an empty and barren commission. My temper is not susceptible of envy, and the view of successful merit has always excited my warmest applause. The miseries of a vacant life were never known to a man whose hours were insufficient for the inexhaustible pleasures of study. But I lamented that at the proper age I had not embraced the lucrative pursuits of the law or of trade, the chances of civil office or India adventure, or even the fat slumbers of the church; and my repentance became more lively as the loss of time was more irretrievable. Experience showed me the use of grafting my private consequence on the importance of a great professional body; the benefits of those firm connections which are cemented by hope and interest, by gratitude and emulation, by the mutual exchange of services and favours. From the emoluments of a profession I might have derived an ample fortune, or a competent income, instead of being stinted to the same narrow allowance, to be increased only by an event which I sincerely deprecated. The progress and the knowledge of our domestic disorders aggravated my anxiety, and I began to apprehend that I might be left in my old age without the fruits either of industry or inheritance.

In the first summer after my return, whilst I enjoyed at Beriton the society of my friend Deyverdun, our daily conversations expatiated over the field of ancient and modern literature; and we freely discussed my studies,

my first *Essay*, and my future projects.   The *Decline and
Fall of Rome* I still contemplated at an awful distance:
but the two historical designs which had balanced my
choice were submitted to his taste; and in the parallel
between the Revolutions of Florence and Switzerland,
our common partiality for a country which was *his* by
birth, and *mine* by adoption, inclined the scale in favour
of the latter.   According to the plan, which was soon
conceived and digested, I embraced a period of two
hundred years, from the association of the three peasants
of the Alps to the plenitude and prosperity of the Helvetic
body in the sixteenth century.   I should have described
the deliverance and victory of the Swiss, who have never
shed the blood of their tyrants but in a field of battle;
the laws and manners of the confederate states;   the
splendid trophies of the Austrian, Burgundian, and
Italian wars; and the wisdom of a nation who, after some
sallies of martial adventure, has been content to guard
the blessings of peace with the sword of freedom.

> —— Manus hæc inimica tyrannis
> Ense petit placidam sub libertate quietem.[1]

My judgment, as well as my enthusiasm, was satisfied
with the glorious theme; and the assistance of Deyverdun
seemed to remove an insuperable obstacle.   The French
or Latin memorials, of which I was not ignorant, are in-
considerable in number and weight; but in the perfect
acquaintance of my friend with the German language I
found the key of a more valuable collection.   The most
necessary books were procured; he translated, for my
use, the folio volume of Schilling, a copious and con-
temporary relation of the war of Burgundy; we read and

[1] This hand hostile to tyrants seeks even by the sword to ensure
peace with liberty.

marked the most interesting parts of the great chronicle of Tschudi; and by his labour, or that of an inferior assistant, large extracts were made from the History of Lauffer and the Dictionary of Lew; yet such was the distance and delay, that two years elapsed in these preparatory steps; and it was late in the third summer (1767) before I entered, with these slender materials, on the more agreeable task of composition. A specimen of my *History*, the first book, was read the following winter in a literary society of foreigners in London; and as the author was unknown, I listened, without observation, to the free strictures, and unfavourable sentence, of my judges. The momentary sensation was painful; but their condemnation was ratified by my cooler thoughts. I delivered my imperfect sheets to the flames,[1] and for ever renounced a design in which some expense, much labour, and more time, had been so vainly consumed. I cannot regret the loss of a slight and superficial essay; for such the work must have been in the hands of a stranger, uninformed by the scholars and statesmen, and remote from the libraries and archives of the Swiss republics. My ancient habits, and the presence of Deyverdun, encouraged me to write in French for the continent of Europe; but I was conscious myself that my style, above prose and below poetry, degenerated into a verbose and turgid declamation. Perhaps I may impute the failure to the injudicious choice of a foreign language. Perhaps I may suspect that the language itself is ill adapted to sustain the vigour and dignity of an important narrative.

---

[1] He neglected to burn them. He left at Sheffield Place the introduction, or first book, in forty-three pages folio, written in a very small hand, besides a considerable number of notes. Mr. Hume's opinion, expressed in a letter in the last note, perhaps may justify the publication of it.—SHEFFIELD.

But if France, so rich in literary merit, had produced a great original historian, his genius would have formed and fixed the idiom to the proper tone, the peculiar mode of historical eloquence.

It was in search of some liberal and lucrative employment that my friend Deyverdun had visited England. His remittances from home were scanty and precarious. My purse was always open, but it was often empty; and I bitterly felt the want of riches and power, which might have enabled me to correct the errors of his fortune. His wishes and qualifications solicited the station of the travelling governor of some wealthy pupil; but every vacancy provoked so many eager candidates, that for a long time I struggled without success; nor was it till after much application that I could even place him as a clerk in the office of the Secretary of State. In a residence of several years he never acquired the just pronunciation and familiar use of the English tongue, but he read our most difficult authors with ease and taste: his critical knowledge of our language and poetry was such as few foreigners have possessed; and few of our countrymen could enjoy the theatre of Shakspeare and Garrick with more exquisite feeling and discernment. The consciousness of his own strength, and the assurance of my aid, emboldened h'm to imitate the example of Dr. Maty, whose *Journal Britannique* was esteemed and regretted; and to improve his model, by uniting with the transactions of literature a philosophic view of the arts and manners of the British nation. Our journal for the year 1767, under the title of *Mémoires Littéraires de la Grande Bretagne,* was soon finished and sent to the press. For the first article, Lord Lyttelton's *History of Henry II.,* I must own myself responsible; but the public has ratified my judgment of that voluminous work, in which sense and learning are not illuminated by a ray of genius. The next specimen was the choice of my friend, *The Bath Guide*, a light and whimsical performance, of local, and even verbal, pleasantry. I started at the attempt: he smiled at my fears: his courage was justified by success; and a master of both languages will applaud the curious felicity with which he has transfused into French prose the spirit, and even the humour, of the English verse. It is not my wish to deny how deeply I was interested in these Memoirs, of which I need not surely be ashamed; but at the distance of more than twenty years, it would be impossible for me to ascertain the respective shares of the two associates. A long and intimate communication of ideas had cast our sentiments and style in the same mould. In our social labours we composed and corrected by turns; and the praise which I might honestly bestow would fall perhaps on some article or passage most properly my own. A second volume (for the year 1768) was published of these Memoirs. I will presume to say that their merit was superior to their reputation; but it is not less true that they were productive of more reputation than emolument. They introduced my friend to the protection, and myself to the acquaintance, of the Earl of Chesterfield, whose age and infirmities secluded him from the world; and of Mr. David Hume, who was under-secretary to the office in which Deyverdun was more humbly employed. The former accepted a dedication (April 12, 1769), and reserved the author for the future education of his successor: the latter enriched the journal with a reply to Mr. Walpole's *Historical Doubts*, which he afterwards shaped into the form of a note. The materials of the third volume were almost completed, when I recommended Deyverdun as governor to Sir Richard Worsley, a youth, the son of my old lieutenant-colonel, who was lately deceased. They set forwards on their travels; nor did they return to England till some time after my father's death.

My next publication was an accidental sally of love and resentment; of my reverence for modest genius, and my aversion for insolent pedantry. The sixth book of the *Æneid* is the most pleasing and perfect composition of Latin poetry. The descent of Æneas and the Sibyl to the infernal regions, to the world of spirits, expands an awful and boundless prospect, from the nocturnal gloom of the Cumæan grot,

> Ibant obscuri solâ sub nocte per umbram,[1]

to the meridian brightness of the Elysian fields;

> Largior hic campos æther et lumine vestit
> Purpureo—— [2]

from the dreams of simple nature to the dreams, alas! of Egyptian theology, and the philosophy of the Greeks. But the final dismission of the hero through the ivory gate, whence

> Falsa ad cœlum mittunt insomnia manes,[3]

seems to dissolve the whole enchantment, and leaves the reader in a state of cold and anxious scepticism. This most lame and impotent conclusion has been variously imputed to the taste or irreligion of Virgil; but, according to the more elaborate interpretation of Bishop Warburton, the descent to hell is not a false, but a mimic scene; which represents the initiation of Æneas, in the character of

[1] Darkling they travelled through the shade under the solitary night.—*Æneid*, B. vi. l. 268.

[2] Here the air they breathe is freer and more enlarged and clothes the fields with radiant light.—*Æneid*, B. vi. 648.

[3] The shades send up lying dreams to the world above.—*Æneid*, B. vi. 896.

a lawgiver, to the Eleusinian mysteries. This hypothesis, a singular chapter in the *Divine Legation of Moses*, had been admitted by many as true; it was praised by all as ingenious; nor had it been exposed, in a space of thirty years, to a fair and critical discussion. The learning and the abilities of the author had raised him to a just eminence; but he reigned the dictator and tyrant of the world of literature. The real merit of Warburton was degraded by the pride and presumption with which he pronounced his infallible decrees; in his polemic writings he lashed his antagonists without mercy or moderation; and his servile flatterers (see the base and malignant *Essay on the Delicacy of Friendship*), [1] exalting the master critic far above Aristotle and Longinus, assaulted every modest dissenter who refused to consult the oracle, and to adore the idol. In a land of liberty such despotism must provoke a general opposition, and the zeal of opposition is seldom candid or impartial. A late professor of Oxford (Dr. Lowth), in a pointed and polished epistle (August 31, 1765), defended himself, and attacked the bishop; and, whatsoever might be the merits of an insignificant controversy, his victory was clearly established by the silent confusion of Warburton and his slaves. *I* too, without any private offence, was ambitious of breaking a lance against the giant's shield; and in the beginning of the year 1770, my *Critical Observations on the Sixth Book of the Æneid* were sent, without my name, to the press. In this short essay, my first English publication, I aimed my strokes against the person and the hypothesis of Bishop Warburton. I proved, at least to my own satisfaction, *that* the ancient lawgivers did not invent the mysteries, and *that* Æneas was never invested with the

[1] By Hurd, afterwards Bishop of Worcester.—See *Dr. Parr's Tracts* by Warburton, and a Warburtonian.

office of lawgiver: *that* there is not any argument, any
circumstance, which can melt a fable into allegory, or
remove the scene from the Lake Avernus to the Temple
of Ceres: *that* such a wild supposition is equally injurious
to the poet and the man: *that* if Virgil was not initiated
he could not, if he were he would not, reveal the secrets
of the initiation: *that* the anathema of Horace (*vetabo qui
Cereris sacrum vulgarit*, etc.)[1] at once attests his own
ignorance and the innocence of his friend.   As the Bishop
of Gloucester and his party maintained a discreet silence,
my critical disquisition was soon lost among the pamphlets
of the day; but the public coldness was overbalanced to
my feelings by the weighty approbation of the last and
best editor of Virgil, Professor Heyne of Gottingen, who
acquiesces in my confutation, and styles the unknown
author *doctus . . . et elegantissimus Britannus*.[2]   But I
cannot resist the temptation of transcribing the favourable
judgment of Mr. Hayley, himself a poet and a scholar:
" An intricate hypothesis, twisted into a long and laboured
chain of quotation and argument, the Dissertation on the
Sixth Book of Virgil, remained some time unrefuted. . . .
At length, a superior, but anonymous, critic arose, who,
in one of the most judicious and spirited essays that our
nation has produced on a point of classical literature,
completely overturned this ill-founded edifice, and exposed
the arrogance and futility of its assuming architect."   He
even condescends to justify an acrimony of style which
had been gently blamed by the more unbiassed German:
" *Paulo acrius quam velis . . . perstrinxit.*"[3]   But I

[1] I shall curse him who discloses the secrets of Ceres.—*Odes*, II. ii. 26.
[2] A learned and most elegant Briton.
[3] He censured a little more sharply than one would wish.

The editor of the Warburtonian tracts, Dr. Parr (p. 192), con-
siders the allegorical interpretation " as completely refuted in a
most clear, elegant, and decisive work of criticism; which could

cannot forgive myself the contemptuous treatment of a
man who, with all his faults, was entitled to my esteem;[1]
and I can less forgive, in a personal attack, the cowardly
concealment of my name and character.

In the fifteen years between my *Essay on the Study of
Literature* and the first volume of the *Decline and Fall*
(1761-1776), this criticism on Warburton, and some
articles in the journal, were my sole publications. It is
more especially incumbent on me to mark the employment, or to confess the waste of time, from my travels to
my father's death, an interval in which I was not diverted
by any professional duties from the labours and pleasures
of a studious life. 1. As soon as I was released from the
fruitless task of the Swiss revolutions (1768), I began
gradually to advance from the wish to the hope, from the
hope to the design, from the design to the execution, of
my historical work, of whose limits and extent I had yet
a very inadequate notion. The classics, as low as Tacitus,
the younger Pliny, and Juvenal, were my old and familiar
companions. I insensibly plunged into the ocean of the
Augustan history; and in the descending series I investigated, with my pen almost always in my hand, the
original records, both Greek and Latin, from Dion Cassius
to Ammianus Marcellinus, from the reign of Trajan to the
last age of the Western Cæsars. The subsidiary rays of
medals and inscriptions, of geography and chronology,

not, indeed, derive authority from the greatest name, but to which
the greatest name might with propriety have been affixed."—
SHEFFIELD.

[1] The *Divine Legation of Moses* is a monument, already crum-
bling in the dust, of the vigour and weakness of the human mind.
If Warburton's new argument proved anything, it would be a
demonstration against the legislator who left his people without
the knowledge of a future state. But some episodes of the work,
on the Greek philosophy, the hieroglyphics of Egypt, etc., are
entitled to the praise of learning, imagination, and discernment.

were thrown on their proper objects; and I applied the collections of Tillemont, whose inimitable accuracy almost assumes the character of genius, to fix and arrange within my reach the loose and scattered atoms of historical information. Through the darkness of the middle ages I explored my way in the *Annals* and *Antiquities of Italy* of the learned Muratori; and diligently compared them with the parallel or transverse lines of Sigonius and Maffei, Baronius and Pagi, till I almost grasped the ruins of Rome in the fourteenth century, without suspecting that this final chapter must be attained by the labour of six quartos and twenty years. Among the books which I purchased, the *Theodosian Code*, with the commentary of James Godefroy, must be gratefully remembered: I used it (and much I used it) as a work of history rather than of juris-prudence: but in every light it may be considered as a full and capacious repository of the political state of the empire in the fourth and fifth centuries. As I believed, and as I still believe, that the propagation of the Gospel, and the triumph of the church, are inseparably connected with the decline of the Roman monarchy, I weighed the causes and effects of the revolution, and contrasted the narratives and apologies of the Christians themselves, with the glances of candour or enmity which the Pagans have cast on the rising sects. The Jewish and Heathen testimonies, as they are collected and illustrated by Dr. Lardner, directed, without superseding, my search of the originals; and in an ample dissertation on the miraculous darkness of the passion, I privately drew my conclusions from the silence of an unbelieving age. I have assembled the preparatory studies, directly or indirectly relative to my history; but, in strict equity, they must be spread beyond this period of my life, over the two summers (1771 and 1772) that elapsed between my father's death and my settlement in London.   2. In a free conversation with books and men it would be endless to enumerate the names and characters of all who are introduced to our acquaintance; but in this general acquaintance we may select the degrees of friendship and esteem.   According to the wise maxim, *Multum legere potius quam multa*,[1] I reviewed, again and again, the immortal works of the French and English, the Latin and Italian classics.   My Greek studies (though less assiduous than I designed) maintained and extended my knowledge of that incomparable idiom.   Homer and Xenophon were still my favourite authors; and I had almost prepared for the press an essay on the *Cyropædia*, which, in my own judgment, is not unhappily laboured.   After a certain age the new publications of merit are the sole food of the many; and the most austere student will be often tempted to break the line, for the sake of indulging his own curiosity, and of providing the topics of fashionable currency.   A more respectable motive may be assigned for the third perusal of Blackstone's *Commentaries*, and a copious and critical abstract of that English work was my first serious production in my native language.   3. My literary leisure was much less complete and independent than it might appear to the eye of a stranger.   In the hurry of London I was destitute of books; in the solitude of Hampshire I was not master of my time.   My quiet was gradually disturbed by our domestic anxiety, and I should be ashamed of my unfeeling philosophy had I found much time or taste for study in the last fatal summer (1770) of my father's decay and dissolution.

The disembodying of the militia at the close of the war (1763) had restored the major (a new Cincinnatus) to a

---

[1] To read the same book many times rather than many books but once.

life of agriculture.   His labours were useful, his pleasures
innocent, his wishes moderate; and my father *seemed* to
enjoy the state of happiness which is celebrated by poets
and philosophers as the most agreeable to nature, and
the least accessible to fortune.

> Beatus ille, qui procul negotiis
>   (Ut prisca gens mortalium)
> Paterna rura bobus exercet suis,
>   Solutus omni fœnore.[1]   Hor. *Epod.* ii.

But the last indispensable condition, the freedom from
debt, was wanting to my father's felicity; and the vanities
of his youth were severely punished by the solicitude and
sorrow of his declining age.   The first mortgage, on my
return from Lausanne (1758), had afforded him a partial
and transient relief.   The annual demand of interest and
allowance was a heavy deduction from his income; the
militia was a source of expense, the farm in his hands was
not a profitable adventure, he was loaded with the costs
and damages of an obsolete lawsuit; and each year
multiplied the number and exhausted the patience of his
creditors.   Under these painful circumstances, I consented
to an additional mortgage, to the sale of Putney, and to
every sacrifice that could alleviate his distress.   But he
was no longer capable of a rational effort, and his reluctant
delays postponed, not the evils themselves, but the
remedies of those evils (*remedia malorum potius quam
mala differebat*).[2]   The pangs of shame, tenderness, and

[1] Like the first mortals, blest is he,
From debts, and usury, and business free,
With his own team who ploughs the soil,
Which grateful once confess'd his father's toil.
                              FRANCIS.

[2] Deferring the remedies of the evils, not checking the evils
themselves.

self-reproach incessantly preyed on his vitals; his constitution was broken; he lost his strength and his sight:
the rapid progress of a dropsy admonished him of his end,
and he sunk into the grave on the 10th of November 1770,
in the sixty-fourth year of his age. A family tradition
insinuates that Mr. William Law had drawn his pupil in
the light and inconstant character of *Flatus*, who is ever
confident and ever disappointed in the chase of happiness.
But these constitutional failings were happily compensated
by the virtues of the head and heart, by the warmest
sentiments of honour and humanity. His graceful person,
polite address, gentle manners, and unaffected cheerfulness, recommended him to the favour of every company;
and in the change of times and opinions, his liberal spirit
had long since delivered him from the zeal and prejudice
of a Tory education. I submitted to the order of nature;
and my grief was soothed by the conscious satisfaction
that I had discharged all the duties of filial piety.

As soon as I had paid the last solemn duties to my
father, and obtained, from time and reason, a tolerable
composure of mind, I began to form a plan of an independent life, most adapted to my circumstances and
inclination. Yet so intricate was the net, my efforts were
so awkward and feeble, that nearly two years (November
1770—October 1772) were suffered to elapse before I
could disentangle myself from the management of the
farm, and transfer my residence from Beriton to a house
in London. During this interval I continued to divide
my year between town and the country; but my new
situation was brightened by hope; my stay in London
was prolonged into the summer; and the uniformity of
the summer was occasionally broken by visits and
excursions at a distance from home. The gratification
of my desires (they were not immoderate) has been

seldom disappointed by the want of money or credit;
my pride was never insulted by the visit of an importunate
tradesman; and my transient anxiety for the past or
future has been dispelled by the studious or social occupation of the present hour. My conscience does not accuse
me of any act of extravagance or injustice, and the
remnant of my estate affords an ample and honourable
provision for my declining age. I shall not expatiate on
my economical affairs, which cannot be instructive or
amusing to the reader. It is a rule of prudence, as well
as of politeness, to reserve such confidence for the ear of
a private friend, without exposing our situation to the
envy or pity of strangers; for envy is productive of hatred,
and pity borders too nearly on contempt. Yet I may
believe, and even assert, that, in circumstances more
indigent or more wealthy, I should never have accomplished the task, or acquired the fame, of an historian;
that my spirit would have been broken by poverty and
contempt; and that my industry might have been relaxed
in the labour and luxury of a superfluous fortune.

I had now attained the first of earthly blessings, independence: I was the absolute master of my hours and
actions: nor was I deceived in the hope that the establishment of my library in town would allow me to divide the
day between study and society. Each year the circle
of my acquaintance, the number of my dead and living
companions, was enlarged. To a lover of books the shops
and sales of London present irresistible temptations; and
the manufacture of my history required a various and
growing stock of materials. The militia, my travels, the
House of Commons, the fame of an author, contributed
to multiply my connections: I was chosen a member of
the fashionable clubs; and, before I left England in 1783,
there were few persons of any eminence in the literary or

political world to whom I was a stranger.[1] It would most assuredly be in my power to amuse the reader with a gallery of portraits and a collection of anecdotes. But I have always condemned the practice of transforming a private memorial into a vehicle of satire or praise. By my own choice I passed in town the greatest part of the year; but whenever I was desirous of breathing the air of the country I possessed an hospitable retreat at Sheffield Place in Sussex, in the family of my valuable friend Mr. Holroyd, whose character, under the name of Lord Sheffield, has since been more conspicuous to the public.

No sooner was I settled in my house and library than I undertook the composition of the first volume of my *History*. At the outset all was dark and doubtful; even the title of the work, the true era of the Decline and Fall of the Empire, the limits of the introduction, the division of the chapters, and the order of the narrative; and I was often tempted to cast away the labour of seven years. The style of an author should be the image of his mind, but the choice and command of language is the fruit of exercise. Many experiments were made before I could hit the middle tone between a dull chronicle and a rhetorical declamation: three times did I compose the first chapter, and twice the second and third, before I was

[1] From the mixed, though polite, company of Boodle's, White's, and Brooks's, I must honourably distinguish a weekly society, which was instituted in the year 1764, and which still continues to flourish, under the title of the Literary Club. (Hawkins's *Life of Johnson*, p. 415; Boswell's *Tour to the Hebrides*, p. 97.) The names of Dr. Johnson, Mr. Burke, Mr. Topham Beauclerc, Mr. Garrick, Dr. Goldsmith, Sir Joshua Reynolds, Mr. Colman, Sir William Jones, Dr. Percy, Mr. Fox, Mr. Sheridan, Mr. Adam Smith, Mr. Steevens, Mr. Dunning, Sir Joseph Banks, Dr. Warton and his brother Mr. Thomas Warton, Dr. Burney, etc., form a large and luminous constellation of British stars.

tolerably satisfied with their effect.   In the remainder of
the way I advanced with a more equal and easy pace; but
the fifteenth and sixteenth chapters have been reduced,
by three successive revisals, from a large volume to their
present size; and they might still be compressed, without
any loss of facts or sentiments.   An opposite fault may
be imputed to the concise and superficial narrative of the
first reigns from Commodus to Alexander; a fault of
which I have never heard, except from Mr. Hume in his
last journey to London.   Such an oracle might have been
consu ted and obeyed with rational devotion; but I was
soon disgusted with the modest practice of reading the
manuscript to my friends.   Of such friends some will
praise from politeness, and some will criticise from vanity.
The author himself is the best judge of his own performance; no one has so deeply meditated on the subject;
no one is so sincerely interested in the event.

By the friendship of Mr. (now Lord) Eliot, who had
married my first-cousin, I was returned at the general
election for the borough of Liskeard.   I took my seat at
the beginning of the memorable contest between Great
Britain and America, and supported, with many a sincere
and silent vote, the rights, though not, perhaps, the
interest, of the mother-country.   After a fleeting illusive
hope, prudence condemned me to acquiesce in the humble
station of a mute.   I was not armed by nature and
education with the intrepid energy of mind and voice,

Vincentem strepitus, et natum rebus agendis.[1]

Timidity was fortified by pride, and even the success of
my pen discouraged the trial of my voice.[2]   But I assisted

[1] Fitted for action and to quell the tumultuous noise of the crowd
—Horace, *De Arte Poetica*, l. 82.

[2] A French sketch of Mr. Gibbon's Life, written by himself,
probably for the use of some foreign journalist or translator, con-

Gibbon's Autobiography 143

at the debates of a free assembly; I listened to the attack
and defence of eloquence and reason; I had a near
prospect of the characters, views, and passions of the
first men of the age. The cause of government was ably
vindicated by *Lord North,* a statesman of spotless integrity,
a consummate master of debate, who could wield with
equal dexterity the arms of reason and of ridicule. He
was seated on the Treasury Bench between his Attorney-
and Solicitor-General, the two pillars of the law and state,
magis pares quam similes; [1] and the minister might indulge
in a short slumber, whilst he was upholden on either hand
by the majestic sense of *Thurlow,* and the skilful eloquence
of *Wedderburne.* From the adverse side of the house an
ardent and powerful opposition was supported by the lively
declamation of *Barré,* the legal acuteness of *Dunning,* the
profuse and philosophic fancy of *Burke,* and the argumentative vehemence of *Fox,* who, in the conduct of a
party, approved himself equal to the conduct of an empire.
By such men every operation of peace and war, every
principle of justice or policy, every question of authority
and freedom, was attacked and defended; and the subject

tains no fact not mentioned in his English Life. He there describes
himself with his usual candour. " Depuis huit ans il a assisté aux dé-
libérations les plus importantes, mais il ne s'est jamais trouvé *le
courage,* ni *le talent,* de parler dans une assemblée publique."
[" During eight years he has taken part in very important delibera-
tions, but he has at no time found either the courage or the knack
of speaking in a public assembly."] This sketch was written before
the publication of his three last volumes, as in closing it he says of
his *History,* " Cette entreprise lui demande encore plusieurs années
d'une application soutenue; mais quelqu'en soit le succès, il trouve
dans cette application même un plaisir toujours varié et toujours
renaissant." [" That undertaking demanded of him during several
years a closely sustained application. But be the success what it
might, he found in the application itself a pleasure always varied
and always renewed."]—SHEFFIELD.
[1] Rather equal than alike.

of the momentous contest was the union or separation of
Great Britain and America.   The eight sessions that I sat
in parliament were a school of civil prudence, the first
and most essential virtue of an historian.

The volume of my *History*, which had been somewhat
delayed by the novelty and tumult of a first session, was
now ready for the press.   After the perilous adventure had
been declined by my friend Mr. Elmsley, I agreed, upon
easy terms, with Mr. Thomas Cadell, a respectable bookseller, and Mr. William Strahan, an eminent printer; and
they undertook the care and risk of the publication, which
derived more credit from the name of the shop than from
that of the author.   The last revisal of the proofs was
submitted to my vigilance; and many blemishes of style,
which had been invisible in the manuscript, were discovered and corrected in the printed sheet.   So moderate
were our hopes, that the original impression had been
stinted to five hundred, till the number was doubled by
the prophetic taste of Mr. Strahan.   During this awful
interval I was neither elated by the ambition of fame, nor
depressed by the apprehension of contempt.   My diligence
and accuracy were attested by my own conscience.
History is the most popular species of writing, since it
can adapt itself to the highest or the lowest capacity.   I
had chosen an illustrious subject.   Rome is familiar to
the schoolboy and the statesman; and my narrative was
deduced from the last period of classical reading.   I had
likewise flattered myself that an age of light and liberty
would receive, without scandal, an inquiry into the human
causes of the progress and establishment of Christianity.

I am at a loss how to describe the success of the work
without betraying the vanity of the writer.   The first
impression was exhausted in a few days; a second and
third edition were scarcely adequate to the demand; and

the bookseller's property was twice invaded by the pirates of Dublin. My book was on every table, and almost on every toilette; the historian was crowned by the taste or fashion of the day; nor was the general voice disturbed by the barking of any *profane* critic. The favour of mankind is most freely bestowed on a new acquaintance of any original merit; and the mutual surprise of the public and their favourite is productive of those warm sensibilities which at a second meeting can no longer be rekindled. If I listened to the music of praise, I was more seriously satisfied with the approbation of my judges. The candour of Dr. Robertson embraced his disciple. A letter from Mr. Hume overpaid the labour of ten years; but I have never presumed to accept a place in the triumvirate of British historians.

That curious and original letter will amuse the reader, and his gratitude should shield my free communication from the reproach of vanity.

" EDINBURGH, 18*th March*, 1776.

" DEAR SIR,—As I ran through your volume of history with great avidity and impatience, I cannot forbear discovering somewhat of the same impatience in returning you thanks for your agreeable present, and expressing the satisfaction which the performance has given me. Whether I consider the dignity of your style, the depth of your matter, or the extensiveness of your learning, I must regard the work as equally the object of esteem; and I own that, if I had not previously had the happiness of your personal acquaintance, such a performance from an Englishman in our age would have given me some surprise. You may smile at this sentiment, but, as it seems to me that your countrymen, for almost a whole

generation, have given themselves up to barbarous and
absurd faction, and have totally neglected all polite letters,
I no longer expected any valuable production ever to
come from them. I know it will give you pleasure (as it
did me) to find that all the men of letters in this place
concur in their admiration of your work, and in their
anxious desire of your continuing it.

" When I heard of your undertaking (which was some
time ago), I own I was a little curious to see how you
would extricate yourself from the subject of your two last
chapters. I think you have observed a very prudent
temperament; but it was impossible to treat the subject
so as not to give grounds of suspicion against you, and
you may expect that a clamour will arise. This, if anything, will retard your success with the public; for in
every other respect your work is calculated to be popular.
But among many other marks of decline, the prevalence
of superstition in England prognosticates the fall of
philosophy and decay of taste; and though nobody be
more capable than you to revive them, you will probably
find a struggle in your first advances.

" I see you entertain a great doubt with regard to the
authenticity of the poems of Ossian. You are certainly
right in so doing. It is indeed strange that any men of
sense could have imagined it possible that above twenty
thousand verses, along with numberless historical facts,
could have been preserved by oral tradition during fifty
generations, by the rudest, perhaps, of all the European
nations, the most necessitous, the most turbulent, and the
most unsettled. Where a supposition is so contrary to
common sense, any positive evidence of it ought never to
be regarded. Men run with great avidity to give their
evidence in favour of what flatters their passions and
their national prejudices. You are therefore over and

above indulgent to us in speaking of the matter with hesitation.

" I must inform you that we are all very anxious to hear that you have fully collected the materials for your second volume, and that you are even considerably advanced in the composition of it.   I speak this more in the name of my friends than in my own, as I cannot expect to live so long as to see the publication of it. Your ensuing volume will be more delicate than the preceding, but I trust in your prudence for extricating you from the difficulties; and, in all events, you have courage to despise the clamour of bigots.—I am, with great regard, dear sir, your most obedient and most humble servant,   DAVID HUME."

Some weeks afterwards I had the melancholy pleasure of seeing Mr. Hume in his passage through London; his body feeble, his mind firm.   On the 25th of August of the same year (1776) he died, at Edinburgh, the death of a philosopher.

My second excursion to Paris was determined by the pressing invitation of M. and Madame Necker, who had visited England in the preceding summer.   On my arrival I found M. Necker Director-General of the Finances, in the first bloom of power and popularity.   His private fortune enabled him to support a liberal establishment; and his wife, whose talents and virtues I had long admired, was admirably qualified to preside in the conversation of her table and drawing-room.   As their friend I was introduced to the best company of both sexes; to the foreign ministers of all nations, and to the first names and characters of France, who distinguished me by such marks of civility and kindness as gratitude will not suffer me to forget, and modesty will not allow me to enumerate. The fashionable suppers often broke into the morning hours; yet I occasionally consulted the Royal Library, and that of the Abbey of St. Germain, and in the free use of their books at home I had always reason to praise the liberality of those institutions. The society of men of letters I neither courted nor declined; but I was happy in the acquaintance of M. de Buffon, who united with a sublime genius the most amiable simplicity of mind and manners. At the table of my old friend M. de Forcemagne I was involved in a dispute with the Abbé de Mably; and his jealous irascible spirit revenged itself on a work which he was incapable of reading in the original.

As I might be partial in my own cause, I shall transcribe the words of an unknown critic, observing only that this dispute had been preceded by another on the English constitution at the house of the Countess de Froulay, an old Jansenist lady.

"Vous étiez chez M. de Forcemagne, mon cher Théodon, le jour que M. l'Abbé de Mably et M. Gibbon y dinèrent en grande compagnie. La conversation roula presque entièrement sur l'histoire. L'Abbé, étant un profond politique, la tourna sur l'administration quand on fut au dessert; et comme par caractère, par humeur, par l'habitude d'admirer Tite Live, il ne prise que le systême républicain, il se mit à vanter l'excellence des républiques; bien persuadé que le savant Anglois l'approuveroit en tout, et admireroit la profondeur de génie qui avoit fait diviner tous ces avantages à un François. Mais M. Gibbon, instruit par l'expérience des inconvéniens d'un gouvernement populaire, ne fut point du tout de son avis, et il prit généreusement la défense du gouvernement monarchique. L'Abbé voulut le convaincre par Tite Live, et par quelques argumens tirés de Plutarque en

faveur des Spartiates.   M. Gibbon, doué de la mémoire
la plus heureuse, et ayant tous les faits présens à la
pensée, domina bientôt la conversation; l'Abbé se fâcha,
il s'emporta, il dit des choses dures; l'Anglois, conservant
le phlegme de son pays, prenoit ses avantages, et pressoit
l'Abbé avec d'autant plus de succès que la colère le
troubloit de plus en plus.   La conversation s'échauffoit,
et M. de Forcemagne la rompit en se levant de table, et
en passant dans le salon, où personne ne fut tenté de la
renouer."   (*Supplément de la Manière d'écrire l'Histoire*,
p. 125, etc.)[1]

Nearly two years had elapsed between the publication
of my first and the commencement of my second volume;

---

[1] You were at the house of M. de Forcemagne, my dear Theodon,
on the day that M. the Abbé de Mably and Mr. Gibbon dined there
among a large party.   The conversation ran at first almost wholly
on history.   The Abbé being a keen politician, turned it on
the administration when the dessert was served, and as by
temperament, inclination, and habit of mind he was an admirer of
Titus Livius, he valued only the republican form of government
and therefore began to praise the excellence of republics, being fully
persuaded that the learned Englishman would altogether approve
of his line of argument and admire the profundity of the genius
which had enabled a Frenchman to perceive all these recommendations.   But Mr. Gibbon, fully informed by experience of the inconvenience arising from a democratic form of government, was
not of his opinion, and warmly espoused the side of monarchical
government.   The Abbé desired to convince him out of Livy and
by certain arguments taken from Plutarch in favour of the Spartans.
Mr. Gibbon, endowed with a fine memory and having all the facts
at his fingers' ends, presently assumed the lead in the conversation.
The Abbé became annoyed, then flew into a passion, and said hard
things; the Englishman, retaining the calmness of his country,
drove home his advantage, and as he pressed the Abbé with more
and more success, choler affected the latter ever more noticeably.
The conversation stopped for a moment; M. de Forcemagne broke
off the discussion by leaving the table, and passed into the salon,
where no one tried to renew it.—*Supplement to the Way to Write
History*, p. 125.

and the causes must be assigned of this long delay. 1.
After a short holiday I indulged my curiosity in some
studies of a very different nature, a course of anatomy,
which was demonstrated by Doctor Hunter, and some
lessons of chemistry, which were delivered by Mr. Higgins.
The principles of these sciences, and a taste for books of
natural history, contributed to multiply my ideas and
images; and the anatomist and chemist may sometimes
track me in their own snow. 2. I dived, perhaps too
deeply, into the mud of the Arian controversy; and
many days of reading, thinking, and writing were consumed in the pursuit of a phantom. 3. It is difficult to
arrange, with order and perspicuity, the various transactions of the age of Constantine; and so much was I
displeased with the first essay, that I committed to the
flames above fifty sheets. 4. The six months of Paris
and pleasure must be deducted from the account. But
when I resumed my task I felt my improvement; I was
now master of my style and subject, and, while the
measure of my daily performance was enlarged, I discovered less reason to cancel or correct. It has always
been my practice to cast a long paragraph in a single
mould, to try it by my ear, to deposit it in my memory,
but to suspend the action of the pen till I had given the
last polish to my work. Shall I add, that I never found
my mind more vigorous, nor my composition more happy,
than in the winter hurry of society and parliament?

Had I believed that the majority of English readers
were so fondly attached even to the name and shadow of
Christianity; had I foreseen that the pious, the timid,
and the prudent would feel, or affect to feel, with such
exquisite sensibility; I might, perhaps, have softened
the two invidious chapters, which would create many
enemies, and conciliate few friends. But the shaft was

shot, the alarm was sounded, and I could only rejoice that, if the voice of our priests was clamorous and bitter, their hands were disarmed from the powers of persecution. I adhered to the wise resolution of trusting myself and my writings to the candour of the public, till Mr. Davies of Oxford presumed to attack, not the faith, but the fidelity, of the historian. *My Vindication*, expressive of less anger than contempt, amused for a moment the busy and idle metropolis; and the most rational part of the laity, and even of the clergy, appear to have been satisfied of my innocence and accuracy. I would not print this *Vindication* in quarto, lest it should be bound and preserved with the *History* itself. At the distance of twelve years I calmly affirm my judgment of Davies, Chelsum, etc. A victory over such antagonists was a sufficient humiliation. They however were rewarded in this world. Poor Chelsum was indeed neglected; and I dare not boast the making Dr. Watson a bishop; he is a prelate of a large mind and liberal spirit: but I enjoyed the pleasure of giving a royal pension to Mr. Davies, and of collating Dr. Apthorpe to an archiepiscopal living. Their success encouraged the zeal of Taylor the Arian, and Milner the Methodist, with many others, whom it would be difficult to remember, and tedious to rehearse. The list of my adversaries, however, was graced with the more respectable names of Dr. Priestley, Sir David Dalrymple, and Dr. White; and every polemic, of either university, discharged his sermon or pamphlet against the impenetrable silence of the Roman historian. In his *History of the Corruptions of Christianity*, Dr. Priestley threw down his two gauntlets to Bishop Hurd and Mr. Gibbon. I declined the challenge in a letter, exhorting my opponent to enlighten the world by his philosophical discoveries, and to remember that the merit of his predecessor Servetus is now reduced to a single passage, which indicates the smaller circulation of the blood through the lungs, from and to the heart. Instead of listening to this friendly advice, the dauntless philosopher of Birmingham continued to fire away his double battery against those who believed too little, and those who believed too much. *From my* replies he has nothing to hope or fear: but his Socinian shield has repeatedly been pierced by the mighty spear of Horsley, and his trumpet of sedition may at length awaken the magistrates of a free country.

The profession and rank of Sir David Dalrymple (now a Lord of Session) has given a more decent colour to his style. But he scrutinised each separate passage of the two chapters with the dry minuteness of a special pleader; and as he was always solicitous to make, he may have succeeded sometimes in finding, a flaw. In his *Annals of Scotland* he has shown himself a diligent collector and an accurate critic.

I have praised, and I still praise, the eloquent sermons which were preached in St. Mary's pulpit at Oxford by Dr. White. If he assaulted me with some degree of illiberal acrimony, in such a place, and before such an audience, he was obliged to speak the language of the country. I smiled at a passage in one of his private letters to Mr. Badcock: " The part where we encounter Gibbon must be brilliant and striking."

In a sermon preached before the university of Cambridge, Dr. Edwards complimented a work " which can only perish with the language itself;" and esteems the author a formidable enemy. He is, indeed, astonished that more learning and ingenuity has not been shown in the defence of Israel; that the prelates and dignitaries of the church (alas, good man!) did not vie with each other whose stone should sink the deepest in the forehead of this Goliath.

" But the force of truth will oblige us to confess that, in the attacks which have been levelled against our sceptical historian, we can discover but slender traces of profound and exquisite erudition, of solid criticism, and accurate investigation; but we are too frequently disgusted by vague and inconclusive reasoning; by unseasonable banter and senseless witticisms; by imbittered bigotry and enthusiastic jargon; by futile cavils and illiberal invectives. Proud and elated by the weakness of his antagonists, he condescends not to handle the sword of controversy."

Let me frankly own that I was startled at the first discharge of ecclesiastical ordnance; but as soon as I found that this empty noise was mischievous only in the intention, my fear was converted into indignation; and every feeling of indignation or curiosity has long since subsided in pure and placid indifference.

The prosecution of my *History* was soon afterwards checked by another controversy of a very different kind. At the request of the Lord Chancellor, and of Lord Weymouth, then Secretary of State, I vindicated, against the French manifesto, the justice of the British arms. The whole correspondence of Lord Stormont, our late ambassador at Paris, was submitted to my inspection, and the *Mémoire Justificatif*, which I composed in French, was first approved by the Cabinet Ministers, and then delivered as a state paper to the courts of Europe. The style and manner are praised by Beaumarchais himself, who, in his private quarrel, attempted a reply; but he flatters me by ascribing the memoir to Lord Stormont; and the grossness of his invective betrays the loss of temper and of wit; he acknowledged that *le style ne seroit pas sans grace, ni la logique sans justesse,*[1] etc., if the facts were true which he undertakes to disprove. For these facts my credit is not pledged; I spoke as a lawyer from my brief; but the veracity of Beaumarchais may be estimated from the assertion that France, by the Treaty of Paris (1763), was limited to a certain number of ships of war. On the application of the Duke of Choiseul he was obliged to retract this daring falsehood.

Among the honourable connections which I had formed, I may justly be proud of the friendship of Mr. Wedderburne, at that time Attorney-General, who now illustrates the title of Lord Loughborough, and the office of Chief Justice of the Common Pleas. By his strong recommendation, and the favourable disposition of Lord North, I was appointed one of the Lords Commissioners of Trade and Plantations; and my private income was enlarged by a clear addition of between seven and eight hundred pounds a year. The fancy of a hostile orator may paint in the strong colours of ridicule " the perpetual virtual adjournment, and the unbroken sitting vacation of the Board of Trade." But it must be allowed that our duty was not intolerably severe, and that I enjoyed many days and weeks of repose without being called away from my library to the office. My acceptance of a place provoked some of the leaders of opposition, with whom I had lived in habits of intimacy; and I was most unjustly accused of deserting a party in which I had never enlisted.

The aspect of the next session of parliament was stormy and perilous; county meetings, petitions, and committees of correspondence, announced the public discontent; and instead of voting with a triumphant majority, the friends

---

[1] The style would not be without elegance nor the logic without point.

of government were often exposed to a struggle and sometimes to a defeat. The House of Commons adopted Mr.
Dunning's motion, " That the influence of the Crown had
increased, was increasing, and ought to be diminished: "
and Mr. Burke's Bill of Reform was framed with skill, introduced with eloquence, and supported by numbers. Our
late president, the American Secretary of State, very
narrowly escaped the sentence of proscription; but the
unfortunate Board of Trade was abolished in the committee by a small majority (207 to 199) of eight votes.
The storm, however, blew over for a time; a large defec-
tion of country gentlemen eluded the sanguine hopes of
the patriots; the Lords of Trade were revived; administration recovered their strength and spirit; and the flames
of London, which were kindled by a mischievous madman,
admonished all thinking men of the danger of an appeal
to the people. In the premature dissolution which
followed this session of parliament I lost my seat. Mr.
Eliot was now deeply engaged in the measures of opposition, and the electors of Liskeard are commonly of the
same opinion as Mr. Eliot.

In this interval of my senatorial life I published the
second and third volumes of the *Decline and Fall*. My
ecclesiastical history still breathed the same spirit of freedom; but Protestant zeal is more indifferent to the
characters and controversies of the fourth and fifth
centuries. My obstinate silence had damped the ardour
of the polemics. Dr. Watson, the most candid of my
adversaries, assured me that he had no thoughts of renew-
ing the attack, and my impartial balance of the virtues
and vices of Julian was generally praised. This truce was
interrupted only by some animadversions of the Catholics
of Italy, and by some angry letters from Mr. Travis, who
made me personally responsible for condemning, with the

best critics, the spurious text of the three heavenly witnesses.

The piety or prudence of my Italian translator has provided an antidote against the poison of his original. The fifth and seventh volumes are armed with five letters from an anonymous divine to his friends, Foothead and Kirk, two English students at Rome; and this meritorious service is commended by Monsignor Stonor, a prelate of the same nation, who discovers much venom in the *fluid* and nervous style of Gibbon. The critical essay at the end of the third volume was furnished by the Abbate Nicola Spedalieri, whose zeal has gradually swelled to a more solid confutation in two quarto volumes.—Shall I be excused for not having read them?

The brutal insolence of Mr. Travis's challenge can only be excused by the absence of learning, judgment, and humanity; and to that excuse he has the fairest or foulest pretension. Compared with Archdeacon Travis, Chelsum and Davies assume the title of respectable enemies.

The bigoted advocate of popes and monks may be turned over even to the bigots of Oxford; and the wretched Travis still smarts under the lash of the merciless Porson. I consider Mr. Porson's answer to Archdeacon Travis as the most acute and accurate piece of criticism which has appeared since the days of Bentley. His strictures are founded in argument, enriched with learning, and enlivened with wit; and his adversary neither deserves nor finds any quarter at his hands. The evidence of the three heavenly witnesses would now be rejected in any court of justice: but prejudice is blind, authority is deaf, and our vulgar bibles will ever be polluted by this spurious text, " *sedet æternumque sedebit.*" [1] The more learned eccle-

---

[1] "It remains and will remain to the end of time."—*Æneid*, vi. 617.

siastics will indeed have the secret satisfaction of reprobating in the closet what they read in the church.

I perceived, and without surprise, the coldness and even prejudice of the town; nor could a whisper escape my ear, that, in the judgment of many readers, my continuation was much inferior to the original attempts. An author who cannot ascend will always appear to sink: envy was now prepared for my reception, and the zeal of my religious, was fortified by the motive of my political, enemies. Bishop Newton, in writing his own Life, was at full liberty to declare how much he himself and two eminent brethren were disgusted by Mr. Gibbon's prolixity, tediousness, and affectation. But the old man should not have indulged his zeal in a false and feeble charge against the historian, who had faithfully and even cautiously rendered Dr. Burnet's meaning by the alternative of sleep or repose. That philosophic divine supposes that, in the period between death and the resurrection, human souls exist without a body, endowed with internal consciousness, but destitute of all active or passive connection with the external world. " Secundum communem dictionem sacræ scripturæ, mors dicitur somnus, et morientes dicuntur *obdormire*, quod innuere mihi videtur statum mortis esse statum quietis, silentii, et ἀεργασίας." (*De Statû Mortuorum*, ch. v. p. 98.)[1]

I was however encouraged by some domestic and foreign testimonies of applause; and the second and third volumes insensibly rose in sale and reputation to a level with the first. But the public is seldom wrong; and I am inclined to believe that, especially in the beginning, they are more

[1] " According to the received language of Holy Scripture, death is called sleep, and those dying are said to fall asleep, which seems to me to intimate that the state of death is one of rest, of silence, and of abstinence from labour."—*Concerning the State of the Dead*, chap. v., p. 98.

prolix and less entertaining than the first; my efforts had not been relaxed by success, and I had rather deviated into the opposite fault of minute and superfluous diligence. On the Continent my name and writings were slowly diffused: a French translation of the first volume had disappointed the booksellers of Paris; and a passage in the third was construed as a personal reflection on the reigning monarch.

Before I could apply for a seat at the general election the list was already full; but Lord North's promise was sincere, his recommendation was effectual, and I was soon chosen on a vacancy for the borough of Lymington, in Hampshire. In the first session of the new parliament the administration stood their ground; their final overthrow was reserved for the second. The American war had once been the favourite of the country: the pride of England was irritated by the resistance of her colonies, and the executive power was driven by national clamour into the most vigorous and coercive measures. But the length of a fruitless contest, the loss of armies, the accumulation of debt and taxes, and the hostile confederacy of France, Spain, and Holland, indisposed the public to the American war, and the persons by whom it was conducted; the representatives of the people followed, at a slow distance, the changes of their opinion; and the ministers, who refused to bend, were broken by the tempest. As soon as Lord North had lost, or was about to lose, a majority in the House of Commons, he surrendered his office, and retired to a private station, with the tranquil assurance of a clear conscience and a cheerful temper: the old fabric was dissolved, and the posts of government were occupied by the victorious and veteran troops of opposition. The Lords of Trade were not immediately dismissed, but the board itself was abolished by Mr.

Burke's bill, which decency had compelled the patriots to revive; and I was stripped of a convenient salary, after having enjoyed it about three years.

So flexible is the title of my *History*, that the final era might be fixed at my own choice: and I long hesitated whether I should be content with the three volumes, the fall of the Western empire, which fulfilled my first engagement with the public. In this interval of suspense, nearly a twelvemonth, I returned by a natural impulse to the Greek authors of antiquity; I read with new pleasure the *Iliad* and the *Odyssey*, the Histories of Herodotus, Thucydides, and Xenophon, a large portion of the tragic and comic theatre of Athens, and many interesting dialogues of the Socratic school. Yet in the luxury of freedom I began to wish for the daily task, the active pursuit, which gave a value to every book, and an object to every inquiry: the preface of a new edition announced my design, and I dropped without reluctance from the age of Plato to that of Justinian. The original texts of Procopius and Agathias supplied the events and even the characters of his reign; but a laborious winter was devoted to the Codes, the Pandects, and the modern interpreters, before I presumed to form an abstract of the civil law. My skill was improved by practice, my diligence perhaps was quickened by the loss of office; and, excepting the last chapter, I had finished the fourth volume before I sought a retreat on the banks of the Leman Lake.

It is not the purpose of this narrative to expatiate on the public or secret history of the times: the schism which followed the death of the Marquis of Rockingham, the appointment of the Earl of Shelburne, the resignation of Mr. Fox, and his famous coalition with Lord North. But I may assert with some degree of assurance, that in their political conflict those great antagonists had never felt

any personal animosity to each other, that their recon-
ciliation was easy and sincere, and that their friendship
has never been clouded by the shadow of suspicion or
jealousy. The most violent or venal of their respective
followers embraced this fair occasion of revolt, but their
alliance still commanded a majority in the House of
Commons; the peace was censured, Lord Shelburne resigned, and the two friends knelt on the same cushion to
take the oath of Secretary of State. From a principle of
gratitude I adhered to the coalition; my vote was counted
in the day of battle, but I was overlooked in the division
of the spoil. There were many claimants more deserving
and importunate than myself: the Board of Trade could
not be restored; and, while the list of places was curtailed,
the number of candidates was doubled. An easy dismission to a secure seat at the Board of Customs or Excise
was promised on the first vacancy: but the chance was
distant and doubtful; nor could I solicit with much ardour
an ignoble servitude, which would have robbed me of the
most valuable of my studious hours: [1] at the same time
the tumult of London, and the attendance on parliament,
were grown more irksome; and, without some additional

[1] About the same time, it being in contemplation to send a secretary of embassy to Paris, Mr. Gibbon was a competitor for that
office. The credit of being distinguished and stopped by government when he was leaving England, the salary of £1200 a year, the
society of Paris, and the hope of a future provision for life, disposed
him to renounce, though with much reluctance, an agreeable
scheme on the point of execution; to engage, without experience,
in a scene of business which he never liked; to give himself a master,
or at least a principal, of an unknown, perhaps an unamiable
character: to which might be added the danger of the recall of the
ambassador, or the change of ministry. Mr. Anthony Storer was
preferred. Mr. Gibbon was somewhat indignant at the preference;
but he never knew that it was the act of his friend Mr. Fox, contrary to the solicitations of Mr. Craufurd, and other of his friends.—
SHEFFIELD.

income, I could not long or prudently maintain the style of expense to which I was accustomed.

From my early acquaintance with Lausanne I had always cherished a secret wish that the school of my youth might become the retreat of my declining age. A moderate fortune would secure the blessings of ease, leisure, and independence: the country, the people, the manners, the language, were congenial to my taste; and I might indulge the hope of passing some years in the domestic society of a friend. After travelling with several English,[1] Mr. Deyverdun was now settled at home, in a pleasant habitation, the gift of his deceased aunt: we had long been separated, we had long been silent; yet in my first letter I exposed, with the most perfect confidence, my situation, my sentiments, and my designs. His immediate answer was a warm and joyful acceptance; the picture of our future life provoked my impatience; and the terms of arrangement were short and simple, as he possessed the property, and I undertook the expense of our common house. Before I could break my English chain it was incumbent on me to struggle with the feelings of my heart, the indolence of my temper, and the opinion of the world, which unanimously condemned this voluntary banishment. In the disposal of my effects, the library, a sacred deposit, was alone excepted. As my post-chaise moved over Westminster Bridge I bade a long farewell to the " fumum et opes strepitumque Romæ." [2] My journey, by the direct road through France, was not attended with any accident, and I arrived at Lausanne nearly twenty years

[1] Sir Richard Worsley, Lord Chesterfield, Broderick Lord Midleton, and Mr. Hume, brother to Sir Abraham.
[2] " The smoke, and the wealth, and the street-noise of Rome."— Horace, *Odes*, B. III., xxix. 12.

after my second departure. Within less than three
months the coalition struck on some hidden rocks: had I
remained on board I should have perished in the general
shipwreck.

Since my establishment at Lausanne more than seven
years have elapsed; and if every day has not been equally
soft and serene, not a day, not a moment, has occurred in
which I have repented of my choice. During my absence,
a long portion of human life, many changes had happened:
my elder acquaintance had left the stage; virgins were
ripened into matrons, and children were grown to the age
of manhood. But the same manners were transmitted
from one generation to another: my friend alone was an
inestimable treasure; my name was not totally forgotten,
and all were ambitious to welcome the arrival of a stranger
and the return of a fellow-citizen. The first winter was
given to a general embrace, without any nice discrimina-
tion of persons and characters. After a more regular
settlement, a more accurate survey, I discovered three
solid and permanent benefits of my new situation. 1. My
personal freedom had been somewhat impaired by the
House of Commons and the Board of Trade; but I was
now delivered from the chain of duty and dependence,
from the hopes and fears of political adventure: my sober
mind was no longer intoxicated by the fumes of party, and
I rejoiced in my escape as often as I read of the midnight
debates which preceded the dissolution of parliament.
2. My English economy had been that of a solitary
bachelor, who might afford some occasional dinners. In
Switzerland I enjoyed, at every meal, at every hour, the
free and pleasant conversation of the friend of my youth;
and my daily table was always provided for the reception
of one or two extraordinary guests. Our importance in
society is less a positive than a relative weight: in London

I was lost in the crowd; I ranked with the first families of Lausanne, and my style of prudent expense enabled me to maintain a fair balance of reciprocal civilities.   3. Instead of a small house between a street and a stable-yard, I began to occupy a spacious and convenient mansion, connected on the north side with the city, and open on the south to a beautiful and boundless horizon.   A garden of four acres had been laid out by the taste of Mr. Deyverdun: from the garden a rich scenery of meadows and vineyards descends to the Leman Lake, and the prospect far beyond the lake is crowned by the stupendous mountains of Savoy. My books and my acquaintance had been first united in London; but this happy position of my library in town and country was finally reserved for Lausanne.   Possessed of every comfort in this triple alliance, I could not be tempted to change my habitation with the changes of the seasons.

My friends had been kindly apprehensive that I should not be able to exist in a Swiss town at the foot of the Alps, after having so long conversed with the first men of the first cities of the world.   Such lofty connections may attract the curious, and gratify the vain; but I am too modest, or too proud, to rate my own value by that of my associates; and, whatsoever may be the fame of learning or genius, experience has shown me that the cheaper qualifications of politeness and good sense are of more useful currency in the commerce of life.   By many, conversation is esteemed as a theatre or a school: but, after the morning has been occupied by the labours of the library, I wish to unbend rather than to exercise my mind; and in the interval between tea and supper I am far from disdaining the innocent amusement of a game at cards. Lausanne is peopled by a numerous gentry, whose companionable idleness is seldom disturbed by the pursuits of avarice or ambition: the women, though confined to a domestic education, are endowed for the most part with more taste and knowledge than their husbands and brothers: but the decent freedom of both sexes is equally remote from the extremes of simplicity and refinement. I shall add, as a misfortune rather than a merit, that the situation and beauty of the Pays de Vaud, the long habits of the English, the medical reputation of Dr. Tissot, and the fashion of viewing the mountains and glaciers, have opened us on all sides to the incursions of foreigners. The visits of Mr. and Madame Necker, of Prince Henry of Prussia, and of Mr. Fox, may form some pleasing exceptions; but, in general, Lausanne has appeared most agreeable in my eyes when we have been abandoned to our own society. I had frequently seen Mr. Necker, in the summer of 1784, at a country house near Lausanne, where he composed his *Treatise on the Administration of the Finances.* I have since, in October 1790, visited him in his present residence, the castle and barony of Copet, near Geneva. Of the merits and measures of that statesman various opinions may be entertained; but all impartial men must agree in their esteem of his integrity and patriotism.

In the month of August 1784, Prince Henry of Prussia, in his way to Paris, passed three days at Lausanne. His military conduct has been praised by professional men; his character has been vilified by the wit and malice of a demon; but I was flattered by his affability, and entertained by his conversation.

In his tour to Switzerland (September 1788) Mr. Fox gave me two days of free and private society. He seemed to feel, and even to envy, the happiness of my situation; while I admired the powers of a superior man, as they are blended in his attractive character with the softness and simplicity of a child. Perhaps no human being was ever more perfectly exempt from the taint of malevolence, vanity, or falsehood.

My transmigration from London to Lausanne could not be effected without interrupting the course of my historical labours. The hurry of my departure, the joy of my arrival, the delay of my tools, suspended their progress; and a full twelvemonth was lost before I could resume the thread of regular and daily industry. A number of books most requisite and least common had been previously selected; the academical library of Lausanne, which I could use as my own, contained at least the fathers and councils; and I have derived some occasional succour from the public collections of Berne and Geneva. The fourth volume was soon terminated, by an abstract of the controversies of the Incarnation, which the learned Dr. Prideaux was apprehensive of exposing to profane eyes. It had been the original design of the learned Dean Prideaux to write the history of the ruin of the Eastern Church. In this work it would have been necessary not only to unravel all those controversies which the Christians made about the hypostatical union, but also to unfold all the niceties and subtle notions which each sect entertained concerning it. The pious historian was apprehensive of exposing that incomprehensible mystery to the cavils and objections of unbelievers; and he durst not, " seeing the nature of this book, venture it abroad in so wanton and lewd an age."

In the fifth and sixth volumes the revolutions of the empire and the world are most rapid, various, and instructive; and the Greek or Roman historians are checked by the hostile narratives of the barbarians of the East and the West.

It was not till after many designs and many trials that

I preferred, as I still prefer, the method of grouping my picture by nations; and the seeming neglect of chronological order is surely compensated by the superior merits of interest and perspicuity.   The style of the first volume is, in my opinion, somewhat crude and elaborate; in the second and third it is ripened into ease, correctness, and numbers; but in the three last I may have been seduced by the facility of my pen, and the constant habit of speaking one language and writing another may have infused some mixture of Gallic idioms.   Happily for my eyes, I have always closed my studies with the day, and commonly with the morning; and a long, but temperate, labour has been accomplished without fatiguing either the mind or body; but when I computed the remainder of my time and my task, it was apparent that, according to the season of publication, the delay of a month would be productive of that of a year.   I was now straining for the goal, and in the last winter many evenings were borrowed from the social pleasures of Lausanne.   I could now wish that a pause, an interval, had been allowed for a serious revisal.

I have presumed to mark the moment of conception: I shall now commemorate the hour of my final deliverance. It was on the day, or rather night, of the 27th of June 1787, between the hours of eleven and twelve, that I wrote the last lines of the last page, in a summer-house in my garden.   After laying down my pen I took several turns in a *berceau*, or covered walk of acacias, which commands a prospect of the country, the lake, and the mountains. The air was temperate, the sky was serene, the silver orb of the moon was reflected from the waters, and all nature was silent.   I will not dissemble the first emotions of joy on recovery of my freedom, and, perhaps, the establishment of my fame.   But my pride was soon humbled, and a sober melancholy was spread over my mind, by the idea that I had taken an everlasting leave of an old and agreeable companion, and that, whatsoever might be the future date of my *History*, the life of the historian must be short and precarious. I will add two facts, which have seldom occurred in the composition of six, or at least of five, quartos. 1. My first rough manuscript, without any intermediate copy, has been sent to the press. 2. Not a sheet has been seen by any human eyes, excepting those of the author and the printer: the faults and the merits are exclusively my own.[1]

I cannot help recollecting a much more extraordinary fact, which is affirmed of himself by Retif de la Bretonne, a voluminous and original writer of French novels. He laboured, and may still labour, in the humble office of corrector to a printing-house; but this office enabled him to transport an entire volume from his mind to the press; and his work was given to the public without ever having been written by the pen.

After a quiet residence of four years, during which I had never moved ten miles from Lausanne, it was not without some reluctance and terror that I undertook, in a journey of two hundred leagues, to cross the mountains and the sea. Yet this formidable adventure was achieved without danger or fatigue; and at the end of a fortnight I found myself in Lord Sheffield's house and library, safe, happy,

---

[1] *Extract from Mr. Gibbon's Commonplace Book.*

The IVth volume of the *History of the Decline and Fall of the Roman Empire*	begun March 1, 1782—ended June 1784.
The Vth volume . . .	begun July 1784—ended May 1, 1786.
The VIth volume . . .	begun May 18, 1786—ended June 27, 1787.

These three volumes were sent to press August 15, 1787, and the whole impression was concluded April following.

and at home.   The character of my friend (Mr. Holroyd) had recommended him to a seat in parliament for Coventry, the command of a regiment of light dragoons, and an Irish peerage.   The sense and spirit of his political writings have decided the public opinion on the great questions of our commercial interest with America and Ireland.[1]

The sale of his *Observations on the American States* was diffusive, their effect beneficial; the Navigation Act, the palladium of Britain, was defended, and perhaps saved, by his pen; and he proves, by the weight of fact and argument, that the mother-country may survive and flourish after the loss of America.   My friend has never cultivated the arts of composition; but his materials are copious and correct, and he leaves on his paper the clear impression of an active and vigorous mind.   His *Observations on the Trade, Manufactures, and Present State of Ireland* were intended to guide the industry, to correct the prejudices, and to assuage the passions of a country which seemed to forget that she could be free and prosperous only by a friendly connection with Great Britain.   The concluding observations are written with so much ease and spirit that they may be read by those who are the least interested in the subject.

He fell [2] (1784) with the unpopular coalition; but his merit has been acknowledged at the last general election, 1790, by the honourable invitation and free choice of the city of Bristol.   During the whole time of my residence in England I was entertained at Sheffield Place and in Down-

---

[1] *Observations on the Commerce of the American States*, by John Lord Sheffield, the 6th edition, London, 1784, in 8vo.

[2] It is not obvious from whence he fell; he never held nor desired any office of emolument whatever, unless his military commissions, and the command of a regiment of light dragoons, which he raised himself, and which was disbanded on the peace in 1783, should be deemed such.

ing Street by his hospitable kindness; and the most pleasant period was that which I passed in the domestic society of the family. In the larger circle of the metropolis I observed the country and the inhabitants with the knowledge, and without the prejudices, of an Englishman; but I rejoiced in the apparent increase of wealth and prosperity, which might be fairly divided between the spirit of the nation and the wisdom of the minister. All party resentment was now lost in oblivion; since I was no man's rival, no man was my enemy. I felt the dignity of independence, and, as I asked no more, I was satisfied with the general civilities of the world. The house in London which I frequented with most pleasure and assiduity was that of Lord North. After the loss of power and of sight he was still happy in himself and his friends, and my public tribute of gratitude and esteem could no longer be suspected of any interested motive. Before my departure from England I was present at the august spectacle of Mr. Hastings's trial in Westminster Hall. It is not my province to absolve or condemn the Governor of India;[1] but Mr. Sheridan's eloquence commanded my applause; nor could I hear without emotion the personal compliment which he paid me in the presence of the British nation.[2]

From this display of genius, which blazed four successive days, I shall stoop to a very mechanical circumstance. As I was waiting in the manager's box I had the curiosity to inquire of the shorthand-writer how many words a ready

---

[1] He considered the *persecution* of that highly respectable person to have arisen from party views.—SHEFFIELD.

[2] He said the facts that made up the volume of narrative were unparalleled in atrociousness, and that nothing equal in criminality was to be traced, either in ancient or modern history, in the correct periods of Tacitus or the luminous page of Gibbon.— *Morning Chronicle*, June 14, 1788.

and rapid orator might pronounce in an hour? From 7000 to 7500 was his answer. The medium of 7200 will afford 120 words in a minute, and two words in each second. But this computation will only apply to the English language.

As the publication of my three last volumes was the principal object, so it was the first care, of my English journey. The previous arrangements with the bookseller and the printer were settled in my passage through London, and the proofs which I returned more correct were transmitted every post from the press to Sheffield Place. The length of the operation, and the leisure of the country, allowed some time to review my manuscript. Several rare and useful books, the *Assises de Jerusalem, Ramusius de Bello C.* P^aro, the Greek *Acts of the Synod of Florence*, the *Statuta Urbis Romæ*, etc., were procured, and I introduced in their proper places the supplements which they afforded. The impression of the fourth volume had consumed three months. Our common interest required that we should move with a quicker pace; and Mr. Strahan fulfilled his engagement, which few printers could sustain, of delivering every week three thousand copies of nine sheets. The day of publication was, however, delayed, that it might coincide with the fifty-first anniversary of my own birthday; the double festival was celebrated by a cheerful literary dinner at Mr. Cadell's house; and I seemed to blush while they read an elegant compliment from Mr. Hayley,[1] whose poetical talents had more than

---

[1] *Occasional Stanzas, by Mr. Hayley, read after the dinner at Mr. Cadell's, May 8, 1788; being the day of the publication of the three last volumes of Mr. Gibbon's History, and his birthday.*

GENII of ENGLAND, and of ROME!
In mutual triumph here assume
    The honours each may claim!

once been employed in the praise of his friend. Before
Mr. Hayley inscribed with my name his epistles on history

This social scene with smiles survey!
And consecrate the festive day
    To Friendship and to Fame!

Enough, by Desolation's tide,
With anguish, and indignant pride,
    Has ROME bewail'd her fate;
And mourn'd that Time, in Havoc's hour,
Defaced each monument of power
    To speak her truly great:

O'er maim'd POLYBIUS, just and sage,
O'er LIVY's mutilated page,
    How deep was her regret!
Touch'd by this Queen, in ruin grand,
See! Glory, by an English hand,
    Now pays a mighty debt:

Lo! sacred to the ROMAN Name,
And raised, like ROME's immortal Fame,
    By Genius and by Toil,
The splendid Work is crown'd to-day,
On which Oblivion ne'er shall prey,
    Not Envy make her spoil!

ENGLAND, exult! and view not now
With jealous glance each nation's brow,
    Where History's palm has spread!
In every path of liberal art,
Thy Sons to prime distinction start,
    And no superior dread.

Science for thee a NEWTON raised;
For thy renown a SHAKSPEARE blazed,
    Lord of the drama's sphere!
In different fields to equal praise
See History now thy GIBBON raise
    To shine without a peer!

Eager to honour living worth,
And bless to-day the double birth,
    That proudest joy may claim,
Let artless Truth this homage pay,
And consecrate the festive day
    To Friendship and to Fame!

I was not acquainted with that amiable man and elegant
poet.   He afterwards thanked me in verse for my second
and third volumes;[1] and in the summer of 1781 the
Roman Eagle[2] (a proud title) accepted the invitation of

[1] SONNET TO EDWARD GIBBON, ESQ., ON THE PUBLICATION OF HIS
SECOND AND THIRD VOLUMES, 1781.

With proud delight th' imperial founder gazed
    On the new beauty of his second Rome,
When on his eager eye rich temples blazed,
    And his fair city rose in youthful bloom:
A pride more noble may thy heart assume,
    O GIBBON! gazing on thy growing work,
In which, constructed for a happier doom,
    No hasty marks of vain ambition lurk:
Thou may'st deride both Time's destructive sway,
    And baser Envy's beauty-mangling dirk;
Thy gorgeous fabric, plann'd with wise delay,
    Shall baffle foes more savage than the Turk;
As ages multiply, its fame shall rise,
And earth must perish ere its splendour dies.

[2] A CARD OF INVITATION TO MR. GIBBON AT BRIGHTHELMSTONE, 1781.

An English sparrow, pert and free,
Who chirps beneath his native tree,
Hearing the Roman eagle's near,
And feeling more respect than fear,
Thus, with united love and awe,
Invites him to his shed of straw.
    Tho' he is but a twittering sparrow,
The field he hops in rather narrow,
When nobler plumes attract his view
He ever pays them homage due;
He looks with reverential wonder
On him whose talons bear the thunder;
Nor could the jackdaws e'er inveigle
His voice to vilify the eagle,
Tho', issuing from the holy towers
In which they build their warmest bowers,
Their sovereign's haunt they slily search,
In hopes to catch him on his perch
(For Pindar says, beside his God

the English Sparrow, who chirped in the groves of Eartham, near Chichester. As most of the former purchasers
were naturally desirous of completing their sets, the sale
of the quarto edition was quick and easy; and an octavo
size was printed to satisfy at a cheaper rate the public
demand. The conclusion of my work was generally read,
and variously judged. The style has been exposed to
much academical criticism; a religious clamour was revived, and the reproach of indecency has been loudly
echoed by the rigid censors of morals. I never could
understand the clamour that has been raised against the
indecency of my three last volumes. 1. An equal degree
of freedom in the former part, especially in the first volume,
had passed without reproach. 2. I am justified in paint-
ing the manners of the times; the vices of Theodora form
an essential feature in the reign and character of Justinian;
and the most naked tale in my history is told by the Rev.
Mr. Joseph Warton, an instructor of youth (*Essay on the
Genius and Writings of Pope*, p. 322-324). 3. My English
text is chaste, and all licentious passages are left in the
obscurity of a learned language. *Le Latin dans ses mots
brave l'honnêteté*, says the correct Boileau, in a country and

> The thunder-bearing bird will nod),
> Then, peeping round his still retreat,
> They pick from underneath his feet
> Some molted feather he lets fall,
> And swear he cannot fly at all.——
>   Lord of the sky! whose pounce can tear
> These croakers, that infest the air,
> Trust him! the sparrow loves to sing
> The praise of thy imperial wing!
> He thinks thou'lt deem him, on his word,
> An honest, though familiar bird;
> And hopes thou soon wilt condescend
> To look upon thy little friend;
> That he may boast around his grove
> A visit from the bird of Jove.

idiom more scrupulous than our own.[1] Yet, upon the
whole, the *History of the Decline and Fall* seems to have
struck root both at home and abroad, and may perhaps
a hundred years hence still continue to be abused. I am
less flattered by Mr. Porson's high encomium on the style
and spirit of my *History* than I am satisfied with his
honourable testimony to my attention, diligence, and
accuracy; those humble virtues which religious zeal had
most audaciously denied. The sweetness of his praise is
tempered by a reasonable mixture of acid. As the book
may not be common in England, I shall transcribe my own
character from the *Bibliotheca Historica* of Meuselius,[2]
a learned and laborious German:—" Summis ævi nostri
historicis Gibbonus sine dubio adnumerandus est. Inter
Capitolii ruinas stans primum hujus operis scribendi
consilium cepit. Florentissimos vitæ annos colligendo
et laborando eidem impendit. Enatum inde monumentum
ære perennius, licet passim appareant sinistrè dicta, minus
perfecta, veritati non satis consentanea. Videmus quidem
ubique fere studium scrutandi veritatemque scribendi
maximum: tamen sine Tillemontio duce, ubi scilicet hujus
historia finitur, sæpius noster titubat atque hallucinatur.
Quod vel maxime fit, ubi de rebus Ecclesiasticis vel de
juris prudentiâ Romanâ (tom. iv.) tradit, et in aliis locis.
Attamen nævi hujus generis haud impediunt quo minus
operis summam et οἰκονομίαν præclarè dispositam, delec-
tum rerum sapientissimum, argutum quoque interdum,
dictionemque seu stylum historico æque ac philosopho
dignissimum, et vix à quoque alio Anglo, Humio ac
Robertsono haud exceptis (*præreptum ?*), vehementer
laudemus, atque sæculo nostro de hujusmodi historiâ
gratulemur. . . . Gibbonus adversarios cum in tum extra

[1] Latin by its terms puts modesty to the blush.
[2] Vol. iv., part 1, p. 342, 344.

patriam nactus est, quia propagationem religionis Christianæ, non, ut vulgo fieri solet, aut more Theologorum, sed ut Historicum et Philosophum decet, exposuerat." [1]

The French, Italian, and German translations have been executed with various success; but, instead of patronising, I should willingly suppress such imperfect copies, which injure the character while they propagate the name of the author. The first volume had been feebly, though faithfully, translated into French by M. Le Clerc de Septchenes, a young gentleman of a studious character and liberal fortune. After his decease the work was continued by two manufacturers of Paris, MM. Desmuniers and Cant-

[1] Beyond question Gibbon must be admitted into the number of the chief historians of our age. To him, standing amid the ruins of the Capitol, first came the idea of undertaking the composition of this work. To the task of gathering the information and of throwing such into literary form he devoted the freshest years of his manhood. Hence there issued a monument more lasting than brass, although here and there statements may appear of questionable taste, statements also less happily expressed than usual, and not in strict accordance with truth. Nevertheless, we observe on the other hand, an outstanding zeal for the investigation and declaration of truth; yet where the help of Tillemont's history ends, there forsooth our author more repeatedly errs and falls into solecisms. This is chiefly apparent when the latter refers to ecclesiastical affairs, or to Roman jurisprudence, though it is also manifest elsewhere. But little imperfections of that character do not prevent the most skilful and artistic arrangement being followed out in the work. Furthermore we may warmly praise the very wise, nay, far-seeing, arrangement of material, the diction and literary style befitting at once the historian and the philosopher, scarcely excelled by any other English writer, Hume and Robertson not excepted. We therefore congratulate our age on the production of such a history. Gibbon has found hostile critics both within and without his own country, because he has criticised the manner in which the Christian religion was propagated throughout the world, not sneeringly as was wont to be done or, on the other hand, not after the methods of Theologians, but as became one who was an historian and a philosopher."

well; but the former is now an active member of the
National Assembly, and the undertaking languishes in the
hands of his associate.   The superior merit of the interpreter, or his language, inclines me to prefer the Italian
version: but I wish that it were in my power to read the
German, which is praised by the best judges.   The Irish
pirates are at once my friends and my enemies.   But I
cannot be displeased with the two numerous and correct
impressions which have been published for the use of the
Continent at Basil in Switzerland.   The conquests of our
language and literature are not confined to Europe alone,
and a writer who succeeds in London is speedily read on
the banks of the Delaware and the Ganges.

In the preface of the fourth volume, while I gloried in
the name of an Englishman, I announced my approaching
return to the neighbourhood of the Lake of Lausanne.
This last trial confirmed my assurance that I had wisely
chosen for my own happiness; nor did I once in a year's
visit entertain a wish of settling in my native country.
Britain is the free and fortunate island; but where is the
spot in which I could unite the comforts and beauties of
my establishment at Lausanne?   The tumult of London
astonished my eyes and ears; the amusements of public
places were no longer adequate to the trouble; the clubs
and assemblies were filled with new faces and young men;
and our best society, our long and late dinners, would soon
have been prejudicial to my health.   Without any share
in the political wheel, I must be idle and insignificant:
yet the most splendid temptations would not have enticed
me to engage a second time in the servitude of parliament
or office.   At Tunbridge, some weeks after the publication
of my *History*, I reluctantly quitted Lord and Lady
Sheffield, and with a young Swiss friend, whom I had
introduced to the English world, I pursued the road of

Dover and Lausanne. My habitation was embellished in
my absence; and the last division of books, which followed
my steps, increased my chosen library to the number of
between six and seven thousand volumes. My seraglio
was ample, my choice was free, my appetite was keen.
After a full repast on Homer and Aristophanes, I involved
myself in the philosophic maze in the writings of Plato,
of which the dramatic is, perhaps, more interesting than
the argumentative part; but I stepped aside into every
path of inquiry which reading or reflection accidentally
opened.

Alas! the joy of my return, and my studious ardour,
were soon damped by the melancholy state of my friend
Mr. Deyverdun. His health and spirits had long suffered
a gradual decline, a succession of apoplectic fits announced
his dissolution, and, before he expired, those who loved
him could not wish for the continuance of his life. The
voice of reason might congratulate his deliverance, but the
feelings of nature and friendship could be subdued only by
time: his amiable character was still alive in my remembrance; each room, each walk was imprinted with our
common footsteps; and I should blush at my own philosophy, if a long interval of study had not preceded and
followed the death of my friend. By his last will he left
to me the option of purchasing his house and garden, or of
possessing them during my life, on the payment either of a
stipulated price, or of an easy retribution, to his kinsman
and heir. I should probably have been tempted by the
demon of property, if some legal difficulties had not been
started against my title; a contest would have been
vexatious, doubtful, and invidious; and the heir most
gratefully subscribed an agreement, which rendered my
life possession more perfect, and his future condition more

advantageous. Yet I had often revolved the judicious
lines in which Pope answers the objections of his long-
sighted friend—

> Pity to build without or child or wife;
> Why, you'll enjoy it only all your life:
> Well, if the use be mine, does it concern one
> Whether the name belong to Pope or Vernon?

The certainty of my tenure has allowed me to lay out a
considerable sum in improvements and alterations: they
have been executed with skill and taste; and few men of
letters, perhaps, in Europe, are so desirably lodged as
myself. But I feel, and with the decline of years I shall
more painfully feel, that I am alone in paradise. Among
the circle of my acquaintance at Lausanne, I have gradually acquired the solid and tender friendship of a respectable family;[1] the four persons of whom it is composed are
all endowed with the virtues best adapted to their age and
situation; and I am encouraged to love the parents as a
brother, and the children as a father. Every day we seek
and find the opportunities of meeting: yet even this
valuable connection cannot supply the loss of domestic
society.

Within the last two or three years our tranquillity has
been clouded by the disorders of France; many families
at Lausanne were alarmed and affected by the terrors of
an impending bankruptcy; but the revolution, or rather
the dissolution, of the kingdom, has been heard and felt in
the adjacent lands.

I beg leave to subscribe my assent to Mr. Burke's creed
on the revolution of France. I admire his eloquence, I
approve his politics, I adore his chivalry, and I can almost
excuse his reverence for church establishments. I have
sometimes thought of writing a dialogue of the dead, in

[1] The family of de Severy.

which Lucian, Erasmus, and Voltaire should mutually acknowledge the danger of exposing an old superstition to the contempt of the blind and fanatic multitude.

A swarm of emigrants of both sexes, who escaped from the public ruin, has been attracted by the vicinity, the manners, and the language of Lausanne; and our narrow habitations, in town and country, are now occupied by the first names and titles of the departed monarchy. These noble fugitives are entitled to our pity; they may claim our esteem, but they cannot, in their present state of mind and fortune, much contribute to our amusement. Instead of looking down as calm and idle spectators on the theatre of Europe, our domestic harmony is somewhat embittered by the infusion of party spirit: our ladies and gentlemen assume the character of self-taught politicians; and the sober dictates of wisdom and experience are silenced by the clamour of the triumphant *democrates*. The fanatic missionaries of sedition have scattered the seeds of discontent in our cities and villages, which have flourished above two hundred and fifty years without fearing the approach of war or feeling the weight of government. Many individuals, and some communities, appear to be infected with the Gallic frenzy, the wild theories of equal and boundless freedom; but I trust that the body of the people will be faithful to their sovereign and to themselves; and I am satisfied that the failure or success of a revolt would equally terminate in the ruin of the country. While the aristocracy of Berne protects the happiness, it is superfluous to inquire whether it be founded in the rights of man: the economy of the state is liberally supplied without the aid of taxes; and the magistrates *must* reign with prudence and equity, since they are unarmed in the midst of an armed nation.

The revenue of Berne, excepting some small duties, is

derived from church lands, tithes, feudal rights, and interest of money. The republic has nearly £500,000 sterling in the English funds, and the amount of their treasure is unknown to the citizens themselves. For myself (may the omen be averted!) I can only declare that the first stroke of a rebel drum would be the signal of my immediate departure.

When I contemplate the common lot of mortality, I must acknowledge that I have drawn a high prize in the lottery of life. The far greater part of the globe is overspread with barbarism or slavery; in the civilised world the most numerous class is condemned to ignorance and poverty; and the double fortune of my birth in a free and enlightened country, in an honourable and wealthy family, is the lucky chance of a unit against millions. The general probability is about three to one that a new-born infant will not live to complete his fiftieth year.[1] I have now passed that age, and may fairly estimate the present value of my existence in the three-fold division of mind, body, and estate.

1. The first and indispensable requisite of happiness is a clear conscience, unsullied by the reproach or remembrance of an unworthy action.

> —— Hic murus aheneus esto,
> Nil conscire sibi, nullâ pallescere culpâ.[2]

I am endowed with a cheerful temper, a moderate sensibility, and a natural disposition to repose rather than to

---

[1] See Buffon, *Supplément à l'Histoire Naturelle*, tom. vii. p. 158-164: of a given number of new-born infants, one half, by the fault of nature or man, is extinguished before the age of puberty and reason.—A melancholy calculation!

[2] "Let this be to thee as it were a brazen wall of defence, to be conscious of no evil that will cause you to grow pale in the presence of others."—Horace, *Epistles*, B. I., i. l. 59.

activity: some mischievous appetites and habits have perhaps been corrected by philosophy or time. The love of study, a passion which derives fresh vigour from enjoyment, supplies each day, each hour, with a perpetual source of independent and rational pleasure; and I am not sensible of any decay of the mental faculties. The original soil has been highly improved by cultivation; but it may be questioned whether some flowers of fancy, some grateful errors, have not been eradicated with the weeds of prejudice. 2. Since I have escaped from the long perils of my childhood, the serious advice of a physician has seldom been requisite. "The madness of superfluous health" I have never known, but my tender constitution has been fortified by time, and the inestimable gift of the sound and peaceful slumbers of infancy may be imputed both to the mind and body. 3. I have already described the merits of my society and situation; but these enjoyments would be tasteless or bitter if their possession were not assured by an annual and adequate supply. According to the scale of Switzerland I am a rich man; and I am indeed rich, since my income is superior to my expense, and my expense is equal to my wishes. My friend Lord Sheffield has kindly relieved me from the cares to which my taste and temper are most adverse: shall I add that, since the failure of my first wishes, I have never entertained any serious thoughts of a matrimonial connection?

I am disgusted with the affectation of men of letters, who complain that they have renounced a substance for a shadow, and that their fame (which sometimes is no insupportable weight) affords a poor compensation for envy, censure, and persecution.[1] My own experience, at least,

---

[1] Mr. d'Alembert relates that, as he was walking in the gardens of Sans Souci with the King of Prussia, Frederic said to him, "Do you see that old woman, a poor weeder, asleep on that sunny bank?

has taught me a very different lesson: twenty happy years have been animated by the labour of my *History*, and its success has given me a name, a rank, a character in the world to which I should not otherwise have been entitled. The freedom of my writings has indeed provoked an implacable tribe; but, as I was safe from the stings, I was soon accustomed to the buzzing of the hornets: my nerves are not tremblingly alive, and my literary temper is so happily framed that I am less sensible of pain than of pleasure. The rational pride of an author may be offended, rather than flattered, by vague indiscriminate praise; but he cannot, he should not, be indifferent to the fair testimonies of private and public esteem. Even his moral sympathy may be gratified by the idea that now, in the present hour, he is imparting some degree of amusement or knowledge to his friends in a distant land; that one day his mind will be familiar to the grandchildren of those who are yet unborn.[1] I cannot boast of the friendship or favour of princes; the patronage of English literature has long since been devolved on our booksellers, and the measure of their liberality is the least

she is probably a more happy being than either of us." The king and the philosopher may speak for themselves; for my part, I do not envy the old woman.

[1] In the first of ancient or modern romances (*Tom Jones*) this proud sentiment, this feast of fancy, is enjoyed by the genius of Fielding—" Come, bright love of fame, etc., fill my ravished fancy with the hopes of charming ages yet to come. Foretell me that some tender maid, whose grandmother is yet unborn, hereafter, when, under the fictitious name of Sophia, she reads the real worth which once existed in my Charlotte, shall from her sympathetic breast send forth the heaving sigh. Do thou teach me not only to foresee but to enjoy, nay even to feed on, future praise. Comfort me by the solemn assurance that, when the little parlour in which I sit at this moment shall be reduced to a worse furnished box, I shall be read with honour by those who never knew nor saw me, and whom I shall neither know nor see."—Book xiii., chap. 1.

ambiguous test of our common success. Perhaps the golden mediocrity of my fortune has contributed to fortify my application.

The present is a fleeting moment, the past is no more; and our prospect of futurity is dark and doubtful. This day may *possibly* be my last: but the laws of probability, so true in general, so fallacious in particular, still allow about fifteen years.[1] I shall soon enter into the period which, as the most agreeable of his long life, was selected by the judgment and experience of the sage Fontenelle. His choice is approved by the eloquent historian of nature, who fixes our moral happiness to the mature season, in which our passions are supposed to be calmed, our duties fulfilled, our ambition satisfied, our fame and fortune established on a solid basis.[2] In private conversation, that great and amiable man added the weight of his own experience; and this autumnal felicity might be exemplified in the lives of Voltaire, Hume, and many other men of letters. I am far more inclined to embrace than to dispute this comfortable doctrine. I will not suppose any premature decay of the mind or body; but I must reluctantly observe that two causes, the abbreviation of time, and the failure of hope, will always tinge with a browner shade the evening of life.[3]

---

[1] Mr. Buffon, from our disregard of the possibility of death within the four-and-twenty hours, concludes that a chance which falls below or rises above ten thousand to one will never affect the hopes or fears of a reasonable man. The fact is true, but our courage is the effect of thoughtlessness, rather than of reflection. If a public lottery were drawn for the choice of an immediate victim, and if our name were inscribed on one of the ten thousand tickets, should we be perfectly easy?

[2] See Buffon.

[3] The proportion of a part to the whole is the only standard by which we can measure the length of our existence. At the age of twenty, one year is a tenth, perhaps, of the time which has elapsed

LAST ILLNESS AND DEATH OF GIBBON

[GIBBON's autobiography only extends to the year 1789. He continued to reside at Lausanne till 1793, when he returned to England to alleviate by his presence and sympathy a domestic affliction of his friend Lord Sheffield. He arrived in England in the beginning of June, and died at London on the 16th of January in the following year. Lord Sheffield has given an account of the last illness and death of his friend, from which the following extracts are taken.]

" Mr. Gibbon arrived in the beginning of June at my house in Downing Street in good health; and after passing about a month with me there, we settled at Sheffield Place for the remainder of summer, where his wit, learning, and cheerful politeness, delighted a great variety of characters. Although he was inclined to represent his health as better than it really was, his habitual dislike to motion appeared to increase; his inaptness to exercise confined him to the library and dining-room, and there he joined my friend Mr. Frederick North in pleasant arguments against

within our consciousness and memory: at the age of fifty it is no more than the fortieth, and this relative value continues to decrease till the last sands are shaken by the hand of death. This reasoning may seem metaphysical; but on a trial it will be found satisfactory and just. The warm desires, the long expectations of youth are founded on the ignorance of themselves and of the world: they are gradually damped by time and experience, by disappointment and possession; and after the middle season the crowd must be content to remain at the foot of the mountain; while the few who have climbed the summit aspire to descend or expect to fall. In old age the consolation of hope is reserved for the tenderness of parents, who commence a new life in their children; the faith of enthusiasts, who sing hallelujahs above the clouds; and the vanity of authors, who presume the immortality of their name and writings.

exercise in general. He ridiculed the unsettled and rest-less disposition that summer, the most uncomfortable, as he said, of all seasons, generally gives to those who have the free use of their limbs. Such arguments were little required to keep society, Mr. Jekyll, Mr. Douglas, etc., within doors, when his company was only there to be enjoyed; for neither the fineness of the season nor the most promising parties of pleasure could tempt the com-pany of either sex to desert him.

" Those who have enjoyed the society of Mr. Gibbon will agree with me that his conversation was still more captivating than his writings. Perhaps no man ever divided time more fairly between literary labour and social enjoyment; and hence, probably, he derived his peculiar excellence of making his very extensive know-ledge contribute, in the highest degree, to the use or pleasure of those with whom he conversed. He united, in the happiest manner imaginable, two characters which are not often found in the same person, the profound scholar and the peculiarly agreeable companion.

" It would be superfluous to attempt a very minute delineation of a character which is so distinctly marked in the Memoirs and Letters. He has described himself without reserve, and with perfect sincerity. The Letters, and especially the Extracts from the Journal, which could not have been written with any purpose of being seen, will make the reader perfectly acquainted with the man.[1]

[1] Elsewhere Lord Sheffield observes—" His [Gibbon's] letters in general bear a strong resemblance to the style and turn of his con-versation; the characteristics of which were vivacity, elegance, and precision, with knowledge astonishingly extensive and correct. He never ceased to be instructive and entertaining; and in general there was a vein of pleasantry in his conversation which prevented its becoming languid, even during a residence of many months with a family in the country.

" It has been supposed that he always arranged what he intended

"Excepting a visit to Lord Egremont and Mr. Hayley, whom he particularly esteemed, Mr. Gibbon was not absent from Sheffield Place till the beginning of October, when we were reluctantly obliged to part with him, that he might perform his engagement to Mrs. Gibbon at Bath, the widow of his father, who had early deserved, and invariably retained, his affection. From Bath he proceeded to Lord Spencer's at Althorp, a family which he always met with uncommon satisfaction. He continued in good health during the whole summer, and in excellent spirits (I never knew him enjoy better); and when he went from Sheffield Place, little did I imagine it would be the last time that I should have the inexpressible pleasure of seeing him there in full possession of health.

"FROM GIBBON TO LORD SHEFFIELD

"'ST. JAMES'S STREET, *Nov. 11th,* 1793.

"'I must at length withdraw the veil before my state of health, though the naked truth may alarm you more than a fit of the gout. Have you never observed, through my *inexpressibles,* a large prominency which, as it was not at all painful, and very little troublesome, I had strangely neglected for many years? But since my departure from

to say before he spoke; his quickness in conversation contradicts this notion: but it is very true that, before he sat down to write a note or letter, he completely arranged in his mind what he meant to express. He pursued the same method in respect to other composition; and he occasionally would walk several times about his apartment before he had rounded a period to his taste. He has pleasantly remarked to me that it sometimes cost him many a turn before he could throw a sentiment into a form that gratified his own criticism. His systematic habit of arrangement in point of style, assisted, in his instance, by an excellent memory and correct judgment, is much to be recommended to those who aspire to perfection in writing."

Sheffield Place it has increased (most stupendously), is increasing, and ought to be diminished.   Yesterday I sent for Farquhar, who is allowed to be a very skilful surgeon. After viewing and palping, he very seriously desired to call in assistance, and has examined it again to-day with Mr. Cline, a surgeon, as he says, of the first eminence.   They both pronounce it a *hydrocele* (a collection of water), which must be let out by the operation of tapping; but, from its magnitude and long neglect, they think it a most extra-ordinary case, and wish to have another surgeon, Dr. Baillie, present.   If the business should go off smoothly, I shall be delivered from my burthen (it is almost as big as a small child), and walk about in four or five days with a truss.   But the medical gentlemen, who never speak quite plain, insinuate to me the possibility of an inflammation, of fever, etc.   I am not appalled at the thoughts of the operation, which is fixed for Wednesday next, twelve o'clock; but it has occurred to me that you might wish to be present, before and afterwards, till the crisis was past; and to give you that opportunity I shall solicit a delay till Thursday or even Friday.   Adieu.'

" Immediately on receiving the last letter, I went the same day from Brighthelmstone to London, and was agree-ably surprised to find that Mr. Gibbon had dined at Lord Lucan's, and did not return to his lodgings, where I waited for him, till eleven o'clock at night.   Those who have seen him within the last eight or ten years must be surprised to hear that he could doubt whether his disorder was apparent.   When he returned to England in 1787, I was greatly alarmed by a prodigious increase, which I always conceived to proceed from a rupture.   I did not under-stand why he, who had talked with me on every other subject relative to himself and his affairs without reserve,

should never in any shape hint at a malady so troublesome; but on speaking to his *valet de chambre*, he told me
Mr. Gibbon could not bear the least allusion to that subject, and never would suffer him to notice it.   I consulted
some medical persons, who, with me supposing it to be a
rupture, were of opinion that nothing could be done, and
said that he surely must have had advice, and of course
had taken all necessary precautions.   He now talked
freely with me about his disorder, which, he said, began
in the year 1761; that he then consulted Mr. Hawkins the
surgeon, who did not decide whether it was the beginning
of a rupture, or a hydrocele; but he desired to see Mr.
Gibbon again when he came to town.   Mr. Gibbon, not
feeling any pain, nor suffering any inconvenience, as he
said, never returned to Mr. Hawkins; and although the
disorder continued to increase gradually, and of late years
very much indeed, he never mentioned it to any person,
however incredible it may appear, from 1761 to November
1793.   I told him that I had always supposed there was no
doubt of its being a rupture; his answer was, that he never
thought so, and that he and the surgeons who attended
him were of opinion that it was a hydrocele.   It is now
certain that it was originally a rupture, and that a
hydrocele had lately taken place in the same part; and
it is remarkable that his legs, which had been swelled about
the ankle, particularly one of them, since he had the
erysipelas in 1790, recovered their former shape as soon
as the water appeared in another part, which did not
happen till between the time he left Sheffield Place, in the
beginning of October, and his arrival at Althorp, towards
the latter end of that month.   On the Thursday following
the date of his last letter Mr. Gibbon was tapped for the
first time; four quarts of a transparent watery fluid were
discharged by that operation.   Neither inflammation nor

fever ensued; the tumour was diminished to nearly half
its size; the remaining part was a soft irregular mass.   I
had been with him two days before, and I continued with
him above a week after the first tapping, during which
time he enjoyed his usual spirits; and the three medical
gentlemen who attended him will recollect his pleasantry,
even during the operation.   He was abroad again in a few
days, but, the water evidently collecting very fast, it was
agreed that a second puncture should be made a fortnight
after the first.   Knowing that I should be wanted at a
meeting in the country, he pressed me to attend it, and
promised that soon after the second operation was performed he would follow me to Sheffield Place.

"GIBBON TO LORD SHEFFIELD AT BRIGHTON

"'ST. JAMES'S STREET, *Nov. 25th*, 1793.

"'Though Farquhar has promised to write a line, I
conceive you may not be sorry to hear directly from me.
The operation of yesterday was much longer, more searching, and more painful than the former; but it has eased
and lightened me to a much greater degree.[1]   No inflammation, no fever, a delicious night, leave to go abroad
to-morrow, and to go out of town when I please, *en
attendant* the future measures of a radical cure. . . .'

"On the 10th of December Mr. Gibbon proceeded to
Sheffield Place; and his discourse was never more brilliant
nor more entertaining than on his arrival.   The parallels
which he drew, and the comparisons which he made,
between the leading men of this country were sketched in
his best manner, and were infinitely interesting.   How-

[1] Three quarts of the same fluid as before were discharged.—
SHEFFIELD.

ever, this last visit to Sheffield Place became far different
from any he had ever made before.   That ready, cheerful,
various, and illuminating conversation, which we had
before admired in him, was not now always to be found in
the library or the dining-room.   He moved with difficulty,
and retired from company sooner than he had been used to
do.   On the 23rd of December his appetite began to fail
him.   He observed to me that it was a very bad sign *with
him* when he could not eat his breakfast, which he had
done at all times very heartily; and this seems to have been
the strongest expression of apprehension that he was
ever observed to utter.   A considerable degree of fever
now made its appearance.   Inflammation arose, from the
weight and the bulk of the tumour.   Water again collected
very fast, and when the fever went off he never entirely
recovered his appetite even for breakfast.   I became very
uneasy at his situation towards the end of the month, and
thought it necessary to advise him to set out for London.
He went to London on the 7th of January, and the next
day I received the following billet, the last he ever wrote:—

"GIBBON TO LORD SHEFFIELD

"'ST. JAMES'S STREET, *four o'clock, Tuesday.*

"' This date says everything.   I was almost killed between Sheffield Place and East Grinsted, by hard, frozen,
long, and cross ruts, that would disgrace the approach to
an Indian wigwam.   The rest was something less painful;
and I reached this place half-dead, but not seriously
feverish or ill.   I found a dinner invitation from Lord
Lucan; but what are dinners to me?   I wish they did not
know of my departure.   I catch the flying post.   What
an effort!   Adieu till Thursday or Friday.'

" By his own desire I did not follow him till Thursday the 9th. I then found him far from well. The tumour more distended than before, inflamed, and ulcerated in several places. Remedies were applied to abate the inflammation; but it was not thought proper to puncture the tumour, for the third time, till Monday the 13th of January, when no less than six quarts of fluid were discharged. He seemed much relieved by the evacuation. His spirits continued good. He talked, as usual, of passing his time at houses which he had often frequented with great pleasure—the Duke of Devonshire's, Mr. Craufurd's, Lord Spencer's, Lord Lucan's, Sir Ralph Payne's, and Mr. Batt's: and when I told him that I should not return to the country, as I had intended, he pressed me to go: knowing I had an engagement there on public business, he said, ' You may be back on Saturday, and I intend to go on Thursday to Devonshire House.' I had not any apprehension that his life was in danger, although I began to fear that he might not be restored to a comfortable state, and that motion would be very troublesome to him; but he talked of a radical cure. He said that it was fortunate the disorder had shown itself while he was in England, where he might procure the best assistance; and if a radical cure could not be obtained before his return to Lausanne, there was an able surgeon at Geneva, who could come to tap him when it should be necessary.

" On Tuesday the 14th, when the risk of inflammation and fever from the last operation was supposed to be passed, as the medical gentlemen who attended him expressed no fears for his life, I went that afternoon part of the way to Sussex, and the following day reached Sheffield Place. The next morning, the 16th, I received by the post a good account of Mr. Gibbon, which mentioned also that he hourly gained strength. In the evening came a letter

by express, dated noon that day, which acquainted me
that Mr. Gibbon had had a violent attack the preceding
night, and that it was not probable he could live till I
came to him.   I reached his lodgings in St. James's Street
about midnight, and learned that my friend had expired a
quarter before one o'clock that day, the 16th of January
1794.

   " After I left him on Tuesday afternoon, the 14th, he
saw some company, Lady Lucan and Lady Spencer, and
thought himself well enough at night to omit the opium
draught which he had been used to take for some time.
He slept very indifferently: before nine the next morning
he rose, but could not eat his breakfast.   However, he
appeared tolerably well, yet complained at times of a pain
in his stomach.   At one o'clock he received a visit of an
hour from Madame de Sylva; and at three his friend Mr.
Craufurd, of Auchinames (for whom he had a particular
regard), called and stayed with him till past five o'clock.
They talked, as usual, on various subjects; and twenty
hours before his death Mr. Gibbon happened to fall into a
conversation, not uncommon with him, on the probable
duration of his life.   He said that he thought himself a
good life for ten, twelve, or perhaps twenty years.   About
six he ate the wing of a chicken, and drank three glasses of
Madeira.   After dinner he became very uneasy and impatient; complained a good deal, and appeared so weak
that his servant was alarmed.   Mr. Gibbon had sent to his
friend and relation Mr. Robert Darell, whose house was
not far distant, desiring to see him, and adding that he had
something particular to say.   But, unfortunately, this
desired interview never took place.

   " During the evening he complained much of his
stomach, and of a disposition to vomit.   Soon after nine
he took his opium draught and went to bed.   About ten

he complained of much pain, and desired that warm napkins might be applied to his stomach. He almost incessantly expressed a sense of pain till about four o'clock in the morning, when he said he found his stomach much easier. About seven the servant asked whether he should send for Mr. Farquhar? he answered, no; that he was as well as he had been the day before. At about half-past eight he got out of bed, and said he was ' *plus adroit* ' than he had been for three months past, and got into bed again without assistance, better than usual. About nine he said that he would rise. The servant, however, persuaded him to remain in bed till Mr. Farquhar, who was expected at eleven, should come. Till about that hour he spoke with great facility. Mr. Farquhar came at the time appointed, and he was then visibly dying. When the *valet de chambre* returned, after attending Mr. Farquhar out of the room, Mr. Gibbon said, ' *Pourquoi est-ce que vous me quittez ?* ' This was about half-past eleven. At twelve he drank some brandy and water from a teapot, and desired his favourite servant to stay with him. These were the last words he pronounced articulately. To the last he preserved his senses; and when he could no longer speak, his servant, having asked a question, he made a sign to show that he understood him. He was quite tranquil, and did not stir; his eyes half-shut. About a quarter before one he ceased to breathe.

" The *valet de chambre* observed that Mr. Gibbon did not at any time show the least sign of alarm or apprehension of death; and it does not appear that he ever thought himself in danger, unless his desire to speak to Mr. Darell may be considered in that light.

" Perhaps I dwell too long on these minute and melancholy circumstances. Yet the close of such a life can hardly fail to interest every reader; and I know that the public has received a different and erroneous account of my friend's last hours.

"I can never cease to feel regret that I was not by his side at this awful period; a regret so strong that I can express it only by borrowing (as Mason has done on a similar occasion) the forcible language of Tacitus: *Mihi præter acerbitatem amici erepti, auget mæstitiam quod assidere valetudini, fovere deficientem, satiari vultu, complexu non contigit.*[1] It is some consolation to me that I did not, like Tacitus, by a long absence, anticipate the loss of my friend several years before his decease.   Although I had not the mournful gratification of being near him on the day he expired, yet, during his illness, I had not failed to attend him with that assiduity which his genius, his virtues, and, above all, our long, uninterrupted, and happy friendship, sanctioned and demanded."

[1] As for me over and above the bitterness of our friend's loss, our sorrow is increased, because it was not permitted to us to watch over thy failing health, to nourish thee in thy weakness, to stamp thine image on our hearts, and to solace ourselves with thine embraces.

INDEX

ABINGDON, Earl of, 126 *note*
Abrollas, 43
Abulfaragius, Pocock's abridgment from, 36
Acton, General, 19
Acton, Richard, 12
Acton, Sir Whitmore, 12
Addison, Joseph, 92, 120
Adolphus, Prince, 29
Æneas, 30, 132, 133
Æneid, 132
Agathias, 159
Age of Sesostris, 47, 48
Ajax, 30
Aldenham, 12
Alembert, Jean le Rond d', 92, 115, 181 *note*
Alexander, Emperor, 142
Algiers, 19
Allamand, Mons., of Bex, 71 *note*, 76
Allesborough, 9
Alton, 89
Alvarez, 78
Alzire, 78
Amsterdam, 68
Anderson, Adam, 36
Annals and Antiquities of Italy, 136
Annals of Scotland, 152
Anne, Queen, 13
Antoninus, 120
Apthorpe, Dr., 151
Arabian Nights Entertainments, 29
Arau, 73
Ardennes, 82
Aristophanes, 177
Aristotle, 100
Arius, 55
Armand, Francis, 115
Ashmole, Elias, 10
Assises de Jerusalem, 170
Athanasian Creed, 52
Athens, 100, 159

Atticus, 26, 100
Aubrey, Sir John, 126 *note*
Augsburg, Congress of, 95
Augustine, St., 5
Augustus, Emperor, 71 *note*
Avernus, Lake, 134

Bacon, Francis, 110
Badcock, Rev. Samuel, 152
Baden, 73
Baillie, Dr., 187
Banks, Sir Joseph, 141 *note*
Bannier, l'Abbé, 67 *note*
Barbeyrac, John, 72
Barthelemy, Jean Jacques, 115
Basle, 73, 176
Bath, 33, 34, 35, 49, 186
Batt, John, 191
Bayle, Peter, 54, 57, 59, 64, 94
Beaufort, Mr. de, 83
Beaumarchais, 153, 154
Beausobre, Isaac de, 106
Behmen, Jacob, 17
Bentley, Dr. Richard, 27, 99, 156
Berkley, Earl of, 126 *note*
Berne, 73, 165, 179
Bernouilli, James, 45
Bertie, Hon. Peregrine, 126 *note*
Besançon, 19, 116
Betts, Dr. John, 10
Bienne, 73
Bigge, Thomas Charles, 126 *note*
Birch, Dr. Thomas, 109, 110
Blackstone, Sir William, 54, 60, 137
Blandford, 103, 105, 106
Bleterie, Abbé de la, 72, 115
Bocage, Mme. du, 115
Boehat, M. de, 67 *note*
Bois le Duc, 83
Bolingbroke, Lord, 13, 100
Bologna, 121, 123
Bolton, Duke of (Lord Lieutenant), 102

Boodle, 141 *note*
Bossuet, Jacques Bénigne, Bishop of Meaux, 52
Bougainville, Jean Pierre de, 115
Bower, Archibald, 35
Brabant, 83
Breitinger, Professor, of Zurich, 71 *note*, 75
Bretonne, Retif de la, 167
Brill, 83
Bristol, 168
Bristol, Earl of, 86
British Museum, 94, 123
Buffon, Conte de, 27, 115, 148, 180 *note*, 183 *note*
Burgundy, 128
Buriton, 28, 32, 34, 47, 48, 87, 88, 90, 93, 106, 108, 109, 110, 125, 127, 139
Burke, Edmund, 102, 141 *note*, 143, 155, 158, 178
Burman, John, 45
Burnet, Dr., 157
Burney, Dr., 141 *note*
Bute, Lord, 89, 126 *note*
Byers, Mr. James, 122

Cade, Jack, 8
Cadell, Mr. Thomas, 144, 170 and *note*
Calais, 124
Cambridge, 37, 40, 44, 152
Canon Chronicus, 47
Caperonnier, Claude, 115
Caroline, Queen, 100
Casaubon, Isaac, 91
Catrou, Francis, 69
Catullus, 71 *note*
Caylus, Count de, 96, 97, 115
Cellarius, Christopher, 36
Cellini, Benvenuto, 5
Cenis, Mount, 121, 123
Charles I., 55
Charles II., 10
Charles V., Emperor, 4, 112
Charles VIII. of France, 108
Charles, Duke of Burgundy, 111
Charles Emanuel III., King of Sardinia, 121
Chelsum, Rev. J., 151, 156
Chesterfield, Lord, 86, 100, 131, 161 *note*
Chichester, 88

Chillingworth, William, 39, 55, 57
Choiseul, Duke of, 154
Christ Church (College), 59
Chrysostom, St., 44, 51
Cibber, Colley, 5
Cicero, 26, 44, 67, 90, 91, 100, 105
Civil History of Naples (Giannone), 73
Clarendon, Lord, 59
Clarke, Mr. Godfrey, of Derbyshire, 126 and *note*
Cleaver, Rev. Mr., 126 *note*
Cline, Dr., 187
Cluverius, 120
College Street, 30, 83
Colman, Mr., 141 *note*
Commodus, 142
Condamine, Charles Marie de la, 115
Confucius, 3
Conic Sections, 71 *note*
Constantine, Emperor, 35, 150
Continuation of Echard's Roman History, 35
Cosmo de Medicis, 111, 112
Coventry, 168
Coventry, Thomas Lord, 9
Cranbrook, 103
Crassy, 78, 79
Craufurd, Mr., 160 *note*, 191
Crevier, Jean Baptiste Louis, 75
Critical Observations on the Sixth Book of the Æneid, 133
Crousaz, Jean Pierre de, 63, 67, 72, 119
Curchod, Mademoiselle Susan, 79, 80

Dacier, Andrew, 69, 71 *note*
D'Aiguillon, Duchesse, 96
Dalrymple, Sir David, 151, 152
Damar, John, 126 *note*
Danaus, 48
Danube, River, 35
D'Anville, 120
Darell, Robert, 192, 193
Davies, Mr., of Oxford, 151, 156
Dean's Yard, 31
Decline and Fall of the Roman Empire, 128, 135, 141, 155, 159, 167, 174, 176, 182
Devizes, 106
Devonshire, Duke of, 191

Deyverdun, Mr., of Lausanne, 62, 69, 125, 127, 128, 129, 130, 131, 161, 163, 177
Dialogues de Amicitiâ, 67 *note*
Diderot, Dionysius, 115
Dijon, 116
Dion Cassius, 71 *note*, 135
Discours Préliminaire à l'Encyclo-pédie, 93
Divine Legation of Moses, 133
Donatus, 120
Dorchester, Earl of, 126 *note*
Douay, 55
Dover, 103, 106, 112, 124, 176
Dresden, 121
Dryden, John, 29, 101 *note*
Dublin, 97, 145
Duclos, Charles Dineau, 115
Ductor Historicus, 34
Dugdale, Sir William, 10
Dumesnil, 116
Dummer, Lord Chancellor, 21
Dunning, Mr., 141 *note*, 143, 155

Eartham, 172
Edgar, Sir Gregory, 9
Edinburgh, 146, 147
Edmonstone, Colonel, 126 *note*
Edwards, Dr., 152
Effingham, Earl of, 103
Einsiedlen, Benedictine Abbey at, 74
Eisenschmidt, John Gasper, 89
Eliot, Lord, 16, 60, 142, 155
Elizabeth, Queen, 51 *note*, 109, 110
Elliston, Edward, 16
Elmsley, Mr. Peter, 144
Elvira, 112
Emmanuel College, Cambridge, 18
Epistles ad Familiares, 67 *note*
Erasmus of Rotterdam, 5, 99, 179
Ernesti, Dr. J. A., 68
Erudits, 92
Esher, 33
Essay on the Delicacy of Friend-ship, 133
Essay on Epic Poetry, 100
Essay on the Genius and Writings of Pope, 173
Essay on the Human Understand-ing, 72
Essay on the Study of Literature, 90, 91, 92, 94, 96, 99, 104, 108, 114, 128, 135

Essex, Earl of, 110
Eton College, 31, 37
Euphemon, 78
Exposition of the Catholic Doctrine, 52

Ferney, 117
Ferrara, 123
Fielding, Henry, 3, 4, 182 *note*
Fiens, James, Baron Say and Seale, 7, 8
Fisher, John, the Jesuit, 55
Florence, 121, 122, 128
Florus, 69 *note*
Foncemagne, Etienne de, 108, 116, 148, 149 and *note*
Fontenelle, Bernard le Bovier de, 94, 115, 183
Foothead, 156
Forum, the, 122
Fox, Charles James, 141 *note*, 143, 159, 160 *note*, 164
Fragmenta Regalia, 109
Francis, Rev. Philip, 33
Frederic the Great, Emperor of Prussia, 100, 121, 181 *note*
Freret, Nicholas, 89
Frey, Mr., of Lausanne, 60, 61
Froulay, Countess de, 148

Gale, Thomas, 107
Garrick, David, 86, 130, 141 *note*
Gascoygne, Sir Thomas, 126 *note*
Geneva, 57, 74, 80, 96, 115, 119, 164, 165, 191
Genoa, 121
Geoffrin, Mme., 115
George I., 15
Gesner, Professor John Matthew, 71 *note*, 75
Giannone, Peter, 72, 73
Gibbon, Edmund, 7, 126 *note*
Gibbon, Edward (1666), 12, 13, 16
Gibbon, Edward the Elder, 16, 19, 21, 28, 33, 34, 46, 52, 58, 59, 79, 81, 82, 83, 86, 87, 88, 89, 90, 94, 96, 102, 124, 125, 132, 136, 138
Gibbon, Mrs. Edward, sen., 85, 88, 89, 125
Gibbon, Mrs. Hester, 17
Gibbon, John, 9, 10, 11, 12

Gibbon, John, architect to Edward III., 6
Gibbon, Matthew, 9, 12
Gibbon, Robert, 8 and *note*, 9
Gibbon, Thomas, Dean of Carlisle, 12
Gloucester, Bishop of, 134
Godefroy, James, 136
Goldoni, Carla, 5
Goldsmith, Dr. Oliver, 141 *note*
Goodwood, 88
Gordon, Thomas, **34**
Gosport, 89
Grævius, 120
Greaves, John, 91
Greek Acts of the Synod of Florence, 170
Grew, Dr. Nehemiah, 10
Gronovius, James, 91
Grotius, Hugo, 72
Guichardt, Mr. C. T., 104
Guignes, M. de, 115
Guise, Sir William, 126 *note*

Hague, 82
Hai Ebn Yokhdan, 25
Hamilton, Count, 100
Hamilton, Sir William, 123
Hardwicke, Lord Chancellor, 7 *note*
Harwich, 83
Hastings, Mr. Warren, 169
Hawkins, Dr., 188
Hawkins's *Life of Johnson*, 141 *note*
Hayley (the poet), 134, 170 and *note*, 171
Hayley, Mr. William, 186
Hearne, Thomas, 34
Hector, 29
Heddington Hill, 47
Helvetius, Claude Adrian, 115
Helvicus, Christopher, 36
Henly, Earl of Northington, 21
Henry III. of England, 108
Henry V. of England, 108
Henry, Prince, of Prussia, 164
Herbelot, Bartholomew d', 36
Hercules, 48
Herodotus, 34, 70 *note*, 159
Hervey, Lady, 86, 97, 114
Heyne, Professor, of Gottingen, 134
Higgins, Mr., 150

Hilsea barracks, 103
Histoire de l'Académie Françoise, 95
Histoire Critique du Manichéisme, 106
Histoire de l'Eglise et de l'Empire, 63
Histoire des grands Chemins de l'Empire Romain, 120
Historical Doubts, 131
History of the Corruptions of Christianity, 151
History of Henry II., 130
History of the Liberty of the Swiss, 111
History of Naples, 67 *note*
History of the Protestant Variations, 51
History of the Republic of Florence, under the House of Medicis, 111
History of the World (Howell's), 35
Hoadley, Bishop, 18
Hoare, Mr., of Wiltshire, 35
Holroyd, Mr., 141, 168
Homer, 70, 106, 107, 137, 177
Hooker, Richard, 39
Hooper, George, 91
Horace, 33, 69, 71 *note*, 94 and *note*, 107, 120, 134, 142 *note*
Hort, Sir John, 126 *note*
Howell, James, 35
Huet, Peter Daniel, 5
Hume, Sir Abraham, 161 *note*
Hume, David, 4, 92, 109, 110, 129 *note*, 131, 142, 145, 147, 161 *note*, 175 *note*, 183
Hunter, Dr., 150
Hurd, Dr., Bishop of Worcester, 107, 110, 133 *note*, 151
Hyde, Dr. Thomas, 47

Iliad, 70, 71 *note*, 106, 159
Introductio ad Latinam Blasoniam (1682), 10
Inverary, 113
Isocrates, 100
Italia Antiqua, 120

James I., 109, 110
Jesus College, Cambridge, 9
John, King of England, 108
Johnson, Samuel (quoted), 73, 107, 141 *note*

ones, Sir William, 141 *note*
ournal Britannique, 94, 130
ournal Etranger, 101 *note*
ulian, 155
ulius Cæsar, 71 *note*
ustin, 69 *note*
ustinian, 159, 173
uvenal, 120, 135

Kingston-upon-Thames, 26, 27, 29
Kirkby, Mr. John, 24, 25

La Barré, 91
La Bruyere, Jean, 18
Lambertini (Pope Benedict XIV.), 123
Lardner, Dr., 136
Lausanne, 10, 60, 61, 62, 63, 65, 66, 69, 70, 73, 74, 75, 77, 78, 79, 80, 81, 82, 86, 87, 93, 96, 98, 116, 118, 119, 125, 138, 161, 162, 163, 164, 165, 166, 167, 176, 178, 179, 191
Law, William, 17, 19, 90, 139
Le Clerc, John, 64, 94
Legge, Chancellor of the Exchequer, 89
Leghorn, 19, 122
Leibnitz, Godfrey William, 98
Leman, Lake, 116, 159, 163
Lewis (the bookseller), 54 and *note*
Lewis of Wurtemburg, Prince, 116, 117
L'Hôpital, Marquis de, 71 and *note*
Liége, 82
Life of Automathes, 25
Life of Julian (Bleterie), 72
Life of Sir Walter Raleigh, 109, 110
Limborch, Philip, 65
Lipsius, Justus, 69, 93
Lipsius ad Germanos et Sallos, 112
Liskeard, 142, 155
Littlebury, 34
Livy, 69 *note*, 74, 75, 91
Locke, John, 39, 65, 69 *note*, 72, 73, 76
Loretto, 123
Lorraine, 83
Loughborough, Lord, 154
Louis XIV., 58, 113
Lowth, Robert, Bishop of London, 38, 39, 43

Luard, Jean Baptiste Antoine, 101 *note*, 115
Lucan, Lord, 187, 191
Lucca, 122
Lucian, 179
Lucretius, 69 *note*
Lucullus, 101 *note*
Lusignan, 78
Lymington, 158
Lyons, 123, 124
Lyttelton, Lord, 130

Mabillon, Jean, 119
Mably, Abbé de, 148, 149 and *note*
Machiavel, Niccolo, 35
Maestricht, 83
Maffei, 136
Magdalen College, 33, 38, 40, 43, 44, 46, 54, 61
Mahomet, 35
Mallet, Mr. David, 60 and *note*, 83, 90, 93, 94, 97, 99, 110, 112, 114
Manetho's *History of Egypt*, 48
Mann, Sir Horace, 122
Marlborough, Duke of, 3
Marli, 113
Marolles, Michael de, 5
Mars, 80 *note*
Marsham, Sir John, 36, 47
Maty, Dr. Matthew, 93, 94, 95, 96, 101, 130
Mayence, 117
Mémoire Justificatif, 153
Mémoires du Comte de Grammont, 9 *note*
Mémoires Littéraires de la Grande Bretagne, 130
Mémoires Militaires, 104
Mémoires sur la Suisse, 67 *note*
Memoirs of the Academy of Inscriptions, 90
Mesery, M. de, 118, 119
Mesery, Mme. de, 118
Mesures Itinéraires, 120
Metamorphoses, 30
Meuse, River, 82
Mezeray, Francis Endes de, 35
Meziriac, Claude Gaspard Bachet Sieur de, 69, 71 *note*
Middleton, Dr., 50, 51, 54, 68
Midleton, Lord Broderick, 161 *note*
Milan, 121, 123

Milner, Joseph, 151
Modena, 121
Moivre, Abraham de, 106
Molesworth, Lord, 13
Molesworth, Mr., 52
Monrepos, 77, 78
Monson, Sir William, 109
Montaigne, Michael de, 5
Montesquieu, 98, 115, 123
Montfaucon, Bernard de, 119
Montmorency, 115
Montrose, Marquis of, 109
Muratori, 136

Nancy, 83
Naples, 121, 122
Nardini, 120
Naunton, Sir Robert, 109
Naval Tracts, 109
Necker, Jacques, 80, 147, 164
Necker, Madam, 147, 164
Nepos, Cornelius, 26
Neufchâtel, 73
New River Company, 16
Newton, Bishop, 5, 157
Newton, Sir Isaac, 36, 47, 98
Nicoll, Dr. John, 30
Nivernois, Duke de, 114
North, Lord, 143, 154, 158, 159, 169, 184
Numatianus, Rutilius, 120

Observations on the American States, 168
Observations on the Trade, Manufactures, and Present State of Ireland, 168
Ockley, Simon, 35
Oder, River, 125
Odiham, 89
Odyssey, 159
Olbach, Baron d', 115
Oldys, William, 109, 110
Opuscula Mythologica, 107
Ossian, 146
Ovid, 30, 69, 71 note, 91, 120
Oxford, 33, 36, 37, 38, 39, 40, 42, 44, 45, 47, 49, 50, 53, 54, 59, 63, 81, 151, 153, 156
Oxford, Lord, 21

Padua, University of, 123
Palæographica, 119

Palayé, Jean Baptiste de la Curri de Ste., 115
Palgrave, Rev. Mr., 126 note
Palladio, 123
Paris, 44, 80, 93, 95, 96, 101, 112 113, 114, 116, 117, 118, 119, 124 147, 150, 153, 158, 160 note, 16.
Paris, Treaty of, 154
Parma, 121
Parr, Dr., 133 note, 134 note
Parsons, Father Robert, 51 note
Pascal's Provincial Letters, 72
Patton, Miss Dorothea (afterwards Mrs. Edward Gibbon sen.), 84
Paul, Father (Pietro Soav Polano), 35
Pavilliard, Rev. Mr., 60, 61, 62 63, 64, 65, 70, 73, 82, 116
Pavilliard, Madam, 88, 118
Payne, Sir Ralph, 191
Pays de Vaud, 62, 65, 74, 79, 117 164
Pelavius, Dionysius, 35
Percy, Dr., 141 note
Petersfield, 19, 87, 89, 93
Petrarch, Giovanni, 5
Phædrus, 27
Piedmont, 121, 123
Pindar, 80
Pisa, 81 note, 122
Pithou, Peter, 27
Pitt, Colonel, 96
Pitt, William, 100
Plato, 38, 159, 177
Plautus, 69 and note
Pliny the Elder, 91, 120
Pliny the Younger, 5, 27, 67, 135
Plutarch, 58
Pocock, Edward, 25, 36, 47
Polignac, Cardinal Melchior de, 58
Pomponius Mela, 120
Pope, Alexander, 29, 63
Porson, Mr., 156, 174
Porten, Mrs. Catherine, 23, 27, 28, 30, 31, 34, 83
Porten, James, 28
Porten, Judith, 20 and note
Portsmouth, 89, 105
Prælectiones, 43
Prideaux, Dr. Humphrey, 36, 165
Priestly, Dr., 151
Procopius, 159

Propertius, 71 note
Ptolemy Philadelphus, 48
Puffendorf, Samuel de, 72
Putney, 20, 24, 26, 28, 32, 34, 60, 138

Queensborough, Castle of, 6
Quintilian, 68, 92
Quintus Curtius, 69 note

Raleigh, Sir Walter, 109, 110, 111
Reading, 89
Reflections on Exile, 100
Religion of a Protestant, 56
Reynal, Guillaume T. F., 115
Reynolds, Sir Joshua, 98, 107, 141 note
Rezzonico (Pope Clement XIII.), 123
Richard Cœur de Lion, 108
Ridley, Major, 126 note
Robertson, Dr. William, 92, 110, 145, 175 note
Robinson Crusoe, 25
Rockingham, Marquis of, 159
Rollin, Charles, 75
Rolvenden, 5, 8
Roman Antiquities, 120
Rome, 93, 99, 120, 121, 122, 123, 124, 136, 144, 150, 161 and note
Romulus, 122
Ross, Bishop, 68
Rotterdam, 58, 83
Round, J. H., 4 note
Rousseau, Jean Jacques, 5, 27, 115

St. Catherine's Cloyster, 10
St. Germain, Abbey of, 148
St. Germain de Prèz, 44
St. Sulpice, Church of (Paris), 114
Salisbury, 103
Sallust, 69 and note
Savonarola, 112
Savoy, Mountains of, 163
Scaliger, Joseph Justus, 36, 106
Schavedt, Margrave of, 125
Scott, George, 106
Scott, Sir William, 59
Seagar, Sir William, 7
Septennial Bill, 15
Serious Call, 18
Servetus, 152
Servius, M. Honoratus, 69

Sethosis, 48
Severy, de (family of), 178 note
Shakspeare, 130
Sheffield, Lord, 119, 126 note, 141, 167, 168 note, 176, 181, 184
Shelburne, Earl of, 159, 160
Sheridan, Mr. Richard Brinsley, 141 note, 169
Sidney, Sir Philip, 108
Sidonius Apollinaris, 95
Sienna, 122
Sigonius, 136
Sirmond, Father, 94, 95
Smith, Dr. Adam, 42, 141 note
Soleurre, 73
Southampton, 103, 106, 125
South Sea Company, 13, 15, 19
Spanheim, Ezechiel, 120
Spedalieri, Abbate Nicola, 156
Spelman, Sir Henry, 34
Spencer, Lord, 186
Spenser, Edmund, 3
Stanislaus, 83
Statuta Urbis Romæ, 170
Stawell, Lord, 87 note
Steevens, Mr., 141 note
Stewart, Sir Simeon, 89
Stockbridge, 89
Stonor, Monsignor, 156
Storer, Mr. Anthony, 160 note
Stormont, Lord, 153
Stourhead, 35
Strabo, 107, 120
Strahan, Mr. William, 144, 170
Strauchius, Egidius, 36 and note
Suetonius, 69 note, 71 note
Swift, Jonathan, 92

Tacitus, 34, 69 and note, 91, 169 note
Taylor, Henry, the Arian, 151
Temple, Sir William, 5, 100
Temple of Ceres, 134
Terence, 46, 67 note, 69
Thanaus, 4
Theodosian Code, 136
Thoulouse, 57
Thucydides, 159
Tibullus, Aulus Albius, 71 note
Tillemont, 136, 175 note
Tissot, Dr., 164
Titus, Emperor, 108
Titus Livius, 149 note

Tom Jones, 4, 182 note
Topham Beauclerc, Mr., 141 note
Torrentius, Lœvinus, 69, 71 note
Tower of London, 9
Trajan, 135
Travis, Mr. George, 155, 156
Traytorrens, M. de, 71 and note
Treatise on the Administration of
    the Finances, 164
Treatise of Government, 72
Tschudi, 129
Tully, 99, 106, 122
Tunbridge, 176
Turin, 121, 123

Ulysses, 30
Universal History, 34
University College, 59
Usher, James (Archbishop), 36

Valerius Maximus, 69 note
Velleius Paterculus, 69 note
Venice, 123
Venus of Medicis, 122
Verburgius, 68
Verona, 123
Versailles, 113
Vertot d'Abœuf, René Aubert de,
    67, 111
Vicenza, 123
Viner, Mr., 60
Virgil, 33, 69 and note, 70, 71 note,
    101 note, 120, 132, 134
Virginia, Colony of, 9, 110
Voltaire, 47, 76, 77, 78, 100, 115,
    117, 179, 183

Wainfleet, Bishop, 43
Waldegrave, Dr., 44, 47, 48, 59
Walpole, Sir Robert, 20, 21,
    131

Warburton, Bishop, 132, 133 and
    note, 135 and note
Warton, Dr., 141 note
Warton, Rev. Joseph, 173
Warton, Mr. Thomas, 141 note
Washington (Sussex), 47
Watson, Dr., Bishop of Llandaff,
    151, 155
Weddal, William, 126 note
Wedderburne, Mr., 143, 154
Wells, Dr. Edward, 36
Wesseling, 120
Westminster School, 18, 32, 34, 3
Weymouth, Lord, Secretary o
    State, 153
Whiston, William, 5
White, Dr., 151, 152
Whitnell, George, 9 note
Wilton, 113
Winchester, 32, 34, 89, 103
Wolfenbuttel, Ducal Library at, 1
Wood, Anthony, 5
Wooddeson, Dr. (Gibbon's school
    master at Kingston), 26
Worsley, Sir Richard, 161 note
Worsley, Lieutenant-Colonel Si
    Thomas, 102, 125, 131

Xenophon, 34, 68, 70, 71 note
    137, 159

York, Duke of, 96
Yorke, Lord Chancellor Charles
    7 note

Zayre, 78
Zocolants (Franciscan Friars), 12
    note
Zuinglius, Ulricus, 74
Zulime, 78
Zurich, 73, 74

MADE AT THE
TEMPLE PRESS LETCHWORTH
IN GREAT BRITAIN

EVERYMAN'S LIBRARY

A LIST OF THE 954 VOLUMES
ARRANGED UNDER AUTHORS

Anonymous works are given under titles.
Anthologies, Dictionaries, etc. are arranged at the end of the list.

Abbott's Rollo at Work, etc., 275
Addison's Spectator, 164–7
Æschylus's Lyrical Dramas, 62
Æsop's and Other Fables, 657
Aimard's The Indian Scout, 428
Ainsworth's Tower of London, 400
  ,,   Old St. Paul's, 522
  ,,   Windsor Castle, 709
  ,,   Rookwood, 870
  ,,   The Admirable Crichton, 894
A Kempis's Imitation of Christ, 484
Alcott's Little Women, and Good
    Wives, 248
  ,,   Little Men, 512
Alpine Club: Peaks, Passes, and
  Glaciers, 778
Andersen's Fairy Tales, 4
  ,,   More Fairy Tales, 822
Anglo-Saxon Chronicle, 624
Anson's Voyages, 510
Aristophanes' Acharnians, etc., 344
  ,,   Frogs, etc., 516
Aristotle's Nicomachean Ethics, 547
  ,,   Politics, 605
  ,,   Poetics, and Demetrius
    on Style, etc., 901
Armour's Fall of the Nibelungs, 312
    Gudrun, 880
Arnold's (Matthew) Essays, 115
  ,,   Poems, 334
  ,,   Study of Celtic Literature,
    etc., 458
Aucassin and Nicolette, 497
Augustine's (Saint) Confessions, 200
Aurelius' (Marcus) Meditations, 9
Austen's (Jane) Sense and Sensi-
    bility, 21
  ,,   Pride and Prejudice, 22
  ,,   Mansfield Park, 23
  ,,   Emma, 24
  ,,   Northanger Abbey, and
    Persuasion, 25

Bacon's Essays, 10
  ,,   Advancement of Learning,
    719
Bagehot's Literary Studies, 520, 521

Baker's (Sir S. W.) Cast up by the
  Sea, 539
Ballantyne's Coral Island, 245
  ,,   Martin Rattler, 246
  ,,   Ungava, 276
Balzac's Wild Ass's Skin, 26
  ,,   Eugénie Grandet, 169
  ,,   Old Goriot, 170
  ,,   Atheist's Mass, etc., 229
  ,,   Christ in Flanders, etc., 284
  ,,   The Chouans, 285
  ,,   Quest of the Absolute, 286
  ,,   Cat and Racket, etc., 349
  ,,   Catherine de Médici, 419
  ,,   Cousin Pons, 463
  ,,   The Country Doctor, 530
  ,,   Rise and Fall of César
    Birotteau, 596
  ,,   Lost Illusions, 656
  ,,   The Country Parson, 686
  ,,   Ursule Mirouët, 733
Barbusse's Under Fire, 798
Barca's (Mme C. de la) Life in
  Mexico, 664
Bates's Naturalist on the Amazon,
  446
Baxter's (Richard) Autobiography,
  868
Beaumont and Fletcher's Selected
  Plays, 506
Beaumont's (Mary) Joan Seaton, 597
Bede's Ecclesiastical History, 479
Belloc's Stories, Essays, and Poems,
  948
Belt's Naturalist in Nicaragua, 561
Bennett's The Old Wives' Tale, 919
Berkeley's (Bishop) Principles of
  Human Knowledge, New Theory
  of Vision, etc., 483
Berlioz (Hector), Life of, 602
Binns's Life of Abraham Lincoln,
  783
Björnson's Plays, 625, 696
Blackmore's Lorna Doone, 304
  ,,   Springhaven, 350
Blackwell's Pioneer Work for
  Women, 667

Blake's Poems and Prophecies, 792
Bligh's A Book of the 'Bounty,' 950
Boccaccio's Decameron, 845, 846
Boehme's The Signature of All
    Things, etc., 569
Bonaventura's The Little Flowers,
    The Life of St. Francis, etc., 485
Borrow's Wild Wales, 49
    ,,   Lavengro, 119
    ,,   Romany Rye, 120
    ,,   Bible in Spain, 151
    ,,   Gypsies in Spain, 697
Boswell's Life of Johnson, 1, 2
    ,,   Tour to the Hebrides, 387
Boult's Asgard and Norse Heroes,
    689
Boyle's The Sceptical Chymist, 559
Bright's (John) Speeches, 252
Brontë's (A.) The Tenant of Wildfell
    Hall, and Agnes Grey, 685
Brontë's (C.) Jane Eyre, 287
    ,,   Shirley, 288
    ,,   Villette, 351
    ,,   The Professor, 417
Brontë's (E.) Wuthering Heights, 243
Brown's (Dr. John) Rab and His
    Friends, etc., 116
Browne's (Frances) Grannie's Won-
    derful Chair, 112
Browne's (Sir Thos.) Religio Medici,
    etc., 92
Browning's Poems, 1833–44, 41
    ,,   ,,   1844–64, 42
    ,,   The Ring and the Book,
        502
Buchanan's Life and Adventures of
    Audubon, 601
Bulfinch's The Age of Fable, 472
    ,,   Legends of Charlemagne,
        556
Bunyan's Pilgrim's Progress, 204
    ,,   Grace Abounding, and
        Mr. Badman, 815
Burke's American Speeches and
    Letters, 340
    ,,   Reflections on the French
        Revolution, etc., 460
Burnet's History of His Own Times,
    85
Burney's Evelina, 352
Burns's Poems and Songs, 94
Burton's East Africa, 500
Burton's (Robert) Anatomy of
    Melancholy, 886–8
Butler's Analogy of Religion, 90
Butler's (Samuel) Erewhon and
    Erewhon Revisited, 881
Butler's The Way of All Flesh, 895
Buxton's Memoirs, 773
Byron's Complete Poetical and
    Dramatic Works, 486–8
    ,,   Letters, 931

Caesar's Gallic War, etc., 702
Calderon's Plays, 819
Canton's Child's Book of Saints, 61
    ,,   Invisible Playmate, etc., 566
Carlyle's French Revolution, 31, 32
    ,,   Letters, etc., of Cromwell,
        266–8

Carlyle's Sartor Resartus, 278
    ,,   Past and Present, 608
    ,,   Essays, 703, 704
    ,,   Reminiscences, 875
Carroll's (Lewis) Alice in Wonder-
    land, etc., 836
Castiglione's The Courtier, 807
Cellini's Autobiography, 51
Cervantes' Don Quixote, 385, 386
Chaucer's Canterbury Tales, 307
Chesterfield's Letters to his Son, 823
Chesterton's Stories, Essays, and
    Poems, 913
Chrétien de Troyes's Arthurian
    Romances, 698
Cibber's Apology for his Life, 668
Cicero's Select Letters and Orations,
    345
Clarke's Tales from Chaucer, 537
    ,,   Shakespeare's Heroines,
        109–11
Cobbett's Rural Rides, 638, 639
Coleridge's Biographia, 11
    ,,   Golden Book of Poetry, 43
    ,,   Lectures on Shakespeare,
        162
Collins's Woman in White, 464
Collodi's Pinocchio, 538
Conrad's Lord Jim, 925
Converse's Long Will, 328
    ,,   House of Prayer, 923
Cook's (Captain) Voyages, 99
Cooper's The Deerslayer, 77
    ,,   The Pathfinder, 78
    ,,   Last of the Mohicans, 79
    ,,   The Pioneer, 171
    ,,   The Prairie, 172
Cowper's Letters, 774
    ,,   Poems, 872
Cox's Tales of Ancient Greece, 721
Craik's Manual of English Litera-
    ture, 346
Craik (Mrs.). See Mulock
Creasy's Fifteen Decisive Battles,
    300
Crèvecœur's Letters from an Amer-
    ican Farmer, 640
Curtis's Prue and I, and Lotus, 413

Dana's Two Years Before the Mast,
    588
Dante's Divine Comedy, 308
Darwin's Origin of Species, 811
    ,,   Voyage of the Beagle, 104
Dasent's Story of Burnt Njal, 558
Daudet's Tartarin of Tarascon, 423
Defoe's Robinson Crusoe, 59
    ,,   Captain Singleton, 74
    ,,   Memoirs of a Cavalier, 283
    ,,   Journal of Plague, 289
    ,,   Tour through England and
        Wales, 820, 821
    ,,   Moll Flanders, 837
De Joinville's Memoirs of the
    Crusades, 333
de la Mare's Stories and Poems, 940
Demosthenes' Select Orations, 546
Dennis's Cities and Cemeteries of
    Etruria, 183, 184

Quincey's Lake Poets, 163
  ,,   Opium-Eater, 223
  ,,   English Mail Coach, etc., 609
Retz (Cardinal), Memoirs of, 735, 36
scartes' Discourse on Method, 70
ckens's Barnaby Rudge, 76
  ,,   Tale of Two Cities, 102
  ,,   Old Curiosity Shop, 173
  ,,   Oliver Twist, 233
  ,,   Great Expectations, 234
  ,,   Pickwick Papers, 235
  ,,   Bleak House, 236
  ,,   Sketches by Boz, 237
  ,,   Nicholas Nickleby, 238
  ,,   Christmas Books, 239
  ,,   Dombey and Son, 240
  ,,   Martin Chuzzlewit, 241
  ,,   David Copperfield, 242
  ,,   American Notes, 290
  ,,   Child's History of England, 291
  ,,   Hard Times, 292
  ,,   Little Dorrit, 293
  ,,   Our Mutual Friend, 294
  ,,   Christmas Stories, 414
  ,,   Uncommercial Traveller, 536
  ,,   Edwin Drood, 725
  ,,   Reprinted Pieces, 744
sraeli's Coningsby, 535
dge's Hans Brinker, 620
nne's Poems, 867
stoevsky's Crime and Punishment, 501
  ,, The House of the Dead, 533
  ,, Letters from the Underworld, etc., 654
  ,, The Idiot, 682
  ,, Poor Folk, and The Gambler, 711
  ,, The Brothers Karamazov, 802, 803
  ,, The Possessed, 861, 862
wden's Life of R. Browning, 701
yden's Dramatic Essays, 568
  ,,   Poems, 910
fferin's Letters from High Latitudes, 499
umas's The Three Musketeers, 81
  ,, The Black Tulip, 174
  ,, Twenty Years After, 175
  ,, Marguerite de Valois, 326
  ,, The Count of Monte Cristo, 393, 394
  ,, The Forty-Five, 420
  ,, Chicot the Jester, 421
  ,, Vicomte de Bragelonne, 593-5
  ,, Le Chevalier de Maison Rouge, 614
u Maurier's Trilby, 863
uruy's Heroes of England, 471
  ,, History of France, 737, 738

ddington's Nature of the Physical World, 922
dgar's Cressy and Poictiers, 17

Edgar's Runnymede and Lincoln Fair, 320
Edgeworth's Castle Rackrent, etc., 410
Eighteenth-Century Plays, 818
Eliot's Adam Bede, 27
  ,,   Silas Marner, 121
  ,,   Romola, 231
  ,,   Mill on the Floss, 325
  ,,   Felix Holt, 353
  ,,   Scenes of Clerical Life, 468
  ,,   Middlemarch, 854, 855
Ellis's (Havelock) Selected Essays, 930
Elyot's Gouernour, 227
Emerson's Essays, 12
  ,,   Representative Men, 279
  ,,   Nature, Conduct of Life, etc., 322
  ,,   Society and Solitude, etc., 567
  ,,   Poems, 715
Epictetus' Moral Discourses, 404
Erckmann-Chatrian's The Conscript and Waterloo, 354
  ,,   Story of a Peasant, 706, 707
Euclid's Elements, 891
Euripides' Plays, 63, 271
Evans's Holy Graal, 445
Evelyn's Diary, 220, 221
Everyman and other Interludes, 381
Ewing's (Mrs.) Mrs. Overtheway's Remembrances, etc., 730
  ,,   Jackanapes, Daddy Darwin's Dovecot, and The Story of a Short Life, 731

Faraday's Experimental Researches in Electricity, 576
Ferrier's (Susan) Marriage, 816
Fielding's Tom Jones, 355, 356
  ,,   Amelia, 852, 853
  ,,   Joseph Andrews, 467
  ,,   Jonathan Wild, and The Journal of a Voyage to Lisbon, 877
Finlay's Byzantine Empire, 33
  ,,   Greece under the Romans, 185
Flaubert's Madame Bovary, 808
  ,,   Salammbo, 869
Fletcher's (Beaumont and) Selected Plays, 506
Ford's Gatherings from Spain, 152
Forster's Life of Dickens, 781, 782
Fox's (George) Journal, 754
Fox's (Charles James) Selected Speeches, 759
Francis's (Saint) The Little Flowers, etc., 485
Franklin's Journey to the Polar Sea, 447
Freeman's Old English History for Children, 540
French Mediaeval Romances. 557
Froissart's Chronicles, 57
Froude's Short Studies, 13, 705
  ,,   Henry VIII, 372-4
  ,,   Edward VI, 375
  ,,   Mary Tudor, 477

Froude's History of Queen Eliza-
    beth's Reign, 583–7
    ,,   Life of Benjamin Disraeli,
        Lord Beaconsfield, 666

Galsworthy's The Country House,
    917
Galt's Annals of the Parish, 427
Galton's Inquiries into Human
    Faculty, 263
Gaskell's Cranford, 83
    ,,   Life of Charlotte Brontë,
        318
    ,,   Sylvia's Lovers, 524
    ,,   Mary Barton, 598
    ,,   Cousin Phillis, etc., 615
    ,,   North and South, 680
Gatty's Parables from Nature, 158
Geoffrey of Monmouth's Histories of
    the Kings of Britain, 577
George's Progress and Poverty, 560
Gibbon's Roman Empire, 434 – 6,
    474–6
    ,,   Autobiography, 511
Gilfillan's Literary Portraits, 348
Giraldus Cambrensis, Wales, 272
Gleig's Life of Wellington, 341
    ,,   The Subaltern, 708
Goethe's Faust, 335
    ,,   Conversations with Ecker-
        mann, 851
    ,,   Wilhelm Meister, 599, 600
Gogol's Dead Souls, 726
    ,,   Taras Bulba, 740
Goldsmith's Vicar of Wakefield, 295
    ,,   Poems and Plays, 415
    ,,   Citizen of the World,
        etc., 902
Goncharov's Oblomov, 878
Gore's Philosophy of the Good Life,
    924
Gorki's Through Russia, 741
Gotthelf's Ulric the Farm Servant,
    228
Gray's Poems and Letters, 628
Green's Short History of the English
    People, 727, 728. The cloth edition
    is in 2 vols. All other editions are
    in 1 vol.
Grettir Saga, 699
Grimm's Fairy Tales, 56
Grote's History of Greece, 186–97
Guest's (Lady) Mabinogion, 97

Hahnemann's The Organon of the
    Rational Art of Healing, 663
Hakluyt's Voyages, 264, 265, 313,
    314, 338, 339, 388, 389
Hallam's Constitutional History,
    621–3
Hamilton's The Federalist, 519
Harte's Luck of Roaring Camp, 681
Harvey's Circulation of Blood, 262
Hawthorne's Wonder Book, 5
    ,,   The Scarlet Letter, 122
    ,,   House of Seven Gables,
        176
    ,,   The Marble Faun, 424
    ,,   Twice Told Tales, 531
    ,,   Blithedale Romance,
        592

Hazlitt's Characters of Shakespear
    Plays, 65
    ,,   Table Talk, 321
    ,,   Lectures, 411
    ,,   Spirit of the Age and L
        tures on English Poe
    ,,   Plain Speaker, 814   [4
Hebbel's Plays, 694
Heimskringla: The Olaf Sagas, 71
    ,,   Sagas of the Nor
        Kings, 847
Heine's Prose and Poetry, 911
Helps's (Sir Arthur) Life of Colu
    bus, 332
Herbert's Temple, 309
Herodotus, 405, 406
Herrick's Hesperides, 310
Hobbes's Leviathan, 691
Holinshed's Chronicle, 800
Holmes's Life of Mozart, 564
Holmes's (O. W.) Autocrat, 66
    ,,   Professor, 67
    ,,   Poet, 68
Homer's Iliad, 453
    ,,   Odyssey, 454
Hooker's Ecclesiastical Polity, 20
    202   [5
Horace's Complete Poetical Worl
Houghton's Life and Letters
    Keats, 801
Howard's (E.) Rattlin the Reef
    857
Howard's (John) State of t
    Prisons, 835
Hudson's (W. H.) A Shepherd's Li
    926   [
Hughes's Tom Brown's Schoolda
Hugo's (Victor) Les Misérables, 36
    ,,   Notre Dame, 422
    ,,   Toilers of the Se
        509
Hume's Treatise of Human Natu
    etc., 548, 549
Hunt's (Leigh) Selected Essays, 82
Hutchinson's (Col.) Memoirs, 317
Huxley's (Aldous) Stories, Essay
    and Poems, 935
Huxley's (T. H.) Man's Place
    Nature, 47
    ,,   Select Lectures and L
        Sermons, 498

Ibsen's The Doll's House, etc., 49
    ,,   Ghosts, etc., 552
    ,,   Pretender, Pillars of Societ
    ,,   Rosmersholm, 659
    ,,   Brand, 716
    ,,   Lady Inger, etc., 729
    ,,   Peer Gynt, 747
Ingelow's Mopsa the Fairy, 619
Irving's Sketch Book, 117
    ,,   Conquest of Granada, 478
    ,,   Life of Mahomet, 513
Italian Short Stories, 876

James's (G. P. R.) Richelieu, 357
James's (Henry) The Turn of t
    Screw, and The Aspern Papers, 9
James (Wm.), Selections from, 739

5

Jefferies's (Richard) After London,
    and Amaryllis at the
              Fair, 951
   ,,   Bevis, 850
Johnson's (Dr.) Lives of the Poets,
    770–1
Jonson's (Ben) Plays, 489, 490
Josephus's Wars of the Jews, 712

Kalidasa's Shakuntala, 629
Kant, Critique of Pure Reason, 909
Keats's Poems, 101
Keble's Christian Year, 690
King's Life of Mazzini, 562
Kinglake's Eothen, 337
Kingsley's (Chas.) Westward Ho! 20
   ,,   Heroes, 113
   ,,   Hereward the Wake, 206
   ,,   Hypatia, 230
   ,,   Water Babies, and
             Glaucus, 277
   ,,   Alton Locke, 462
   ,,   Yeast, 611
   ,,   Madam How and Lady
             Why, 777
   ,,   Poems, 793
Kingsley's (Henry) Ravenshoe, 28
   ,,   Geoffrey Hamlyn, 416
Kingston's Peter the Whaler, 6
   ,,   Three Midshipmen, 7
Kirby's Kalevala, 259, 260
Koran, 380

Lamb's Tales from Shakespeare, 8
   ,,   Essays of Elia, 14
   ,,   Letters, 342, 343
Landor's Imaginary Conversations
   and Poems, 890
Lane's Modern Egyptians, 315
Langland's Piers Plowman, 571
Latimer's Sermons, 40
Law's Serious Call, 91
Lawrence's The White Peacock, 914
Layamon's (Wace and) Arthurian
   Chronicles, 578
Lear (Edward). See under Antho-
   logies
Leibniz' Philosophical Writings, 905
Le Sage's Gil Blas, 437, 438
Leslie's Memoirs of John Constable,
   563
Lessing's Laocoön, etc., 843
Lever's Harry Lorrequer, 177
Lewes's Life of Goethe, 269
Lincoln's Speeches, etc., 206
Livy's History of Rome, 603, 609,
   670, 749, 755, 756
Locke's Civil Government, 751
Lockhart's Life of Napoleon, 3
   ,,   Life of Scott, 55
   ,,   Life of Burns, 156
Longfellow's Poems, 382
Lönnrott's Kalevala, 259, 260
Loti's Iceland Fisherman, 920
Lover's Handy Andy, 178
Lowell's Among My Books, 607
Lucretius's Of the Nature of Things,
   750
Lützow's History of Bohemia, 432

Lyell's Antiquity of Man, 700
Lytton's Harold, 15
   ,,   Last of the Barons, 18
   ,,   Last Days of Pompeii, 80
   ,,   Pilgrims of the Rhine, 390
   ,,   Rienzi, 532

Macaulay's England, 34–6
   ,,   Essays, 225, 226
   ,,   Speeches on Politics, etc.,
             399
   ,,   Miscellaneous Essays, 439
MacDonald's Sir Gibbie, 678
   ,,   Phantastes, 732
Machiavelli's Prince, 280
   ,,   Florence, 376
Maine's Ancient Law, 734
Malory's Le Morte D'Arthur, 45, 46
Malthus on the Principles of
   Population, 692, 693
Mandeville's Travels, 812
Manning's Sir Thomas More, 19
   ,,   Mary Powell, and De-
            borah's Diary, 324
Marlowe's Plays and Poems, 383
Marryat's Mr. Midshipman Easy, 82
   ,,   Little Savage, 159
   ,,   Masterman Ready, 160
   ,,   Peter Simple, 232
   ,,   Children of New Forest,
            247
   ,,   Percival Keene, 358
   ,,   Settlers in Canada, 370
   ,,   King's Own, 580
   ,,   Jacob Faithful, 618
Martineau's Feats on the Fjords, 429
Martinengo - Cesaresco's Folk - Lore
   and other Essays, 673
Marx's Capital, 848, 849
Maugham's (Somerset) Cakes and
   Ale, 932
Maupassant's Short Stories, 907
Maurice's Kingdom of Christ, 146–7
Mazzini's Duties of Man, etc., 224
Melville's Moby Dick, 179
   ,,   Typee, 180
   ,,   Omoo, 297
Meredith's The Ordeal of Richard
   Feverel, 916
Mérimée's Carmen, etc., 834
Merivale's History of Rome, 433
Mickiewicz's Pan Tadeusz, 842
Mignet's French Revolution, 713
Mill's Utilitarianism, Liberty, Repre-
   sentative Government, 482
   ,,   Rights of Woman, 825
Miller's Old Red Sandstone, 103
Milman's History of the Jews, 377,
   378
Milton's Areopagitica and other
       Prose Works, 795
   ,,   Poems, 384
Mitford's Our Village, 927
Molière's Comedies, 830, 831
Mommsen's History of Rome, 542–5
Montagu's (Lady) Letters, 69
Montaigne's Essays, 440–2
Moore's (George) Esther Waters, 933
More's Utopia, and Dialogue of
   Comfort against Tribulation, 461

Morier's Hajji Baba, 679
Morris's (Wm.) Early Romances, 261
　　,, 　　Life and Death of Jason, 575
Morte D'Arthur Romances, 634
Motley's Dutch Republic, 86-8
Mulock's John Halifax, 123

Neale's Fall of Constantinople, 655
Newcastle's (Margaret, Duchess of) Life of the First Duke of Newcastle, etc., 722 　　　[636
Newman's Apologia Pro Vita Sua, On the Scope and Nature of University Education, and a Paper on Christianity and Scientific Investigation, 723
Nietzsche's Thus Spake Zarathustra, 892

Oliphant's Salem Chapel, 244
Omar Khayyám, 819
Osborne (Dorothy), Letters of, 674
Owen's (Robert) A New View of Society, etc., 799

Paine's Rights of Man, 718
Palgrave's Golden Treasury, 96
Paltock's Peter Wilkins, 676
Park's (Mungo) Travels, 205
Parkman's Conspiracy of Pontiac, 302, 303
Pascal's Pensées, 874
Paston Letters, 752, 753
Pater's Marius the Epicurean, 903
Peacock's Headlong Hall, 327
Pearson's The Grammar of Science, 939
Penn's The Peace of Europe, Some Fruits of Solitude, etc., 724
Pepys's Diary, 53, 54
Percy's Reliques, 148, 149
Pinnow's (H.) History of Germany, [929
Pitt's Orations, 145
Plato's Republic, 64
　　,, 　Dialogues, 456, 457
Plutarch's Lives, 407-9
　　,, 　　Moralia, 565
Poe's Tales of Mystery and Imagination, 336
　　,, 　Poems and Essays, 791
Polo's (Marco) Travels, 306
Pope's Complete Poetical Works, 760
Prescott's Conquest of Peru, 301
　　,, 　Conquest of Mexico, 397, 398
Prévost's Manon Lescaut etc., 834
Priestley's Angel Pavement, 938
Procter's Legends and Lyrics, 150
Pushkin's The Captain's Daughter, etc., 898

Quiller-Couch's Hetty Wesley, 864

Rabelais's Gargantua and Pantagruel, 826, 827
Radcliffe's (Mrs. Ann) The Mysteries of Udolpho, 865, 866
Ramayana and Mahabharata, 403

Reade's The Cloister and the Hearth, 29
　　,, 　Peg Woffington, 299
Reid's (Mayne) Boy Hunters of the Mississippi, 582
　　,, 　The Boy Slaves, 797
Renan's Life of Jesus, 805
Reynolds's Discourses, 118
Ricardo's Principles of Politica Economy and Taxation, 590
Richardson's Pamela, 683, 684
　　,, 　　Clarissa, 882-5
Roberts's (Morley) Western Avernus, 762
Robertson's Religion and Life, 37
　　,, 　Christian Doctrine, 38
　　,, 　Bible Subjects, 39
Robinson's (Wade) Sermons, 637
Roget's Thesaurus, 630, 631
Rossetti's (D. G.) Poems, 627
Rousseau's Emile, 518
　　,, 　Social Contract and other Essays, 660
　　,, 　Confessions, 859, 860
Ruskin's Seven Lamps of Architecture, 207
　　,, 　Modern Painters, 208-12
　　,, 　Stones of Venice, 213-15
　　,, 　Unto this Last, etc., 216
　　,, 　Elements of Drawing, etc., 217
　　,, 　Pre-Raphaelitism, etc., 218
　　,, 　Sesame and Lilies, 219
　　,, 　Ethics of the Dust, 282
　　,, 　Crown of Wild Olive, and Cestus of Aglaia, 323
　　,, 　Time and Tide, etc., 450
　　,, 　The Two Boyhoods, 683
Russell's Life of Gladstone, 661

Sand's (George) The Devil's Pool, and François the Waif, 534
Scheffel's Ekkehard, 529
Scott's (M.) Tom Cringle's Log. 710
Scott's (Sir W.) Ivanhoe, 16
　　,, 　Fortunes of Nigel, 71
　　,, 　Woodstock, 72
　　,, 　Waverley, 75
　　,, 　The Abbot, 124
　　,, 　Anne of Geierstein, 125
　　,, 　The Antiquary, 126
　　,, 　Highland Widow, and Betrothed, 127
　　,, 　Black Dwarf, Legend of Montrose, 128
　　,, 　Bride of Lammermoor, 129
　　,, 　Castle Dangerous, Surgeon's Daughter, 130
　　,, 　Robert of Paris, 131
　　,, 　Fair Maid of Perth, 132
　　,, 　Guy Mannering, 133
　　,, 　Heart of Midlothian, 134
　　,, 　Kenilworth, 135
　　,, 　The Monastery, 136
　　,, 　Old Mortality, 137
　　,, 　Peveril of the Peak, 138
　　,, 　The Pirate, 139
　　,, 　Quentin Durward, 140
　　,, 　Redgauntlet, 141
　　,, 　Rob Roy, 142

Scott's (Sir W.) St. Ronan's Well, 143
  ,,   The Talisman, 144
  ,,   Lives of the Novelists, 331
  ,,   Poems and Plays, 550, 551
Seebohm's Oxford Reformers, 665
Seeley's Ecce Homo, 305
Sewell's (Anna) Black Beauty, 748
Shakespeare's Comedies, 153
  ,,   Histories, etc., 154
  ,,   Tragedies, 155
Shchedrin's The Golovlyov Family, 908
Shelley's Poetical Works, 257, 258
Shelley's (Mrs.) Frankenstein, 616
  ,,   Rights of Women, 825
Sheppard's Charles Auchester, 505
Sheridan's Plays, 95
Sienkiewicz's Tales, 871
Sismondi's Italian Republics, 250
Smeaton's Life of Shakespeare, 514
Smith's Wealth of Nations, 412, 413
Smith's (George) Life of Wm. Carey, 395
Smollett's Roderick Random, 790
  ,,   Peregrine Pickle, 838, 839
Sophocles' Dramas, 114
Southey's Life of Nelson, 52
Spectator, 164–7
Speke's Source of the Nile, 50
Spencer's (Herbert) Essays on Education, 503
Spenser's Faerie Queene, 443, 444
  ,,   The Shepherd's Calendar, [1879
Spinoza's Ethics, etc., 481
Spyri's Heidi, 431
Stanley's Memorials of Canterbury, Eastern Church, 251 [89
Steele's The Spectator, 164–7
Stendhal's Scarlet and Black, 945,
Sterne's Tristram Shandy, 617 [946
  ,,   Sentimental Journey, and Journal to Eliza, 796
Stevenson's Treasure Island, and Kidnapped, 763
  ,,   Master of Ballantrae, and The Black Arrow, 764
  ,,   Virginibus Puerisque, and Familiar Studies of Men and Books, 765
  ,,   An Inland Voyage, Travels with a Donkey, and Silverado Squatters, 766
  ,,   Dr. Jekyll and Mr. Hyde, The Merry Men, etc., 767
  ,,   Poems, 768
  ,,   In the South Seas, and Island Nights' Entertainments, 769
  ,,   St. Ives, 904 [etc., 485
St. Francis, The Little Flowers of, 589
Stow's Survey of London, 589
Stowe's Uncle Tom's Cabin, 371
Strickland's Queen Elizabeth, 100
Surtees's Jorrocks's Jaunts, 817
Swedenborg's Heaven and Hell, 379
  ,,   Divine Love and Wisdom, 635
  ,,   Divine Providence, 658
  ,,   The True Christian Religion, 893

Swift's Gulliver's Travels, 60
  ,,   Tale of a Tub, etc., 347
  ,,   Journal to Stella, 757
Swinnerton's The Georgian Literary Scene, 943
Swiss Family Robinson, 430

Tacitus's Annals, 273
  ,,   Agricola and Germania, 274
Taylor's Words and Places, 517
Tchekhov's Plays and Stories, 941
Tennyson's Poems, 44, 626
Thackeray's Esmond, 73
  ,,   Vanity Fair, 298
  ,,   Christmas Books, 359
  ,,   Pendennis, 425, 426
  ,,   Newcomes, 465, 466
  ,,   The Virginians, 507, 508
  ,,   English Humorists, and The Four Georges, 610
  ,,   Roundabout Papers, 687
Thierry's Norman Conquest, 198, 199
Thoreau's Walden, 281
Thucydides' Peloponnesian War, 455
Tolstoy's Master and Man, and Other Parables and Tales, 469
  ,,   War and Peace, 525–7
  ,,   Childhood, Boyhood, and Youth, 591
  ,,   Anna Karenina, 612, 613
Trench's On the Study of Words and English Past and Present, 788
Trollope's Barchester Towers, 30
  ,,   Framley Parsonage, 181
  ,,   The Warden, 182
  ,,   Dr. Thorne, 360 [361
  ,,   Small House at Allington,
  ,,   Last Chronicles of Barset, 391, 392 [761
  ,,   Golden Lion of Granpere,
  ,,   Phineas Finn, 832, 833
Trotter's The Bayard of India, 396
  ,,   Hodson of Hodson's Horse,
  ,,   Warren Hastings, 452 [401
Turgenev's Virgin Soil, 528
  ,,   Liza, 677
  ,,   Fathers and Sons, 742
Tyndall's Glaciers of the Alps, 98
Tytler's Principles of Translation, 168

Vasari's Lives of the Painters, 784–7
Verne's (Jules) Twenty Thousand Leagues under the Sea, 319
  ,,   Dropped from the Clouds, 367
  ,,   Abandoned, 368
  ,,   The Secret of the Island, 369
  ,,   Five Weeks in a Balloon, and Around the World in Eighty Days, 779
Virgil's Æneid, 161
  ,,   Eclogues and Georgics, 222
Voltaire's Life of Charles XII, 270
  ,,   Age of Louis XIV, 780
  ,,   Candide and Other Tales, 936

Wace and Layamon's Arthurian Chronicles, 578 [1828
Wakefield's Letter from Sydney, etc.,

8

Walpole's Letters, 775
Walpole's (Hugh) Mr. Perrin and Mr. Traill, 918
Walton's Compleat Angler, 70
Waterton's Wanderings in South America, 772 [899
Webster and Ford's Selected Plays,
Wells's The Time Machine, and The Wheels of Chance, 915
Wesley's Journal, 105–8
White's Selborne, 48
Whitman's Leaves of Grass, and Democratic Vistas, etc., 573
Whyte-Melville's Gladiators, 523
Wilde's Plays, Prose Writings and Poems, 858 [84
Wood's (Mrs. Henry) The Channings,
Woolf's To the Lighthouse, 949
Woolman's Journal, etc., 402
Wordsworth's Shorter Poems, 203
„   Longer Poems, 311

Xenophon's Cyropaedia, 67

Yellow Book, 503
Yonge's The Dove in the Eagle's Nest, 329
„   The Book of Golden Deeds, 330
„   The Heir of Redclyffe, 362
„   The Little Duke, 470
„   The Lances of Lynwood, 579
Young's (Arthur) Travels in France and Italy, 720

Zola's Germinal, 897

Anthologies, Dictionaries, etc.

A Book of English Ballads, 572
A Book of Heroic Verse, 574
A Book of Nonsense, by Edward Lear, and Others, 806
A Century of Essays, An Anthology, 653
American Short Stories of the Nineteenth Century, 840
A New Anthology of Sense and Nonsense, 813
An Anthology of English Prose: From Bede to Stevenson, 675
An Encyclopaedia of Gardening, by Walter P. Wright, 555
Ancient Hebrew Literature, 4 vols., 253–6
Anglo-Saxon Poetry, 794
Annals of Fairyland, 365, 366, 541
Anthology of British Historical Speeches and Orations, 714
Atlas of Classical Geography, 451
Atlases, Literary and Historical: Europe, 496; America, 553; Asia, 633; Africa and Australasia, 662

Dictionary, Biographical, of English Literature, 449
„   Biographical, of Foreign Literature, 900
„   of Dates, 554
„   Everyman's English, 776
„   of Non-Classical Mythology, 632
„   Smaller Classical, 495
„   of Quotations and Proverbs, 809, 810
English Religious Verse, Edited by G. Lacey May, 937
English Short Stories. An Anthology, 743
Fairy Gold, 157
Fairy Tales from the Arabian Nights,
French Short Stories, 896 [249
Ghost Stories, Edited by John Hampden, 952
Golden Book of Modern English Poetry, 921 [746
Golden Treasury of Longer Poems,
Hindu Scriptures, Edited by Dr. Nicol Macnicol, 944
Minor Elizabethan Drama, 491, 492
Minor Poets of the Eighteenth Century, 844
Minor Poets of the Seventeenth Century, 873
Modern Plays, 942
Modern Short Stories, Edited by John Hadfield, 954
Mother Goose, 473
Muses' Pageant, The, 581, 606, 671
New Golden Treasury, 695
New Testament, The, 93
Poetry Book for Boys and Girls, 894
Political Liberty, a Symposium, 745
Prayer Books of King Edward VI, First and Second, 448
Prelude to Poetry, 789
Reader's Guide to Everyman's Library, revised edition, covering the first 950 vols., 889
Restoration Plays, 604
Russian Short Stories, 758
Selections from St. Thomas Aquinas. Edited by The Rev. Father M. C. D'Arcy, 953
Shorter Novels: Elizabethan, 824
„   Jacobean and Restoration, 841
„   Eighteenth Century, 856
Story Book for Boys and Girls, 934
Table Talk, 906
Tales of Detection, 928
Theology in the English Poets, 493
Thesaurus of English Words and Phrases, Roget's, 630, 631
Twenty One-Act Plays, Selected by John Hampden, 947

NOTE—The following numbers are at present out of print:
89, 109, 110, 111, 146, 147, 228, 244, 275, 346, 350, 376, 390, 418, 480, 493, 540, 541, 574, 597, 641–52, 664, 679

LONDON: J. M. DENT & SONS LTD.
NEW YORK: E. P. DUTTON & CO. INC